Frederick Gard Fleay

A Chronicle History of the Life and Work of William Shakespeare

Frederick Gard Fleay

A Chronicle History of the Life and Work of William Shakespeare

ISBN/EAN: 9783337338084

Printed in Europe, USA, Canada, Australia, Japan

Cover: Foto ©Thomas Meinert / pixelio.de

More available books at **www.hansebooks.com**

A CHRONICLE HISTORY

OF THE

·LIFE AND WORK

OF

WILLIAM SHAKESPEARE·

PLAYER, POET, AND PLAYMAKER

BY

FREDERICK GARD FLEAY

With Two Etched Illustrations.

LONDON
JOHN C. NIMMO
14, KING WILLIAM STREET, STRAND, W.C.
1886

[*All rights reserved*]

Dedication.

TO

THE SHAKESPEARE OF OUR DAYS,

ROBERT BROWNING,

A PERMITTED TRIBUTE

FROM

HIS EVER-DEVOTED LIEGEMAN,

FREDERICK GARD FLEAY.

To him, whose craft, so subtly terse,
   (While lesser minds, for music's sake,
   From single thoughts whole cantos make),
Includes a poem in a verse ;—

To him, whose penetrative art,
   With spheric knowledge only his,
   Dissects by keen analysis
The wiliest secrets of the heart ;—

To him, who rounds us perfect wholes,
   Where wisdom, wit, and love combine ;
   Chief praise be this :—he wrote no line
That could cause pain in childlike souls.

CONTENTS.

	PAGE
INTRODUCTION	1

SECTION I.
THE PUBLIC CAREER OF SHAKESPEARE 7

SECTION II.
THE PERSONAL CONNECTIONS OF SHAKESPEARE WITH OTHER POETS 73

SECTION III.
ANNALS ON WHICH THE PRECEDING SECTIONS ARE FOUNDED 83

SECTION IV.
THE CHRONOLOGICAL SUCCESSION OF SHAKESPEARE'S PLAYS 175

SECTION V.
ON THE MARLOWE GROUP OF PLAYS 255

SECTION VI.
ON THE PLAYS BY OTHER AUTHORS ACTED BY SHAKESPEARE'S COMPANY 284

INTRODUCTION.

It is due to the reader of a new work on a subject already so often handled as the Life of Shakespeare to tell him at the outset what he may expect to find therein, and to state the reasons for which I have thought it worth while to devote nearly ten years to its production. Previous investigators have with industrious minuteness already ascertained for us every detail that can reasonably be expected of Shakespeare's private life. With laborious research they have raked together the records of petty debts, of parish assessments, of scandalous traditions, of idle gossip; and they have shown beyond doubt that Shakespeare was born at Stratford-on-Avon, was married, had three children, left his home, made money as an actor and play-maker in London, returned to his native town, invested his savings there, and died. I do not think that when stript of verbiage, and what the slang of the day calls padding, much more than this can be claimed as the result of the voluminous writings on this side of his career. For one I am thankful that things are so; I have little sympathy with the modern inquisitiveness that peeps over the garden wall to see in what array the great man smokes his pipe, and chronicles the shape and colour of his head-covering. But on the public side of Shakespeare's career little has been adequately ascertained; and with this we are deeply concerned. Not for a mere personal interest, but in its bearings on the history of English literature, we ought to ascertain so far as is possible what companies of actors Shakespeare belonged to, at what theatres they acted, in what plays besides his own he was a performer, what authors this brought him into personal contact with, what influence he exerted on or received from them, what relations, friendly or unfriendly, they had with rival companies, and finally, in what order his own works were produced, and what if any share other hands had in their production. All these matters have been treated carelessly and inaccurately by biographers of the peeping school; and in the last of these we are gravely referred for the chronology of Shakespeare's plays to a schoolboy compilation the author of which is so ignorant as to speak of *Lust's Domi-*

INTRODUCTION.

nion as a play of *Jonson's*, the *News from Hell* as a *play* of Dekker's, and Achilles as Laertes' son. This marvel of inefficiency we are told is the best work on the subject; and this while Malone and Drake are accessible to any student. In the present treatise this hitherto neglected side of Shakespeare's career has been chiefly dwelt on. The facts of his private life are also given; but not the documents on which they are founded, these having been excellently well collected and arranged in the recent *Outlines of the Life of Shakespeare*, by J. O. Halliwell-Phillipps, F.R.S., F.S.A., Hon. M.R.S.L., Hon. M.R.I.A. This book is a treasure-house of documents, and it is greatly to be regretted that they are not published by themselves, apart from hypotheses founded on idle rumour or fallacious mis-reasoning. I do not know any work so full of fanciful theories and *" ignes fatui"* likely to entice *"a deluded traveller out of the beaten path into strange quagmires."* * There is much else besides documents not given in the present treatise; discussions as to who might have been Shakespeare's schoolmaster, whether he was apprenticed to a butcher, whether he stole a deer out of a non-existent park, whether he held horses

---

* "These phrases to their owner I resign,
For God's sake, reader, take them not for mine."

at the theatre door or "was employed in any other equine capacity," whether he went to Denmark or to Venice, and whether Lord Bacon wrote his plays for him. On all these points I must refer to earlier and less sceptical treatises. What the reader will find here is—(1.) A continuous narrative in which the statements are mostly taken for granted in accordance with my own view of the evidence accessible to us ; (2.) Annals or chronological arrangement of the same facts, with discussion of their mutual interrelations ; (3.) Discussion of the evidence on which the chronological succession of Shakespeare's plays is based ; (4.) Similar discussions for plays in which he was not main author but only "coadjutor, novice, journeyman, tutor," or even merely one of the possible actors ; (5.) A few remarks on the German versions of his plays acted on the Continent ; and (6.) Tables of quarto editions of his plays, &c., with a list of all plays entered on the Stationers' Registers from the first opening of theatres to their closing in 1640–42. This last item may seem to be somewhat beyond the scope of this book, but it is greatly needed, and it is better that so difficult a task should be performed by one acquainted with dramatic literature than by some scissors-and-paste compiler who cannot distinguish a play from a prose tract. As to the preparation for the whole work it has been to me a labour of love, not, I trust, altogether lost. I have read and re-read for it every play accessible to me that dates earlier than 1640, have compiled annals for every known writer of that period and discussions of the dates of his plays, and have compared the results and corrected and re-corrected until a consistent whole has been obtained. Of this whole only the part relating to Shakespeare is here issued. I have to thank the editors of *Anglia*, *Englische Studien*, and *Shakespeariana* for enabling me to print some portions relating to other authors, which will, however, require some minor corrections. I have also to thank Dr. Furnivall and Mr. Swinburne for some wholesome criticism upon my earlier work; Dr. Ingleby, Miss Lee, Mr. Boyle, Mr. A. H. Bullen, and especially Dr. H. H. Furness, for kindly sympathy and copies of their own writings, some of which might otherwise have escaped my notice ; and above all Mr. P. A. Daniel, for ever-ready help when asked for, and for judicious strictures on received hypotheses or points debatable. The main regret for the earnest student is that so many of these still exist ; as any attempt to give a biography of Shakespeare the form which is æsthetically its due must fail so long as the true order of the facts on which it rests is still esteemed matter of argument. If the reader would wish to judge before proceeding further of the quality of such argument in the present work I would refer him to the discussion on *Mucedorus* or that on *Henry VI.* in subsequent Sections.

One other point requires notice, if not apology. The plan followed in this volume requires much repetition in order that the separate arguments as to the chronological succession of the plays, and as to the order of events in Shakespeare's life, should be presented in intelligible sequence. This is an evil only to be avoided either by mixing up the two, as is usually done, or by numerous cross-references. Either of these methods leads to greater evils, both by interrupting the logical connection of each series (for unfortunately the evidences are mostly independent of each other), and, which is still more important, by obliterating the mutual support given to the arguments in the twofold lines of evidence by their leading in each division to compatible results. The inconvenience of these repetitions has therefore been submitted to.

LIFE OF SHAKESPEARE.

SECTION I.

THE PUBLIC CAREER OF SHAKESPEARE.

ON or about Saturday 22d April 1564, William Shakespeare, son of John Shakespeare, glover and dealer in wool, and his wife Mary, *née* Arden, was born in Henley Street, Stratford-on-Avon, and was baptized on the 26th. Nothing whatever is known of his early life, and the few meagre details ascertained as to the condition of his family will be found in a subsequent division of this work. Tradition and imagination have supplied untrustworthy materials, with which his biographers have endeavoured to fill up the gap in our information; but it is not until 28th November 1582 that we find any further reliable fact established concerning him. On that day his marriage bond is dated, he being in his nineteenth year, and his bride, Anne

Hathaway, in her twenty-sixth. Their first child, Susanna, was baptized 26th May 1583. To account for this young lady's premature arrival a pre-contract is assumed, but not proved, by recent writers. On 2d February 1585 their twin children, Hamnet and Judith, were baptized; and in 1587, in the spring, Shakespeare gave his assent to a proposed settlement of a mortgage on his mother's Asbies estate. For ten years after there is no vestige of any communication with his family. It is at this point that his public life begins.

In 1587 Leicester's players visited Stratford for the first time. The company, under the same name, that had performed there in 1576 had as well as Warwick's been dissolved in 1583, in order that the Queen's men might be selected from them. In 1586, during the prevalence of the plague in London, this more recent company had been travelling on the Continent, and on their return to England made a provincial tour. Shakespeare probably joined them during or immediately after their visit to Stratford, and during their travels received his earliest instruction in comic acting from Kempe and Pope, who soon after became noted performers; Bryan also belonged to the company at this date. They probably acted mere interludes, not regular five-act plays. On 4th September 1588 the Earl of Leicester died; and his players soon after found a new patron in Lord Strange. They then settled in London, and acted at the Cross Keys in Bishopsgate Street. The head of the company, in its altered constitution, was "Famous Ned Allen," who on 3d January 1588–9 bought up for £37, 10s. Richard Jones' share of "playing apparels, play-books, instruments, &c.," in order to set up his new company. These properties had belonged to Worcester's men under Robert Brown, and were no longer needed by him, as he and his players were about to visit the Continent.

It was in this way that Shakespeare came to London as a poor strolling player, but nevertheless his position was not without its advantages; he was associated already with the most noted comedians of the time, Kempe and Pope; and in Alleyn he had the advantage of studying the method of the greatest tragic actor that had yet trod the English stage. But he did not remain content with merely acting; he now commenced as author. In order to ascertain under what conditions, it will be necessary to briefly state what was the position of the companies and authors in London in 1589.

At that date there were two theatres in London: the better of the two, the Theater, was occupied by the Queen's men, for whom Greene was the principal play-writer. Marlowe, Kyd, and R. Wilson had also contributed plays to their *repertoire*, but just at this time left them and joined Pembroke's, which, like Leicester's, had been a strolling company, but were now settling in London. On the other hand, Peele and Lodge, who had previously written for the Admiral's company, acting at the other theatre, the Curtain, had also joined, and still remained with, the Queen's. Nearly all these writers, if not quite all, were actors as well as authors. Greene, the Johannes Factotum of the Queen's men, had evidently expected to establish a monopoly of play-acting in their favour, and was indignant at the arrival of vagrant troops of Thespians from the country, just when he had practically succeeded in crippling the rival company in London, by enlisting some of their best authors in the service of his own. Hence on 23d August 1589 his publication of *Menaphon*, with Nash's address, containing a virulent attack on Kyd and Marlowe, then writing for Pembroke's men, together with a glorification of Peele, then writing in conjunction with Greene. The absence of any allusion in this tract to Shakespeare or Lord Strange's company conclusively proves that they were not as yet dangerous rivals to the Queen's. Pembroke's men were, and there is indirect evidence that they had from their first settlement in London obtained possession of the second theatre, the Curtain. This evidence is connected with the first direct mention which is extant of Shakespeare's company. For in this same year, 1589, the Martinist controversy had been raging in London; Lyly, Nash, Greene, Monday, and Cooper were the anti-Martinist champions; the Martinists had been ridiculed on the stage in April, probably by Greene at the Theater, possibly by the Paul's children in some play of Lyly's, or by the Earl of Oxford's boys in one of Monday's. The authorities did not interfere. But in November certain players "within the city," to wit, Lord Strange's and the Admiral's, were silenced for "abuses or indecent reflexions" (Strype). A comparison of the *worthies* in *Love's Labour's Lost* with the anti-Martinist writers, of the Euphuist Armado with Lyly, the boy-satirist Mote with Nash, the curate with the Reverend Robert Greene, the schoolmaster-pedant with the pedagogue Cooper, and Antony Dull with Antony Monday, will I think confirm the theory developed by me in a separate essay, that this was the play suppressed on this occasion. It is characteristic of the independence of action shown by Shakespeare's company throughout the reign of Elizabeth that they refused to obey the injunction, and went and played at the Cross-Keys that same afternoon, while the subservient Admiral's company dutifully submitted. I do not suppose, however, that the play as then performed was in all parts from the hand of Shakespeare. It is extremely unlikely that he should have commenced his career by independent writing, and there is not a play of his that can be referred even on the rashest conjecture to a date anterior to 1594, which does not bear the plainest internal evidence to its having been refashioned at a later time. In all probability he began to compose plays, as we know so many of his contemporaries did, as an assistant to some experienced dramatist. It may seem idle, in the absence of any positive evidence, to guess who was his original tutor in composition, and yet, as the careers of Peele, Greene, and Marlowe conclusively show that none of them were in 1589 connected with Lord Strange's company, I venture to suggest that it was Robert Wilson. That dramatist is not heard of in connection with Pembroke's or any other company after August 1589, and he certainly continued to write for the stage. That Shakespeare was greatly influenced by him and Peele is evident from the metrical character of Shakespeare's earliest work, which abounds in heroic rhyme like Peele's in tragedy, and in doggerel and stanza like Wilson's in comedy. It is not till the Historic plays that the influence of Marlowe's blank verse is fully perceptible, and in the earliest of these, *Richard II.*, rhyme is still dominant. Wilson was in this view a better teacher for the inexperienced Shakespeare than a greater man. Marlowe, for instance, might have biassed him on the tragic side, and deferred or prevented his comedy from its earlier pastoral development. *Love's Labour's Won* must have been written at about the same time as *Love's Labour's Lost*, and before the end of 1590 *The Comedy of Errors* probably appeared in its original form. In this same year was produced a play in which, although I cannot detect Shakespeare's hand as coadjutor with its probable author, R. Wilson, he most likely appeared as an actor—*Fair Em;* and that this comedy contained a satirical attack on Greene is evident from the offence he took at it, as shown in his virulent address prefixed to his *Farewell to Folly*. Up to this date Greene's chief attacks had been directed against Kyd in *Menaphon* and in *Never too late*, but as yet there has been found no allusion to Shakespeare in his writings anterior to 1592. Yet Shakespeare must have been known to him as at least part author of the plays acted by Lord Strange's men in 1589 and 1590. Of *Romeo and Juliet*, originally acted in 1591, we also possess a version anterior to Shakespeare's final remodelling, which palpably contains scenes not written by him. These scenes, however, seem due to a finer artist than Kyd, and there is independent evidence that George Peele had by 1591 also become a playwright for Lord Strange's men. One of the plays acted by them in this year was probably Peele's *Edward I.*, here mentioned on account of a curious allusion which would seem to fix the character performed by Shakespeare. In scene 3 Elinor says to Baliol—

" *Shake* [thou] thy *spear* in honour of *his name*
Under whose royalty thou wear'st the same."

Shakespeare is known to have acted "kingly parts," and this of Edward I. was probably one of them. To this same year may probably be assigned the original production of *The Two Gentlemen of Verona*.

The Court festivities of Christmas 1591–2 mark an important epoch in the fortunes of Lord Strange's company, and consequently of Shakespeare, now rapidly coming to the front as their chief writer. During the period we have been considering, 1587–1591, the Queen's and the Admiral's were the only men's companies who performed at Court, but at Christmas 1591–2 the Admiral's did not act at all, and the Queen's, after one performance, gave place to Lord Strange's, and until the death of that nobleman in 1594, his players enjoyed almost a monopoly of Court performances. One presentation by the Earl of Hertford's men, of whom nothing else is recorded, one by the Earl of Sussex', and two by the Earl of Pembroke's, are all that can be balanced with six by Lord Strange's in 1591–2, and three in 1592–3. This pre-eminence at Court was retained by the company under all its changes of constitution far beyond Shakespeare's time, until the closing of the theatres in 1642. Possibly the influence of Lord Southampton, who had come to town and entered at Gray's Inn in 1590, and was stepson to Sir Thomas Heneage, the treasurer, may have had something to do with this. He does not yet, however, appear to have come into direct communication with Shakespeare.

Immediately after this first appearance at Court, Alleyn arranged with Henslow, his father-in-law, to give his company a local habitation in a permanent theatre. This was of no small importance to them; they had hitherto had to play in the inn-yard at the Cross-Keys. Henslow's new theatre was the Rose on the Bankside, which opened in February 1591 2. The singular fact that every old play (*i.e.*, every play that had been previously performed) there acted in this season had been with one possible exception derived from the Queen's players, shows that the hitherto most successful company were reduced to sell their copies, and were probably on the verge of bankruptcy. Among these we find Greene's *Orlando* and *Friar Bacon*, Greene and Lodge's *Looking-glass for London*, Marlowe's *Jew of Malta*, and Kyd's two plays of *Jeronymo*. The only play traceable to another company is Peele's *Battle of Alcazar*, called by Henslow *Mulomorco*. In fact, the Queen's company were now practically without a play-writer. Of their formerly numerous staff Marlowe was writing for Pembroke's men, Kyd and Peele for Lord Strange's, Lodge was abroad, Wilson had left them, and Greene had also quitted them for the Earl of Sussex'. Besides the plays above enumerated, Lord Strange's players acted a dozen others of which only the titles are known, and produced as new plays the following :—On March 3, *Henry VI.* (a re-fashioning by Shakespeare of an old Queen's play, into which he introduced the Talbot scenes, celebrated by Nash, which drew such crowded audiences); on April 11, *Titus and Vespasian* (a version of the Andronicus story extant in a German translation, and probably written by Kyd; on April 28, the second part of *Tamburlane* (not

HIS PUBLIC CAREER.

extant); on June 10, *A Merry Knack to Know a Knave* (probably by Peele and Wilson); and after an interval, during which the theatres were closed on account of the plague, on 5th January 1592-3, *The Jealous Comedy* (probably *The Merry Wives of Windsor*); and finally, January 30, *The Guise* (Marlowe's *Massacre of Paris*).

I have brought together this enumeration of the new plays of Strange's men that the reader may better appreciate the often quoted but sadly misunderstood address by Greene to his fellow-dramatists in his *Groatsworth of Wit*, not published till September after its author's death, but manifestly written and probably circulated in manuscript in the early months of 1592. Its aim is directed against a company of players, "burs, puppets, antics, apes, grooms, painted monsters, peasants," among whom is "an upstart crow, a Johannes Factotum, a Shakescene," who supposes he can bombast out a blank verse. This is palpably directed against Shakespeare and Lord Strange's players, for whom he was then writing and with whom he was then acting. But Greene also says that they had all been beholding to him and to his fellow writers whom he addresses; that is, to Marlowe, Peele, "young Juvenal" (Lodge), and two more (Kyd and Wilson) "that both have writ," whom he might "insert against these buckram gentlemen." This can only apply to the Queen's players, for which company alone Greene had written up to 1591, having supplied them with a play every quarter and purveyed more plays for them than other four (Marlowe, Peele, Kyd, and Lodge), as Nash tells us in his *Piers Penniless*. There must then have been an amalgamation of the better portions of the two companies, the Queen's and Lord Strange's, just before the opening of the Rose Theatre, a conclusion confirmed by the fact that the Queen's plays had passed into the hands of the other company, and, as will be seen when I treat of the Henry VI. plays, deduced by me on other and independent grounds. This attack of Greene's was, I think, answered by Shakespeare in his *Midsummer Night's Dream*, produced in its first form c. June 1592. Bottom and his scratch company have long been recognised as a personal satire, and the following marks would seem to indicate that Greene and the Sussex' company were the butts at which it was aimed. Bottom is a Johannes Factotum who expects a pension for his playing; his comrades are unlettered rustics who once obtain an audience at Theseus' court. The Earl of Sussex' men were so inferior a company that they acted at Court but once, viz., in January 1591–2, and the only new

HIS PUBLIC CAREER.   19

play which can be traced to them at this date is *George a Greene*, in which Greene acted the part of the Pinner himself. This only shows that the circumstances of the fictitious and real events are not discrepant; but when we find Bottom saying that he will get a ballad written on his adventure, and "it shall be called Bottom's Dream, because it hath no bottom" (iv. i. 212) and that peradventure he shall "sing it at her (?) death," we surely may infer an allusion to Greene's *Maiden's Dream* (S. R. 6th December 1591), apparently so called because it hath no maiden in it, and sung at the death of Sir Christopher Hatton. This play of *Midsummer Night's Dream* was produced after the closing of the theatres, c. 12th June 1592, on account of the plague; it and the *Jealous Comedy*, produced 5th January 1592–3, when the theatres reopened for that month only, were almost the last in which Shakespeare worked as a journeyman or with a coadjutor. When he revived these earlier plays for the Chamberlain's men he carefully replaced in almost every instance the work of his quondam companions by other and certainly not weaker lines of his own. Some of his own work of this date, apparently left unfinished on account of the sudden closure of the playhouses, he appears to have taken up and completed in his 1601–2 plays. But no doubt the greater part of this autumn was occupied in writing *Venus and Adonis*, dedicated to Lord Southampton (S. R. 18th April 1593) as "the first heir of his invention," a product of "idle hours:" idle because during the plague no new plays were required of him, nor even rehearsals; the players travelled and acted old plays only. In these circuits a whole company did not usually journey together; it was more profitable to separate into parties of half-a-dozen, and of course to cut down their plays so as to be capable of representation by this small body of actors. One part of Lord Strange's men, consisting of Alleyn, Pope, Bryan, Hemings, Phillips, and Kempe, so travelled in 1593; but no document has been preserved respecting the remainder of the company, which included probably Burbadge, Sly, Condell, Holland, Cowley, and Shakespeare. It appears from Alleyn's correspondence that Cowley was the bearer of a letter to him from London to Bristol; that his section of the company had been at Chelmsford in May, were at Bristol in August, and afterwards visited Shrewsbury, Chester, and York. Meanwhile, on June 1, Marlowe had been killed in a brawl, and his version of the Andronicus story was acted by Sussex' men at the Rose, 23d January 1594. From their hands this play passed to Pembroke's

HIS PUBLIC CAREER.

men c. 8th February, when Sussex' company broke up and went into the country, and from them to the Earl of Derby's before 16th April. But this company of Derby's was no other than Lord Strange's. After Henry Earl of Derby died, 25th September 1593, Ferdinand, his son, who succeeded him, and who had previously borne the title of Lord Strange, was called either Strange or Derby indifferently, he having no son to whom the title of Lord Strange could be, in accordance with custom, assigned in courtesy, although by strict right this title appertained to the Earls of Derby and not to their sons. Along with this Andronicus play the following can be traced as passing from Pembroke's company to Lord Strange's at this date: *The Taming of a Shrew, Edward III., Hamlet, 3 Henry VI.;* and besides this transfer of playbooks there was also a partial transfer of the company itself. Beeston, Cooke, Sinkler, Holland, and others were among these new members. The cause of this arrangement was no doubt poverty; already on 28th September 1593 they could not "save their charges to travel, and were fain to pawn their apparel." So writes Henslowe to Alleyn.

I must now recur to 1593. Immediately after Christmas the theatres reopened; but at the Rose the Earl of Sussex' men acted instead of Lord

Strange's, who played about the city, at the Cross-Keys for example. When Sussex' men broke up, on the 8th April, the Rose remained empty except for three days, 14–16th May, when the Admiral's company acted there, no doubt under Alleyn, who was servant to the Admiral as well as to Lord Strange. The Admiral, however, had himself laid a restraint on the Rose theatre (probably c. 8th April), and ordered that Lord Strange's players should play "three days" (*i.e.*, three days a week) at Newington Butts. This was petitioned against by the watermen, whose calling was greatly in request when the Rose was open, and by Lord Strange's players themselves. No redress appears to have been granted during the life of Lord Strange, who died on 16th April, but when the company had found a new patron in Lord Hunsdon the Chamberlain, and had submitted to the order by playing on alternate days with the Admiral's at Newington Butts, then the restraint on the Rose was removed. The Chamberlain's players, however, did not act there, but under Shakespeare and Burbadge reopened the old Theater, while Alleyn left them and acted with the Admiral's at the Rose.

Before passing to notice the poems written by Shakespeare during this period of "travelling," I may note that these plays acquired from Pembroke's men appear to have been written by Marlowe or Kyd. *Edward III.*, by Marlowe, was, with alterations by Shakespeare, acted about the city in 1594. *Titus Andronicus* and *3 Henry VI.* were also acted by the Chamberlain's company; but they show no evidence of extensive alterations at Shakespeare's hand; he probably merely corrected them. Another play of this date, *Richard III.*, bears strong internal evidence of Marlowe's craftmanship, but was no doubt completed and partly rewritten by Shakespeare. The Kyd plays, on the other hand, were not utilised in this way. New plays on the same plots as the old *Hamlet* and *The Taming of a Shrew* were afterwards produced by the Chamberlain's men—*Hamlet* by Shakespeare, *The Taming of the Shrew* by Lodge (most likely), but greatly altered by Shakespeare some years after. Another play performed by Derby's men contemporaneously with these was *The Seven Deadly Sins*. This play had not been derived from Pembroke's men, but from the Queen's, for whom Tarleton had originally plotted it. The plot as acted in 1594 still exists, and is especially valuable as showing the composition of Lord Strange's company at that date. Shakespeare, however, took no part in it. The large number of performers singularly agrees with the statement in the players'· petition above alluded to that "our company is great." There was also a play *Locrine*, published S. R. 20th July 1594, as revised by W. S., which has been interpreted William Shakespeare. I do not think he could in any way have been concerned in this revival of Peele and Tilney's stilted performance, and suspect that W. S. means William Sly; nor do I think that any other play of Shakespeare's, save those already mentioned, can be assigned to a date anterior to the formation of the Chamberlain's company except *Troylus and Cressida* in its original form, which was probably acted c. 1593. In fact, Shakespeare was from the breaking out of the plague in 1592 until the settlement of his reconstituted company in 1594 chiefly occupied, not with plays, but with poems. His *Venus and Adonis* has already been noticed, and on 9th May 1594 his *Rape of Lucrece* was published. In the Dedication to Lord Southampton, Shakespeare speaks of "the warrant I have of your honourable disposition:" in what especial way Southampton had shown his favour to Shakespeare has been the subject of many conjectures. My own opinion is that he had introduced him as representative of his fellow-actors to Lord Hunsdon, and procured them their new patron; but in a scandalous book called *Willobie his Avisa*, published 3d September 1594, the version of the connection between the nobleman and the "old player" is that W. S. had parted with a mistress to H. W. and been rewarded accordingly; and it would be useless to deny that the *Sonnets* written between 1594 and 1598 distinctly allude to some circumstance of this kind. The *Avisa* book was, however, suppressed or "called in" on 4th June 1599, as a libellous production.

This year may be regarded as the turning-point in Shakespeare's public career. Until the establishment of the Chamberlain's company, he had been an actor gradually rising in the esteem of his fellows, but often obliged to travel and to act about town in inn-yards, and his play-writing had been confined to vamping old plays by other men, or at best to assisting such writers as Wilson or Peele in producing new ones. He had served, as it were, a seven years' apprenticeship. But henceforward he takes his place as one of the chief actors in the principal company in London, acting in a licensed theatre; he is also, with occasional assistance, the sole purveyor of plays to this company, and he is the acknowledged writer of the most popular love poems of his time. For it is to the author of *Lucrece* and *Adonis* that his contemporaries assign their praises far more than to the writer of *Lear* or *Hamlet*. Poems were in their opinion fit work for a prince; but plays were only congruous with strolling vagabondism. It is just at this turning-point that the first nominal mention of Shakespeare is found as acting before the Court at Greenwich on December 26 and 28, along with Kempe and Burbadge.

The performance on 26th December was on the same day that Shakespeare and his company had acted *The Comedy of Errors* at Gray's Inn—the earliest of his plays in their present form, but founded on a previous version, in which another pen was concerned.

On 26th January 1594-5, *Midsummer Night's Dream* was, I conjecture, acted at Greenwich at the marriage of W. Stanley, Earl of Derby, and afterwards on the public stage; it was evidently written for a marriage, but, like the preceding play, had been altered for this special occasion. Its original production was probably in 1592, at the marriage of Robert Carey, afterwards Earl of Monmouth. In both instances the bridegrooms were close connections of the patrons of the actors; W. Stanley being brother to Ferdinand, Lord Strange, and Robert Carey son to Henry, Lord Hunsdon, the Chamberlain. Another 1595 play was *Richard II.*, evidently an imitation of Marlowe's *Edward II.*

Marlowe was Shakespeare's first model in Historical Plays, as Kyd was in Tragedy and Lyly in

HIS PUBLIC CAREER.

Comedy, but he followed Marlowe much more closely than either of the other two. If any other author contributed plays to the Chamberlain's company this year it must have been Lodge, to whom *Mucedorus* and *A Larum for London* may probably be attributed. At Christmas they acted five plays at Court.

In 1596, there is little doubt that Shakespeare produced his *King John*, founded on two old plays on the same subject which were written for the Queen's men in 1589 by Peele, Marlowe, and Lodge. Their plot has been very closely followed by Shakespeare and a few lines borrowed. At some time between 23d July 1596 and 5th March 1597 he also revived *Romeo and Juliet*, at the Theater; this new version was founded on the old play of 1591, in which Shakespeare was only part writer. Of plays by other authors only one can be traced to his company in this year, namely, *Sir Thomas More* (? by Drayton and Lodge). This play was severely handled by the Master of the Revels for its allusions to contemporary events, and the alterations made by him afford instructive study to dramatic critics. On August 5, immediately after the appearance of *Romeo and Juliet*, a ballad on the story was entered S. R., and on August 27, T. Millington was fined for printing ballads on *The Taming of a Shrew* and *Macbeth*. This indicates the existence of a Macbeth play at this time, but probably, like the older *Hamlet* and *Lear*, one in whose production Shakespeare had no share. Kempe mentions the Macbeth ballad as the first production of its author in his *Nine Days' Wonder*. In February this same year James Burbadge bought the property in Blackfriars, on which he began in November to build the Blackfriars Theatre, wherein in 1597, after some opposition, he succeeded in establishing the Chapel children under Evans. The Chamberlain's company did not act at this theatre in Shakespeare's time. There were six Court performances at Christmas 1596–7.

It is necessary now to recur to Shakespeare's private life. On 5th August 1596 his son Hamnet died, and he unquestionably visited Stratford and renewed relations with his family at this time. John Shakespeare having applied to the Heralds' College for a grant of arms, obtained this concession in October, and in the Easter term 1597 William Shakespeare purchased the property called New Place in Stratford. In November 1597 the Asbies business was revived in a Chancery suit brought by Shakespeare's parents against John Lambert, son of Edmond. In the bill of complaint the Shakespeares describe themselves as "of small wealth, and very few friends;" but it is clear that their wealth must have had a recent accession, or they would not now have renewed a dispute which, on their own statement, had lain in abeyance since 1580. All these proceedings alike, the acquisition of a residence in Stratford, the obtaining a grant of arms, the endeavour to establish old claims to family property, point to Shakespeare's desire, now that he had succeeded in London and made money, to settle in Stratford as a country gentleman, and found a family. He may have hoped for the birth of another son, his wife being in 1596 still under forty years of age. But the inferences usually drawn from the incidents of this time, that Shakespeare had constantly held communication with his family, whom he had supported during his theatrical career in London, and that he was, on this occasion, largely indebted to the bounty of Lord Southampton, are mere fancies. The natural interpretation of such records as have reached us is that it was not till touched by the hand of the great reconciler Death, in the person of the expected heir to his new-founded fortunes, that he ever visited his family at all during the nine years since he left them to carve his own way as a strolling player. If conjecture is to be allowed at all, I would rather suggest that his family were offended at his choice of an occupation, and that it was not till he had made a marked success that they were reconciled to him.

Returning to Shakespeare's public career—on 5th March 1597 George Carey, Lord Hunsdon, was created Chamberlain, and his players resumed the title of "The Lord Chamberlain's." Early in this year was almost certainly produced *The Merchant of Venice*, founded on an old play of Dekker's called *Joseph the Jew of Venice*, written c. 1592, and acted in 1594 by the Admiral's men, but not now extant. In the same year was performed *1 Henry IV*. The comic powers of Shakespeare appear in these plays in their highest development in Shylock and Falstaff, and endeavours have been made by several (myself included) to mark this as the beginning of a new period in his manner of work. In such attempts, however, it is necessary to assign specific single dates to each play, and consequently to neglect the proved fact of frequent alterations of considerable extent having been made at revivals. I think it better to regard as Shakespeare's first period the time anterior to the formation of the Chamberlain's company, 1587–93, during which he was employed only as "journeyman or coadjutor," and not to separate the series of Comedies and

HIS PUBLIC CAREER. 31

Histories which were produced in their perfected forms from 1594 to 1602. It may, however, be noted that at this time, 1597, he had entirely discarded the doggerel couplets and the excessive use of rhyme that mark his early work, and that this fact is useful in analysing plays which, though produced later in the form in which they have reached us, were founded on earlier versions in which he was probably only a part writer. Another play acted by Shakespeare's company this year was Drayton's *Merry Devil of Edmonton*. In this, as well as in *Henry IV.*, Sir John Oldcastle was originally one of the characters. This name was adopted from the old Queen's play of *The Famous Victories of Henry V.*, from which the main plot of Shakespeare's Henry V. series was taken, and certainly was not intended to give offence to the Cobhams, his descendants. They took offence, however, and the name was altered to that of Sir John Falstaff, taken from another Queen's play, *1 Henry VI.*, which I have already noticed, and which, with the addition of the scene of the Temple Garden, was acted by the Chamberlain's company.

Between August and October, the Theater having become ruinous, and litigation between James Burbadge, its lessee, and Giles Alleyn, the ground landlord, being imminent, the Chamberlain's company removed to the Curtain. The Earl of Pembroke's company, who have for controversial purposes been unjustifiably confused with the Chamberlain's, in August acted as strollers at Rye, in September at Dover, and on their return to London amalgamated with the Admiral's, and acted at the Rose. Among the plays acted by Shakespeare's company at the Curtain was *Romeo and Juliet*, as appears from a singular allusion in Marston's *Satires*, which also serves to show that this play then, as now, was one of the most popular of his productions. But his popularity is shown in another way this year. Coincidently with the removal to the Curtain, we find the first appearance of authorised publication of his plays, *Richard II.* having been entered S. R. on 29th August, and *Richard III.* on 20th October. The *Romeo and Juliet* printed this year was neither entered nor authorised. On 26th December *Love's Labour's Lost* was acted at Court, being one of four plays provided for the Christmas festivities by this company. It was probably specially commanded, and the alterations from the 1589 version, which were very hurriedly done, were almost certainly made on this occasion.

On 25th February 1598, the first part of *Henry IV.* was printed, and the second part was acted

HIS PUBLIC CAREER.   33

soon after. The popularity of these plays caused a re-issue in this year of the old Queen's play of *The Famous Victories of Henry V.*, brought out in order that the purchaser might imagine he was procuring a copy of Shakespeare's plays. The genuine *Henry IV.*, for this and reasons alluded to above connected with the elimination of Oldcastle's name, was published earlier after its production on the stage than usual. For the same reason this alteration was expressly alluded to in the Epilogue to *2 Henry IV.*, "Oldcastle is not the man." In this same year *Much Ado about Nothing* (probably a recast of *Love's Labour's Won*) was performed. On 7th September was entered S. R., Meres' *Wit's Treasury*, which contains, among many encomiums of Shakespeare, a list of twelve of his plays. This tract was demonstrably not written till June, and the plays are manifestly those that had been produced by Shakespeare during the existence of the Chamberlain's company. These are: *Gentlemen of Verona* (1595), *Errors* (1594), *Love's Labour's Lost* (1597), *Love's Labour's Won* (1598), *Midsummer Night's Dream* (1595), and *Merchant of Venice* (1597); *Richard II.* (1595), *Richard III.* (1594), *Henry IV.* (1597), *King John* (1596), *Titus Andronicus* (1594), and *Romeo and Juliet* (1596). Plays produced before or in 1594 that had not been recast after that

c

year are not mentioned; for instance, *1 Henry VI.* (1592), *Troylus and Cressida* (1593), *The Merry Wives of Windsor* (1592), and *Edward III.* (1594). This list is of the highest value, when rightly understood, in determining the order of production of the plays. Another event, important to the welfare of the Chamberlain's company, was the introduction of Ben Jonson as a play-writer for their stage. This took place in September, and there is no reason for doubting the tradition that he was introduced to them by Shakespeare, who acted in *Every Man in his Humour,* as it was published in the Quarto, before the end of the year. The fact that the Chamberlain's men acted three plays at Court during the Christmas festivities, closes the theatrical record for 1598, but one or two other details remain to be noticed. The establishment of peace on May 2 by the treaty of Vervins, compared with *Sonnet* 107, "olives of endless age," fixes the conclusion of these effusions as about this time, and Southampton's marriage at the end of the year precluded the need of their continuance. They probably were finished before Meres' mention of them in *Wit's Treasury* (written c. July) as Shakespeare's "sugared sonnets among his private friends." Little details of evidence are also extant, showing that since his purchase of New Place,

Shakespeare's residence was partly in the country. On 4th February he appears as third largest owner of corn in his ward at Stratford, and in October we find him procuring a loan of £30 in London, for his friend and countryman Richard Quiney. His London residence at this time was in St. Helen's, Bishopsgate; but still earlier than this, on 24th January, he was in negotiation about the purchase of some thirty acres of land at Shottery, and Abraham Sturley wrote from Stratford to his brother-in-law, the same Richard Quiney, urging him to suggest to Shakespeare the purchase of the corporation tithe-lease; it "would advance him indeed, and would do us much good," says Sturley.

In January 1598-9 James Burbadge brought his dispute with Giles Alleyn about the Theater to a practical conclusion by removing the materials of that structure from Shoreditch to the Bankside, and erecting the Globe with them. This "round" was opened in the spring, and in it all the plays of Shakespeare not hitherto noticed were originally produced. Before quitting the Curtain, however, *A Warning for Fair Women* was there acted by the Chamberlain's men. This was in my opinion Lodge's last play. Another play of the same date was Shakespeare's *Henry V.*, reproduced, with additions and alterations, at the Globe in the autumn of the same year. Other Globe plays of this year were *As You Like It*, and Jonson's *Every Man out of his Humour*. This latter was the first of his comical satires, in which he introduces on the stage Marston, Dekker, Monday, the Globe players, &c. Only this one was acted by Shakespeare's company, and it is specially remarkable that Shakespeare did not take a part in it, although he had acted in *Every Man in his Humour* in 1598. It is pretty clear that he disliked Jonson's personalities, and it is certain that Jonson had to remove them from the Globe Theatre to the Blackfriars, where the Children of the Revels acted under Evans *The Case is Altered* (1599), *Cynthia's Revels* (1600), and *The Poetaster* (1601). Chapman supported Johnson with *Sir Giles Goosecap* (1601). The Paul's Children retaliated with Marston's *Jack Drum's Entertainment* (1600), and *Antonio and Mellida* (1600); the Admiral's at the Rose with Marston's *Histriomastix*, and *Patient Grissel* by Dekker, Haughton, and Chettle (December 1599); and the Chamberlain's with Dekker's *Satiromastix* (1601). All these plays, and the list is not exhaustive, are filled with personal allusions. The quarrel was known as the "War of the theatres." The prevalent dislike to regard Shakespeare as less than angelic has prevented due attention being given to the direct state-

HIS PUBLIC CAREER. 37

ment in *The Return from Parnassus* (acted 1602–3) that he had put down all the playwrights of the University press and administered a purge to Jonson in return for the emetic which he administers to Marston in *The Poetaster*. Shakespeare certainly did take part in this controversy, and it is in the plays dating 1599–1602 that we must look for his contributions to it. One thing, however, is certain, that he did not act as a violent partisan. If he purged Jonson he did not spare Dekker, who had written for his own company in this quarrel; "when rank Thersites opes his Mastick jaws" (*Troylus*, i. 3) identifies him clearly enough. In fact, when the Globe company wanted a thorough party advocate in this matter it was not to Shakespeare that they applied. They took the very unusual course of hiring a poet from a rival company, and hence Dekker's *Satiromastix* was written for them. I venture to add that this would not have been allowed by Shakespeare had he been in London at the time, and that it had to be transferred to the sole use of the Paul's children, probably at his instance. Recurring to *Every Man out of his Humour*, the beginning of all this strife, a comparison of the actor list with that of Jonson's preceding play shows that Kempe, Beeston, and others had left the Chamberlain's company on the opening of the Globe. They no doubt remained at the Curtain, where a company called Lord Derby's soon began to act. This secession did not injure the Globe men, who became very popular. In October, for instance, we hear of Lord Southampton going to plays every day, of course at his old player *protégé's* house. But that some serious quarrel had taken place is, I think, evident from the exclusion of so important a name as Beeston's from the list of chief actors in the first Folio edition of Shakespeare. Duke, Pallant, &c., who seceded at the same time with Beeston, are equally excluded, so that the omission is not accidental.

In this year a perfect edition of *Romeo and Juliet* was published, probably on leaving the Curtain; and *The Passionate Pilgrim* was impudently issued by W. Jaggard as by William Shakespeare. Beyond two sonnets and a few lines from *Love's Labour's Lost*, published in 1598, there is nothing in this book that can be shown to be Shakespeare's, but much that cannot. Somewhere about this date an unsuccessful application was made to impale the arms of Shakespeare with those of Arden. The Chamberlain's men performed three plays at Court during the Christmas festivities, viz.: on 26th December, probably *As You Like It;* 5th January, probably *Henry V.;* and another play on 4th Feb-

HIS PUBLIC CAREER. 39

ruary. I think this was the occasion for which *The Merry Wives of Windsor* was written, or rather rewritten on the foundation of *The Jealous Comedy* of 1592. The Queen, whose admiration for the character of Falstaff is well known, was sorely disappointed that Shakespeare had not fulfilled his promise made in the Epilogue to *2 Henry IV.*, that he would again introduce him on the stage; and there is no reason to doubt the tradition that, wishing to see him under new conditions, she ordered Shakespeare to represent him in love, which order he obeyed by writing *The Merry Wives* within a fortnight. The dates all suit this hypothesis, and in any case there can be no doubt that this comedy stands apart from the Henry V. histories, and was last in point of time. Another play of this year was *Julius Cæsar*. There is no evidence of any other writer than Shakespeare for the company this year, in which the *2* and *3 Henry VI.* (alluded to as recast in Jonson's Prologue to his revised version of *Every Man in his Humour*, acted by the Chapel children early in 1601) were revised and partly rewritten by him. As usual in such cases, the old abridged acting copies of the plays in their earlier shape were reprinted. But there is more interesting matter connected with the publishers in the 1600 entries. On August 4, *As You Like It*,

Henry V., Much Ado about Nothing, and *Every Man in his Humour*, all Chamberlain's plays, were ordered to be "stayed;" they were probably suspected of being libellous, and reserved for further examination. Since the "war of the theatres" was at its height, they may have been restrained as not having obtained the consent of the Chamberlain, on behalf of his company, to their publication. Subsequently, *Every Man in his Humour* was licensed on 14th August, but not printed till 1601. *Much Ado* was also licensed 23d August, and printed; *As You Like It* was not allowed to appear, the company probably objecting that it had only been on the stage for one year, but *Henry V.* was printed surreptitiously by T. Millington and T. Busby before 14th August, on which date it appears in S. R. as the property of T. Pavier, who reprinted it in 1602. The peculiarity of this Quarto issue is, that it contains no matter which does not also appear in the complete Folio version, whereas, in the somewhat similar cases of *Romeo and Juliet*, *The Merry Wives*, and *Hamlet*, there is in every instance some portion of the Quarto which is palpably by another hand. This agrees with my view that these three plays, as in the Folio, were founded on earlier plays, in which Shakespeare was at most a coadjutor, while the Folio

Henry V. is a revision of his own play, produced not long before. Another entry in S. R. is interesting. On October 28, *The Merchant of Venice* was entered to T. Hayes, with Pavier's consent; Roberts had already entered it 22d July 1598, but it had not been allowed to appear, probably because, like those mentioned above, it had then been only one year on the stage. On October 8, *Midsummer Night's Dream* was also entered. Of the editions of these two plays published in this year information will be found in another part of this book. On 11th August the two plays on *Sir John Oldcastle*, of which only one has reached us, were entered. They had been acted in 1599 at the Rose by the Admiral's men, and were directed against the presumed scandal thrown on the "martyr" in Shakespeare's Henry V. series. It should be especially noted that the principal author of these plays was Drayton, formerly fellow-worker with Shakespeare for the Chamberlain's men, and introducer of *Sir John Oldcastle* as a profligate parson in *The Merry Devil of Edmonton*. Of Shakespeare's personal movements during this year we merely know that he was in London in April recovering a debt of £7 of one Clayton, and no doubt acting in the three plays performed at Court in the winter.

In March 1601 the Chamberlain's company were

in disgrace for having publicly acted "the outdated play of *Richard II.*," no doubt inclusive of the deposition scene (which had been omitted in the published copies, under the censorship of the Master of the Revels), for the entertainment of the Essex conspirators. They consequently "travelled," having previously produced Shakespeare's *All's Well that Ends Well*, a considerable portion of which is of much earlier date (c. 1592), but which, in the Parolles scenes, has distinct allusion to Marston's *Jack Drum's Entertainment* of the preceding year, and to the "war of the theatres," not yet concluded. They also acted the play of *Cromwell*, Earl of Essex, by W. S., in which the parallel between the careers of Cromwell and the lately executed Earl is strongly brought out. I believe W. S. to have been William Sly, the well-known actor of the Chamberlain's company. In their travels this year the company visited the Universities of Oxford and Cambridge, where they performed *Julius Cæsar* and *Hamlet*. The version of this last play so acted was not the old play by Kyd, but one hurriedly remodelled by Shakespeare, which we possess in an imperfect form in the first Quarto. Among the Shakespearian additions occur passages alluding to the theatrical war and the popularity of the Chapel Children, to which the travelling of the company

HIS PUBLIC CAREER. 43

is attributed. This proves that Shakespeare was one of the strolling detachment. Jonson seized on this defence in his *Poetaster*, and represented that the travelling was due to the inefficiency of their play-writers, and makes Tucca tell Histrio, the Globe player, that if they will employ Marston, who "pens high lofty in a new stalking strain," they "shall not need to travel with thy pumps full of gravel after a blind jade and a hamper, and stalk upon boards and barrel-heads to an old cracked trumpet." The travels, however, were not confined to England. In October they had reached Aberdeen, where they received the title of "the King's Servants," and Laurence Fletcher, their manager, was admitted burgess of guild of the borough. In all probability a version of the old *Macbeth* play was produced before King James—such a version as that of *Hamlet* acted at the Universities. Its plot would fit more aptly with the circumstances of the Gowry conspiracy of 1600 than that of *Richard II.* would with Essex, and anything more pleasing to the King and people of Scotland could not have been selected. During the absence of this strolling detachment Jonson's *Poetaster* was produced, containing a vigorous attack on the Globe company; and they, in Shakespeare's absence, hired Dekker to reply in his *Satiromastix*, which, with the aid of the Paul's children, they represented in the public theatre of the Globe, and in the private convocation-room of Paul's. During this same absence, on 8th September Shakespeare's father was buried at Stratford. He apparently died intestate. After the return from Scotland, the appearance of Shakespeare's name, as fellow-contributor to Chester's *Love's Martyr* with Jonson, Marston, and Chapman, marks the conclusion of the theatrical quarrel, and the reconciliation of all the principal combatants, except Dekker. But although this book bears the date 1601, it could not, I think, have been issued earlier than March 1601-2, after the production of *Twelfth Night* on February 2 at the Middle Temple. Such presentations as this at Inns of Court were usually of new plays; and there is in this play fairly conclusive internal evidence that the theatrical quarrel was not over when it was acted. With regard to Shakespeare's other play of this year, *Troylus and Cressida*, it was as clearly produced after the reconciliation. ' The entry in S. R., " as it *is* acted by the Lord Chamberlain's men," is absolutely conclusive that it was still on the stage on 1st February 1602-3, and was therefore produced, in all probability, in the later half of 1602. In this play the Prologue, the love story of Troylus, and all the scenes after v. 4, are taken from the old play of c. 1593, in which Shakespeare only wrote as a coadjutor. The Prologue and the later scenes—v. 5–10—are manifestly by the second pen in the main, and printed by mistake, the end of the revised version being shown by the repetition of the lines "Why, but hear you," &c., at the end of v. 3. That the 1602 version of the play was intended to refer to the theatrical quarrel of 1599–1602 is clear from the line "*Rank* Thersites with his *mastick* tooth," who is evidently Dekker, of whom Jonson says in the *Poetaster* (iii. 1), "He has one of the most overflowing *rank* wits in Rome; he will slander any man that breathes if he disgust him." Dekker had produced the *Satiro*MASTIX shortly before *Troylus* was acted; and it has been noted that he was not one of the contributors to Chester's *Martyr*. I believe the Troylus play to have been the one in which Shakespeare put down all the University men, and purged Ben Jonson's pride, as we learn that he did from the University play of *The Return from Parnassus*, acted in January 1602–3; the character of Ajax, "*Slow* as the elephant, into whom nature hath so crowded *humours*," &c. (i. 2), hits off Jonson exactly, and is a good-humoured reply to Jonson's self-estimate as Crites in *Cynthia's Revels* (ii. 1), "A creature of a most divine temper, one in whom the elements and *humours* are peaceably met," &c.

In May 1602 Gilbert Shakespeare (his brother being probably in London) concluded the purchase on his behalf of 107 acres of land in Old Stratford, bought of the Coombes for £320, and on 28th September Walter Getley transferred to him (not in person), at a Court Baron of the Manor of Rowington, a cottage and garden in Chapel Lane. The lady of the manor retained possession until personal completion of the purchase. The Chamberlain's company were re-admitted to act at Court in the winter, not having performed there in 1601–2, probably on account of the *Richard II.* affair. They acted, however, only two plays. In the following March, 1603, Shakespeare remodelled *The Taming of the Shrew* by the rewriting of the Katherine and Petruchio scene. The play before he altered it was one written, I think, by Lodge about 1596, and founded on the old Kyd play of 1589 acted by Pembroke's men. On March 29 Queen Elizabeth died, and whether it be due to the different requirements of the new Court, or to a natural development of Shakespeare's mind, there can be no doubt that a marked change of style and method took place at this epoch in his work. It should not be forgotten that the primary object for which theatres were established was that stage-players "might be the better enabled and prepared to show such plays to her [or his] Majesty as they shall be required," and that the "honest recreation" of the citizens was a secondary matter. For proof of this see the Privy Council documents quoted by Collier in his *Annals, passim,* and specially in i. 309. Hence the succession of a new sovereign had greater influence on the tone of the drama than we can well realise. In Shakespeare's case it inaugurated a period in which Tragedy was predominant in place of Comedy and History. All his greatest tragedies were produced during the next four years 1603-6.

Before quitting the reign of Elizabeth, I call attention to the significant fact that the Chamberlain's company performed at Court before the accession of James exactly twenty-eight plays, and that the number of Shakespeare's plays known to have been produced during the same period by that company is twenty, and of other men's eight. I do not press this exact agreement as showing absolute identity between the two lists; one or two of the Court plays may have been merely revivals, one or two of the stage plays may not have been brought before her Majesty at all, but I think the following inferences justifiable. The Queen, evidently as a general rule, only allowed new plays, or plays so largely reconstructed as to be reckoned as new, to be presented to her. So far as the Chamberlain's company were concerned, these plays consisted on an average of two of Shakespeare's and one of another author's—these numbers, however, being rather exceeded in the earlier years, and diminished in the later. Shakespeare consequently was to this company in the same position as Greene to the Queen's men before his time, purveying to their use "more than four other," which explains his rapid advance in popularity and accumulation of property. And finally, the number of plays supposed to have been lost has been grossly exaggerated by modern critics, who have based their calculations on the Diary of Henslowe, whose policy was quantity rather than quality, and who was continually deceived by his hack-writers presenting to his illiterate ignorance old plays new vamped as if they were completely new.

In 1603 the plague raged in London. In March before the Queen's death, the theatres were closed, and in the license of May 19, which adopted the Chamberlain's men as the King's Servants (a title already conferred on them in Scotland in 1601), a special clause was inserted allowing them to act "when the infection of the plague shall decrease."

HIS PUBLIC CAREER.   49

The infection did not decrease, yet the theatres were reopened, but probably only for a few days. Doubtless the authorities closed them on account of the continuance of the sickness. The plays acted at this reopening were probably *The Miseries of Enforced Marriage*, by George Wilkins, a new author, which was founded on contemporaneous events in Yorkshire, and certainly the perfected *Hamlet* as we now have it in the Folio. The older version, which had been entered S. R. on 26th July 1602, was now published, having probably been "stayed," as was frequently the case with plays printed by J. Roberts (for example *The Merchant of Venice, Troylus and Cressida*), but not till the copyright had been transferred to N. Ling and J. Trundell. In 1604 Ling issued the second Quarto, which in some instances supplies passages omitted in the Folio for stage purposes, and in others presents alternative versions and additions evidently made for the Court performance (one of nine) in the winter 1603-4. It was a common practice to utilise the altered copies of plays acted at Court by allowing their publication. Yet another play acted by the King's men this year was Jonson's *Sejanus*, for which he was accused of Popery and treason by Northampton. When he published it (2d November 1604, S. R.), he stated that "this book in all numbers is not the same with that which was acted on the public stage; wherein a second pen had good share: in place of which I have rather chosen to put weaker, and no doubt less pleasing of mine own, than to defraud so happy a genius of his right by my loathed usurpation." The only known writers for the King's men at this date were Wilkins, W. S. (? Sly), Shakespeare, and possibly Tourneur. Of these there can be no doubt that Shakespeare is the only one that could have been the second pen alluded to. Not that necessarily he was a coadjutor to Jonson in this play. It is more likely that as he acted one of the principal parts in it he inserted or altered scenes in which he himself appeared. It is clear that "the second pen," whoever he was, objected to his share in the play being published, and no wonder, seeing how its main author had been accused on account of it. This probably explains why the book was kept in the press six months, from November 1604 to April 1605. When it was issued Jonson's *Volpone* was just coming on the stage, and it is noticeable that Shakespeare did not act in that play, and that immediately after Jonson quitted the King's men and joined Chapman and Marston in writing *Eastward Ho* for the Revels children, in which *Hamlet* is ridiculed. All this seems to point to a quarrel between Jonson and Shakespeare, and certainly Jonson's behaviour in the Sejanus matter is not, as Gifford calls it, manly. To drag in unnecessarily an allusion to a friend whose personality must have been known to the public of that time, into an address prefixed to a work accused of Popery and sedition was unmanly; and, as his friend had objected to it, was discreditable. No intercourse can be shown between Shakespeare and Jonson after 1603.

On 30th January 1603–4, the new company of the Revels children replaced the Chapel boys at Blackfriars. They were, however, in the main composed of the same actors, and were not unfrequently mentioned under their old name. On March 15, we find that among the King's train, at his entry into London, were nine of the King's company, dressed in the scarlet cloth allowed for the occasion. As these nine are identical with those in the license of 19th May 1603, which is statedly incomplete, they must have been in some way distinguished from the rest of their fellows. They were, no doubt, shareholders in the Globe. Cooke and Lowin, who acted in *Sejanus* and *Volpone*, do not appear among them; nor do Tooley, Gough, and Sinkler, who were at this time members of the company. The nine were Shakespeare, Phillips, Fletcher, Hemings, Burbadge, Sly, Lowin, Condell, and Cowley. In July, Shakespeare was in Stratford, recovering in the local court some £2 odd for malt, &c., sold to one Rogers. In August he was summoned to London, the King's men having to attend at Somerset House to play at the reception of the Spanish ambassador. During this year he produced *Othello* and *Measure for Measure*, which were acted at Court in the winter festivities, along with five old plays of his, and two of Jonson's. *Hamlet* does not occur in this list, as it undoubtedly would have done if produced in 1604. It was, in fact, published this year as it had been acted at Court in the previous winter. Another play acted by the King's men was Marston's *Malcontent*, with an Induction by Webster, in which the reason of its appearance is explained. The Blackfriars children had acted *Jeronymo* in 1600, an old play of Kyd's, which had passed to the King's men from Lord Strange's, by whom it had been purchased of the Queen's. It had probably been taken from the Chamberlain's men to the Chapel children by Jonson, who in 1601, September 25, transferred it to the Admiral's, and wrote additions to it for Henslowe. This appropriation of their property irritated the Globe players, and when they got the chance, at the reconstitution of the Blackfriars children in 1604, they procured *The Malcontent*, which had been acted by these pigmies, and produced it on their own stage as "one for another." They also in December acted "the tragedy of Gowry with all action and actors," so Chamberlain writes to Winwood, December 18, "with exceeding concourse of all sorts of people," but he adds, "some great councillors are much displeased with it, and so 'tis thought it shall be forbidden." It probably was forbidden, as the play has disappeared. Another mysterious play is *The Spanish Maz*, said to have been one of the eleven performed in the winter at Court. Nothing is known of such a play; but much is known of forgery connected with such statements.

In 1605, the tragedy of *King Lear* was acted about 7th May, when the old *Leir*, on which it was founded, but which was a *comedy*, was entered S. R. as a "*Tragical* History" of Leir, &c., "as it was lately acted." Another play of very dubious authorship was acted by the King's men before 3d July, when the ballad on the same events was entered S. R.; this was *The Yorkshire Tragedy*. It was a continuation of the story of *The Miseries of Enforced Marriage*, but treated more realistically and more powerfully. It was published 2d May 1608 as by Shakespeare, as in 1605 *The London Prodigal* had already been, but in the latter instance the publication was unlicensed and surreptitious, while the *Yorkshire Tragedy* was entered S. R. as "written by William Shakespeare." The entry, however, was made for T. Pavier, an unscrupulous piratic printer, who on other occasions tried to establish rights in "Shakespeare's plays" which were not Shakespeare's; and no weight can be assigned to his assertions. Another play acted by the King's men, in March 1605, was Jonson's *Volpone, or The Fox*. This was anterior in production to the plays already mentioned. Immediately afterwards we find Jonson in connection with the Blackfriars children again, and in prison for writing *Eastward Ho*. Shakespeare did not act in *The Fox;* perhaps Jonson was offended at this; he at any rate did not return to the King's men till 1610. On 4th May, Phillips, Shakespeare's fellow-actor, made his will, and died shortly after. We learn from this document, which gives us many other valuable particulars respecting the members of the company, that Shakespeare and Condell were the two of "his fellows" whom, next to Hemings, Burbadge, and Sly, his executors, Phillips most highly appreciated; he left them each a 30s.-piece in gold, but to Fletcher, Armin, Cowley, Cooke, and Tooley a 20s.-piece. He also left legacies to Gilburne and Sands his apprentices, and to Beeston his servant. "His fellows" here means the shareholders in the Globe, as contrasted with the "hired servants," to whom he left "£5 amongst them." There were then in 1605 eleven shareholders, Cooke and Tooley having been added since 15th March 1604. On 24th July Shakespeare invested £40 in a lease of the tithes of Stratford, Old Stratford, Bishopton, and Welcombe, as had been suggested to him in 1598. In August King James was at Oxford, and among the entertainments presented to him were speeches by three young men of St. John's, who personated the three Sibyls who had prophesied to Banquo. This interlude would necessarily recall to the King's mind the old Macbeth play, which had been probably presented to him in Scotland by the Globe players, and if, as there is little reason to doubt, he did write an autograph letter to Shakespeare, it was most likely on this occasion, commanding a fuller version of *Macbeth*. This play was certainly produced at Court, probably at Shrovetide in March 1605-6, but it has been altered since, condensed and interpolated by dances and songs and a new scene with Hecate in it, no doubt by Middleton in 1622, from whose *Witch* the songs are taken. On 9th October the Globe company acted before the Mayor and Corporation at Oxford, and then, if not from the King, Shakespeare would be sure to hear of the Sybils interlude. In all, ten plays were acted at Court this winter by the Globe company. Among them was a version of *Mucedorus*, with additions. This version has only come down to us in imprints of 1610 and later; but there was an edition in 1606 mentioned in Beauclerc's Catalogue, 1781, from which the later title-pages were copied. From the title it appears that it had been revived before the King on Shrove-Sunday night at Whitehall. The original play had been acted about the city, and therefore not later than 1594, before the Chamberlain's men settled at the Theater. The additions are directed against Jonson, whose strictures on monopolies, and sneer at "the miraculous effects of the Oglio del Scoto" in *Volpone*, ii. 1, must have grievously offended James, who had revived the touching for the king's evil. Jonson had subsequently joined Chapman and Marston in writing *Eastward Ho* for the Chapel boys, in which the Scots were still more severely satirised, and was evidently, as may be seen from the address prefixed to *Volpone*, at daggers drawn with the Globe men. Hence, in the *Mucedorus*

HIS PUBLIC CAREER.

additions, the allusions to the "meagre cannibal," the "scrambling raven with his meagre beard" (certainly Jonson, the "thin-bearded Hermaphrodite" in *Satiromastix*), who had, stirred up by Envy, written a comedy for the Globe filled with "dark sentences pleasing to factious brains;" which would have led to their restraint, as *Eastward Ho* did for the Chapel boys, had not the King's players been staid and discreet, and begged pardon of His Majesty on bended knee "for their unwilling error." The threatened information must have been in the autumn of 1605.

To 1606 no other play than *Macbeth* can with certainty be traced: and the marked change of metrical style at this epoch points to a period of rest. In all his subsequent plays, many lines end with unemphatic words, such as *and, if, which, but* and the like, and this change was not introduced gradually but suddenly and decisively. Hence its value as indisputably separating the Fourth Period plays from the preceding. On this ground it is pretty certain that *Timon* was Shakespeare's next production; he only wrote the chief scenes in it, however, and it was finished for the stage by another hand. At this time also, in my opinion, Shakespeare began to write *Cymbeline*, which he afterwards completed himself. This arrangement of his work seems natural; *Lear, Macbeth, Cymbeline* closing the series founded on Holinshed, and *Timon, Antony, Coriolanus*—the series from Plutarch—succeeding them. A minuter examination of the question will be found in a later part of this work. Of other play-writers' contributions to the Globe in 1606 there is only one—*Pericles*, as originally produced by Wilkins, which was ridiculed in *The Puritan* by Middleton—acted by the Paul's children of this year. Wilkins left writing for the King's men, and (1607) joined the Queen's men at the Curtain. This was probably rumoured to have been caused by some quarrel with Shakespeare, for on 6th August 1607, S. R., *The Puritan Widow* was published as by W. S., evidently meaning William Shakespeare. Of all the instances in which Shakespeare's name or initials were fraudulently inserted on title-pages, this play and *Sir John Oldcastle* were the only two in which they were prefixed to plays not even acted by his company. At the Court in the 1606-7 season three Globe plays were presented to the King of Denmark on the occasion of his visit to England, and nine others in the usual course. *Antony and Cleopatra* may be confidently assigned to 1607. It was entered for publication S. R. on 20th May 1608 with *Pericles* (no doubt as originally written by Wilkins), but both plays were stayed;

the former as having been on the stage only one year, the latter to be superseded by the issue in 1609 of the version as altered by Shakespeare. On 22d October *The Merry Devil of Edmonton* was entered S. R. for A. Johnson. The entry for Hunt and Archer on 5th April 1608 is that of the prose story by Thomas Brewer. The initials T. B. in this latter entry have misled Mr. Halliwell and others to assign the authorship of the play to Tony Brewer. On 26th November Shakespeare's *King Lear* was entered S. R. as it was played before the King on 26th December 1606, " Saint Stephen's Night at Christmas last." This settles two important questions ; first, the relation of the Quarto text to the Folio—the Quarto being the version played at Court, the Folio that retained by the players for the public stage ; secondly, the existence of a custom in the Globe company of allowing, in cases of altered or revised plays, the version not required for future stage purposes to be issued to the public in print. Many instances of this custom are brought to light in the present treatise. On October 7, Cyril Tourneur's (?) *Revenger's Tragedy* was entered S. R. The date of production on the stage is uncertain. It had " been sundry times acted by the King's players." Nor am I aware of the grounds on which the authorship is assigned to Tourneur. It was published anonymously. On 25th June, Susanna, Shakespeare's daughter, married John Hall, M.A., physician at Stratford. There were thirteen performances this winter at Court by the King's men. In 1608 Shakespeare probably produced *Coriolanus*. On 21st February Elizabeth Hall was baptized, within eight months from her parents' marriage. The prospect of a continuation of his family, though not of his family name, was some alleviation for Shakespeare of the loss of his youngest brother Edmund, "a player," buried at St. Saviour's, Southwark, 31st December 1607, "with a forenoon knell of the great bell," *ætatis* 27. Of Edmund's career in London we *know* nothing; but surely he must have belonged to the Globe company. His absence from the actors' lists offers no obstacle to this supposition; they are, after that of *The Seven Deadly Sins* in 1594, confined to names of shareholders and principal actors. And if player for the Globe, why not author? May he not, for instance, have written *The Yorkshire Tragedy* under his brother's superintendence, and may not this account for its being published as William Shakespeare's? All attempts to assign it to any known author have egregiously failed. However this may be, and however poignantly William felt the loss of the

Benjamin of the family, a severer bereavement awaited him in the death of his mother, buried at Stratford 9th September 1608. It has always been a favourite hypothesis with me that Volumnia was drawn from her as a model of matronly virtue, and it is certain that at this date a final change took place in Shakespeare's manner of writing. His plays since the accession of James had been, with scarcely an exception, tragedies; from this time they are really, under whatever head they may have hitherto been classed, tragi-comedies, and all turn, as I pointed out many years ago, on the re-uniting of separated members of families. The first of this final group is *Marina*, the part of *Pericles* which replaced Wilkins' work, and which was written in this winter and hurriedly printed in 1609 as a practical answer to Wilkins' prose version, published in 1608, in which he claimed the story as an "infant of his brain." Shakespeare's version must, I think, be placed after his return to London from Stratford, where he remained after his mother's funeral till 16th October, when he stood godfather for William Walker. The Court performances this winter were twelve. On 28th January 1609, *Troylus and Cressida* was entered S. R., not for Roberts, whose intended publication in 1603 had been stayed, but for Bonian and Whalley, who issued it with a preface stating that it had never been "staled with the stage." This false statement was withdrawn in their subsequent reissue during the same year, but it proves that the period during which the play had been performed in 1602 must have been a very short one; such a statement could not have otherwise been put forward with any plausibility. On 20th May the *Sonnets* were published, with a dedication to their "only begetter," Mr. W. H. ⁂ I think that these initials designate Sir William Hervey, to whom Lord Southampton's mother left at her death in November 1607 the greatest part "of her stuff." He was her third husband, and may have been the original suggester to Shakespeare, as a friend to Lord Southampton, that he should write a series of Sonnets to him recommending marriage in 1594, when Southampton had not yet become devoted to "the fair Mrs. Vernon," and was entangled in the affair of the frail Avisa. In 1609 he was busily occupied with the Virginian company, and promoting voyages for American discovery, an allusion to which underlies the Dedication "wisheth the well-wishing adventurer in setting forth," *adventurer* being the current phrase for explorer of unknown regions. On 7th June Shakespeare's cousin, Thomas Green, then residing at New Place, Stratford, issued a final precept in his behalf against one Hornby, who had become bail for John Addenbroke, in a matter of debt for £6. This litigation had begun in August 1608: juries had been summoned on 21st December and 15th February, and then Addenbroke absconded, leaving Hornby to be answerable. The plague being prevalent this year, there were no Christmas performances at Court, and not many on the public stage. *Cymbeline* was Shakespeare's only production. In its present state it has evidently been subjected to revision and to alteration for some revival after Shakespeare's death, when the doggerel in the vision in iv. 4 was inserted; originally, no doubt, the ghosts appeared in dumb show to music. The Globe players received £30 as a compensation for being restrained from playing in London during six weeks, *i.e.*, during August and September, when the bills of mortality show the plague to have been at its height.

In January 1610 the Revels children left the Blackfriars Theatre, and set up with a new organisation under Rossiter at Whitefriars the new private stage. It appears from the statement of C. Burbadge, in the 1635 documents discovered by Mr. Halliwell, that that family then bought up the remainder of the lease from Evans, and took some of the Revels boys, now grown up, to strengthen the Globe company. Among these were Underwood and Ostler; but as C. Burbadge also names Field, who did not join the King's men till 1615 or 1616, his subsequent statement that they set up men-players, Shakespeare, Hemings, Condell, &c., in Blackfriars *at that date*, is not to be taken as necessarily exact. The King's men undoubtedly took possession of Blackfriars for their own performances in 1614 or 1615, after the Globe had been burned and rebuilt; but there is not a trace of them until then in connection with this private house except this *ex parte* statement of C. Burbadge, made for a special purpose, in a plea which is studiously ambiguous. But there is evidence that other companies acted there. Field's *Amends for Ladies* was performed there by the Lady Elizabeth's company and the Duke of York's (afterwards Prince Charles'). This performance must have taken place during a temporary union between the Prince's men and the Lady Elizabeth's, to which latter the play and its author were properly attached; but that the Duke of York's acted continuously at Blackfriars from 1610 to 1615, is very probable. It is not likely that a company under such patronage, and admitted to Court performances every Christmas, should have been merely a strolling company, and there was no other theatre for them to perform in. The King's men held the Globe, Prince Henry's (afterwards the Palgrave's) the Fortune, the Queen's the Bull and the Curtain, the Queen's Revels' boys Whitefriars, and Lady Elizabeth's at first the Swan till 1612, and after its abandonment the newly renovated Hope in 1614, and then the rebuilt Cockpit or Phœnix. There is no proof that Shakespeare ever acted at Blackfriars; there is strong presumption to the contrary as to his supposed shares in that theatre: it was the "private inheritance" of the Burbadges, and that the King's men had shares in it at this time rests on the evidence of forged documents and mischievously fertile imaginations, to which the purchase of twenty acres of land at Stratford by Shakespeare from the Combes in June seems to require access of capital to make this new acquisition feasible. *Winter's Tale* was certainly produced early this year, before Jonson's *Alchemist*, which was acted and entered S. R., October 3, but was, however, "stayed" for the usual reasons, and did not get published till 1612. The Address to the Reader (no doubt dating 1610) contains one of Jonson's numerous allusions to the "dance of antics" in *Winter's Tale*. Jonson, who had produced *Epicene* for the Chapel children in 1609, had returned to the King's men when the boys left Blackfriars. Shakespeare's last play this year, and final finished contribution to the stage, was *The Tempest*, produced about November, after the news that the ships of Sir T. Gates at the Bermudas had not been destroyed. This play as we have it has unfortunately been abridged for Court performances, probably by Beaumont in 1612 or 1613, to whom the insertion of the Masque may confidently be attributed. There were fifteen winter performances at Court in 1610–11.

The loss of Shakespeare was repaired as well as circumstances would permit by the accession of Beaumont and Fletcher to the King's company in 1611. In that year they produced their masterpieces *Philaster, a King and no King* and *The Maid's Tragedy*: in 1612 *The Woman's Prize* (by Fletcher alone), the play of *Cardenas* (probably the original form of *Love's Pilgrimage*), and *The Captain*. Jonson contributed *Catiline* in 1611, and Webster *The Duchess of Malfi* in 1612. *The Second Maiden's Tragedy* (by the author of *The Revenger's Tragedy*, I think) was also produced in 1611. At Court the unusual number of twenty-two plays was acted in the 1611 winter and twenty-eight in 1612. These must have included nearly every play they possessed; and the fact that the whole, or nearly so, of Shakespeare's plays were revived at Court in these two years makes his retirement in 1610 to my mind nearly a certainty, and accounts for the not very felicitous praise of his " copious industry " by Webster in the Dedication of his *White Devil* in 1612. Webster couples the retired Shakespeare with Dekker and Heywood: but Jonson's works he speaks of as " laboured and understanding," Beaumont's and Fletcher's as " no less worthy composures." This higher praise is given to the writers who like himself were then contributing to the Globe repertory. He mentions no one else but Chapman of " full and heightened style." Are we to attribute to this mention of him the tradition that Chapman wrote *The Second Maiden's Tragedy?* On 11th September 1611 Shakespeare's name occurs " in the margin, as if a later insertion " (says Mr. Halliwell) of a list of Stratford donors " towards the charge of prosecuting the bill in Parliament for the better repair of the highways." In 1612 Lane, Greene, and Shakespeare filed a bill before Lord Ellesmere complaining that some of the lessees of the Stratford tithes refused to contribute their proper shares of a reserved rent. It appears from this document that Shakespeare's income from this source was £60. In the same year Heywood, in his *Apology for Actors*, complained of W. Jaggard's having printed in *The Passionate Pilgrim*, 3d edition, two love epistles taken from his *Troia Britannica,* as by W. Shakespeare, "which might put the world in opinion I might steal them from him;" he adds that he knows the author was much offended for Jaggard's presuming to make bold with his name. The name was in consequence withdrawn *altogether* from the title-page. Notwithstanding this, many modern editors print *The Passionate Pilgrim* as Shakespeare's. On 4th February 1613 Richard Shakespeare was buried at Stratford; whether the Gilbert Shakespeare, "adolescens," who was buried 3d February 1612, was also a brother of William's, is doubtful, but likely. On 10th March 1613 Shakespeare bought of Henry Walker a house and yard near Blackfriars Theatre for £140, of which £60 remained on mortgage (one of the trustees being in 1618 John Heming, Shakespeare's fellow-actor): he leased the house to John Robinson for ten years. On 29th June the Globe was burned down. It caught fire during the performance of *All is True* (*Henry VIII.*) This was not the play as we have it—which is a later version by Massinger and Fletcher, written for the Blackfriars Theatre, and containing only three scenes that can be attributed to Shakespeare—but a play in which there was a fool's part. Wotton describes it as " the play of *Henry VIII.,*" but Lorkin says it was a new play called *All is True*, representing some principal pieces of *Henry VIII*. Whether new play or not it was probably by Shakespeare, written c. 1609, and portions of it remain imbedded in that now extant by Fletcher and Massinger c. 1617, the original MS. having perished in the fire. Just at the same time one Lane had been maligning Mrs. Hall, Shakespeare's daughter, in connection with Ralph Smith. Lane was summoned before the Ecclesiastical Court at Worcester on 15th July and excommunicated on the 27th. There were only seven plays performed at Court by the King's men in the winter 1613–14, all their principal writers—Fletcher, Beaumont, Jonson, Webster—having left them after the Globe fire. Surely this is not consistent with the statement of C. Burbadge that they had taken the Blackfriars building to their own use. No new play can be traced to them till 1615, when the Globe had been* rebuilt, and the Prince Charles' men had gone to the Curtain. Then they certainly did take the Blackfriars to themselves, and with an excellent staff of writers—Jonson, Fletcher, Massinger, and Field—they occupied it as well as the new Globe. A letter of John Chamberlain's to Sir Dudley Carleton, 5th January 1615, says of the stage in general: " Of

* It had been reopened in June 1614.

five new plays there is not one that pleases, and therefore they are driven to furbish over their old." Yet Jonson's *Bartholomew Fair* was one of these 1614 plays acted at Court. I suspect that Lady Elizabeth's players were not so well liked as the King's, and that Shakespeare and Beaumont were greatly missed. Fletcher and Massinger were not yet able to replace them even at Court.

In July 1614 John Combe left a legacy of £5 to Shakespeare; this fact disposes of the silly story of Shakespeare having satirised him in infantile doggerel. In the autumn William Combe, the squire of Wilcombe, originated a proposal to enclose common fields in the neighbourhood; he was supported by Shakespeare, who had been guaranteed against prospective loss by Replingham, Combe's agent. The corporation, through his cousin Greene, the town-clerk, remonstrated with him in November when he was in London, and again in December wrote to him representing the inconveniences and loss that would be caused. The matter dragged on to September 1615, and then fell through. This is the last notice of Shakespeare's action in any public matter. On 10th February 1616 his daughter Judith was married to Thomas Quiney, vintner, four years her junior, without licence, whence a fine and threat of excommunication at the Worcester

Ecclesiastical Court: and on 25th April Shakespeare was buried. His will had been executed on 25th March. It was not regularly engrossed, but a corrected draft, originally prepared for copying and completion on 25th January, but evidently neglected until the sudden emergency of Shakespeare's illness. It appears from this document that Judith's marriage portion was to have been £100, on condition of her husband's settling on her £150 in land; if this condition was fulfilled within three years he was left £150 to his own use, if not it was strictly settled on her and her children. This £150 is independent of £100 in discharge of her marriage portion, and £50 conditional on her surrendering her interest in the Rowington manor to Susanna Hall. To Joan Hart, his sister, whose husband had been buried on 17th April, was left wearing apparel, £20, a life-interest in Henley Street, and £5 each to her sons. To Susanna Hall he left all his real estate settled in tail male, with the usual remainders over. To Elizabeth Hall all his plate except the broad silver-gilt bowl, which went to Judith Quiney. To his fellows, Hemings, Burbadge, and Condell, £1, 6s. 8d. each for rings; the usual legacies to the executors, poor, &c.; and to his wife his second best bed. Of course she was fully provided for by freebench in the Rowington copyhold, and dower on the rest of the property; nevertheless, it is strange that she does not appear as executrix, that she had no life-interest left her in house or furniture, and that in the draft of the will, as made in January, her name does not appear to have been mentioned at all. It is only in the subsequent interlineations that her bequest appears.

SECTION II.

THE PERSONAL CONNECTIONS OF SHAKESPEARE WITH OTHER POETS.

ONE of the objects of the present treatise is to bring into clearer light the relations of Shakespeare with contemporary dramatists. Strangely enough this has scarcely been attempted in earlier biographies. His dealings in malt have been carefully chronicled: his connections with poets have been slurred over. It will be useful, therefore, to gather up the scattered notices of personal contact between him and his fellows in dramatic production. Mere allusions to his works, whether complimentary or otherwise, will not come under this category. Such will be found collected, and well collected, in Dr. Ingleby's *Century of Praise;* but they consist almost entirely of slight references to his published works, and have no bearing of importance on his career. Nor, indeed, have we any extended material of any kind to aid us in this investigation; one source of information, which is abundant for most of his contemporaries, being in his case entirely absent. Neither as addressed to him by others, nor by him to others, do any commendatory verses exist in connection with any of his or other men's works published in his lifetime—a notable fact, in whatever way it may be explained. Nor can he be traced in any personal contact beyond a very limited circle, although the fanciful might-have-beens so largely indulged in by his biographers might at first lead us to an opposite conclusion.

With John Lyly, the founder of English Comedy, he seems to have had no personal intercourse, although the reproduction by him of many of Lyly's puns and conceits, and some few of his dramatic situations, distinctly prove that he had carefully examined his published plays. Nor does the solitary reference to Shakespeare in Greene's *Groatsworth of Wit*, however it may display strong personal feeling, lead us to suppose that there had been any personal relations between these dramatists; in fact, the very wording of the passage properly understood distinctly disproves the existence of such relations. Of all the dramatists who had preceded him on the London stage the only two with whom he can be even conjecturally brought in personal contact before the opening of the Rose Theatre in

HIS PERSONAL CONNECTIONS. 75

1592 are Robert Wilson and George Peele. It is unlikely that he should have begun his career as a novice and journeyman independent of tutor or coadjutor, and a minute examination of the careers of these two dramatists leads me to infer that they were connected with the same company as Shakespeare in 1590–1. In any case, they were his immediate models in his early work in several respects. It is from Wilson that his liking for doggerel rhymes and alternately rhyming stanzas was derived: it is from Peele that his love tragedy of *Romeo and Juliet*—his only early tragedy—derived, in its earliest form, as acted in 1591, whatever in it was not Shakespeare's own. Wilson was probably his tutor or coadjutor in Comedy and Peele in Tragedy. But this is after all conjecture; on the other hand, it is certain that in 1592–3 a greater than Peele or Wilson was writing for the same company as Shakespeare, and necessarily in close connection with him. For Marlowe he certainly had a sincere regard: from his poem of *Hero and Leander* Shakespeare makes the only direct quotation to be found in his plays; on his historical plays Shakespeare, after his friend's decease, bestowed in addition, revision, and completion, a greater amount of minute work than on his own; and the earlier of his own histories were distinctly built on lines similar to those of *Edward II.* and *Edward III.* The relation of Shakespeare's Histories to Marlowe's is far more intimate than that of his Comedies or of *Romeo* to any predecessor's productions. I cannot find a trace of direct connection between Shakespeare and any other poet than these mentioned, during the life of Lord Strange. His connection with Lord Southampton seems to have been more intimate than any with his fellow-poets. In the *Sonnets* addressed to him there is mention of other pens who have dedicated poems to his lordship, and whom Shakespeare for poetical purposes professes to regard as dangerous rivals. The only persons known to have *dedicated* anything to Southampton are Nash and Markham, although George Peele had written a high eulogy of him in his *Honour of the Garter* in 1593. Markham's dedication is one of four prefixed to his poem on *The Tragedy of Sir Richard Grenvile* (S. R. 9th September 1595); (1.) to Charles Lord Montjoy (in prose); (2.) to Robert Earl of Sussex (Sonnet); (3.) to the Earl of Southampton (Sonnet); (4.) to Sir Edward Wingfield (Sonnet). I am not aware of any previous attempt to identify Markham with the rival alluded to in the *Sonnets* of Shakespeare, and yet there are many coincidences of language which would lead to this conclusion. Take Sonnet 78, for instance.

"*Thine eyes* . . . have added feathers to the learned's *wing* and given *grace* a double majesty." In Markham we find in 1, "hath given *wings* to my youngling Muse;" and in 3, "whose *eyes* doth crown the most victorious pen" (*cf.* in 1, "that thine *eyes* may lighten," &c.); and in 4, the *double* majesty of the grace, "vouchsafe to *grace* my work and me, *Gracing* the soul beloved of heaven and thee." I do not find in Markham the "affable familiar ghost" of Sonnet 86, but this and other allusions may have referred to his *Thyrsis and Daphne* (S. R. 23d April 1593, five days after the entry of *Venus and Adonis*) which is now unfortunately lost; and there is something like it in the Grenvile Tragedy, in which Markham calls on Grenvile's soul to "sit on his hand" while he writes, which the ghost apparently does until it is dismissed to its "rest" at the end of the poem. Markham was an exceedingly *learned* man and the "proud full sail of his great verse" would well apply to his stilted and conceited effusion. He does not in it allude to Southampton's beauty, though he may have done so in his *Thyrsis*, but he calls him "Bright lamp of *virtue*," with which compare Sonnet 79: "He lends thee *virtue*, and he stole that word from thy behaviour." On the whole I incline to regard Markham as the rival poet of Shakespeare's

Sonnets. As to Nash, his supposed satirical allusions to Shakespeare, as set forth by the fertile fancy of Mr. Simpson, have no more real existence than the allusions discovered by other like imaginations in the writings of Spenser. His only notice of Shakespeare's writings is the well-known mention of the representation of Talbot on the stage, and that is highly complimentary. He may be included under the "every alien pen" of Sonnet 78, but he is not (as I once thought he was) the rival poet alluded to. It may be of interest in connection with this matter to note that in *The Dumb Knight*, in which Markham certainly wrote i. 2, ii. 1, iii. 4, and iv. 2, *Venus and Adonis* is satirised as a lascivious poem.

Of intercourse with other dramatists while a member of the Chamberlain's company, the first instance is that with Lodge and Drayton. That the connection with Drayton terminated in a misunderstanding is clear from the excision of the favourable notice of Shakespeare's *Lucrece* from his *Matilda*, and from Drayton's taking the chief part in writing *Sir John Oldcastle*, the object of which was to keep alive the ill-feeling produced by the unfortunate adoption of that name from the old play of *Henry V.* for the character afterwards called Sir John Falstaff. This connection with Drayton ended in 1597, that with Lodge in 1599. If I am right in my attribution of part authorship to Lodge in *Henry VI.* and *The Taming of the Shrew* in its original form, Shakespeare revised and altered his plays, but not till after Lodge's retirement from connection with the Chamberlain's company. Soon after this, in 1601, he founded his *Hamlet* on Kyd's, but with Kyd himself I have not been able to find that he was at any time personally connected. Nevertheless, as regards mere outward form, Kyd was the chief model for the great tragedies of *Hamlet, Lear,* &c. Of course, as regards all poetic essentials, his influence on Shakespeare cannot for a moment be compared to Marlowe's.

With Marston, Chapman, and Dekker, Shakespeare's relations were ephemeral, in connection with the great stage quarrel of 1599-1601, and in no respect personal, unless we suppose that he had a hand in hiring Dekker to oppose Jonson. My own belief is that he was away in Scotland when *Satiromastix* was produced, and that the division of the company left in London did this without his knowledge. With Jonson his relations were evidently personal and of very varied nature. He probably introduced him to the Chamberlain's company in 1598; he certainly acted in his play of *Every Man in his Humour:* he did not act in *Every Man out of his Humour*—and then Jonson joined the

Chapel children, and entered on his three years' struggle with Marston, Dekker, &c. In 1601 Shakespeare satirised these children in *Hamlet*, and about the same time administered the "purge" to Jonson mentioned in *The Return from Parnassus*: at the end of the same year, he, Jonson, Chapman, and Marston were contributors to Chester's *Love's Martyr*. In 1603 Jonson, who had again joined the Chamberlain's men, wrote *Sejanus* in conjunction with some one (with Shakespeare in my opinion), and got into trouble for it. Shakespeare certainly acted in this play, and must at that time have been on good terms with Jonson. All the allusions to Shakespeare's *Henry V.*, &c., in the Prologue at the revival of *Every Man in his Humour* in 1601 by the Chapel children, and the purge administered to Jonson, had been forgiven and forgotten on both sides. But in 1605 Jonson wrote *Volpone*, in which Shakespeare did not act, and which gave offence at Court: and this caused a new disagreement between him and the King's men (formerly the Chamberlain's). He left them, and with Chapman and Marston wrote *Eastward Ho*, in which *Hamlet* is ridiculed, and for allusions to Scotland in which, similar to those in *Volpone*, the authors were imprisoned. The King's men retaliated with the additions to *Mucedorus*, of which more elsewhere, and Jonson did not join them

HIS PERSONAL CONNECTIONS.   81

again for years. He wrote for the Chapel children in 1609, and not till 1610, at the end of the year, when Shakespeare's dramatic career was just expiring, did he produce *The Alchemist* for them at the Globe. It is to be hoped that these two great dramatists were not at open enmity during the later part of Shakespeare's life; but all record of any real friendship between them ends in 1603, and little value is to be attributed either to the vague traditions of Jonson's visiting him at Stratford, or to the abundant praise lavished on him by Jonson in commendatory verses after his death. Much more important for ascertaining the real relations existing between them are the allusions to *The Tempest* and *Winter's Tale* so abundantly scattered through all Jonson's plays from 1609 to 1616, while Shakespeare was yet alive.

Of other dramatists who were connected with Shakespeare in King James's time I know only of Tourneur and Wilkins—the former simply as an author writing for Shakespeare's company, the latter as the playwright who wrote *Pericles* in its original form: the history of the production of this play has already been given.

As to Beaumont, Fletcher, Webster, &c., who after 1610 wrote for the King's men, and the numerous contemporaries who wrote for other companies, no

F

trace of any intercourse with Shakespeare, personal or otherwise, remains to us, though abundant guesses and hypotheses utterly foundationless[*] will be found in the voluminous Shakespearian literature already existing. The truth appears to be that Shakespeare at no time sought for a large circle of acquaintance, and that his position as almost sole provider of plays for his company relieved him of that miscellaneous comradeship which was the bane of Dekker, Heywood, and many other gifted writers of the time. Of any one of these a far larger personal connection can be proved than I believe ever existed in the case of Shakespeare: and to this we no doubt are greatly indebted for the depth and roundness of those great plays, which could never have been conceived without much solitude, much suffering, and much concentration.

[*] The reader should especially beware of a most absurd identification of Shakespeare with the Crispinus of Jonson's *Poetaster*, recently put forth by Mr. J. Feis in his *Shakspere and Montaigne*. It is a pity that an essay, of which the first four chapters are so valuable, should be disfigured by the palpable chronological and other blunders in the latter portions of the volume.

SECTION III.

ANNALS ON WHICH THE PRECEDING SECTIONS ARE FOUNDED.

Until April 1564.

On 26th April 1564 was baptized William, son of John Shakespeare of Stratford-on-Avon and Mary Arden, at that time an only child, two girls born previously having died in their infancy. John Shakespeare was son of Richard Shakespeare of Snitterfield, where his brother Henry also resided: he was a glover, who speculated in wool, corn, &c. He lived in Henley Street, Stratford, as early as 29th April 1552, having left his father about 1550, and in October 1556 purchased two small estates in that town—one that is now shown as the birthplace, the other in Greenhill Street. In 1557 he married Mary Arden, whose father, Robert, a yeoman, had contracted a second marriage with Agnes Hill, widow, and in the settlement then made had reserved to Mary the reversion to estates at Wilmecote and Snitterfield. Some part of this land was occupied by Richard Shakespeare's grandfather. Mary Arden also received under her father's will, dated 24th November 1556, a considerable sum in money, and the fee-simple of Asbies at Wilmecote, a house with sixty acres of land. In 1557 John was a burgess, a member of the corporation, and by choice of the Court Leet ale-taster to the borough, sworn to look to the assize and goodness of bread, ale, or beer. In September 1558 he was one of the four constables under the rules of the Court Leet. On 6th October 1559 he was again chosen constable and one of the four affeerors for determining fines under the borough bye-laws. In 1561 he was again chosen affeeror, and one of the borough chamberlains, which office he held till the end of 1563.

1564.

In July the plague broke out in Stratford, and continued to December. There died 238 in that half-year, no Shakespeares among them. John Shakespeare had had an early lesson in sanitation by way of a fine of 12d. in April 1552 for having a muck heap in front of his door in Henley Street, within a stone's-throw of one of the public stores of filth. He now contributed fairly to relieve the poor and plague-stricken; about 12d. per month.

1565.

In March John Shakespeare with his former colleague made up the chamberlain's accounts from September 1563 to 1564. Neither of them could sign their names.

1566.

In February he again made up these accounts, and was paid £3, 2s. 7d. "for a rest of old debt" by the corporation. On 13th October his son Gilbert was baptized.

1567.

In September, Ralph Perrot, brewer, John Shakespeare, and Ralph Cawdrey, butcher, were nominated for the office of High Bailiff or Mayor. Cawdrey was elected. For the first time the name appears as "Mr." John Shakespeare.

1568.

On 4th September "Mr. John Shakysper" was chosen High Bailiff. He was succeeded the next year by Robert Salisbury.

1569.

On 15th April John Shakespeare's third daughter (named Joan after her deceased elder sister) was baptized.

1571.

On 28th September John Shakespeare's fourth daughter Anne was baptized. William was now seven, then the usual age for the commencement of grammar-school education, the use of the Absey book and horn-book having been acquired at home. Lily's *Accidence* and the *Sententiæ Pueriles* were the usual text-books for beginners in Latin. Shakespeare had some knowledge of Latin, and a little French; all beyond this is very problematical.

1573.

On 11th March, Richard, John Shakespeare's third son, was baptized.

1575.

John Shakespeare bought two houses in Stratford.

1578.

In January John Shakespeare paid only the amount of borough taxes paid by other aldermen.

William was then fourteen, the usual age for commencing apprenticeship. There is a tradition given by Aubrey that he was apprenticed to a butcher. I believe this to be a myth, originating in the epithet "kill-cow," often applied to tragic actors. Some writers still think that the tradition may be relied on. Another story traced to the parish clerk of 1693 is that he followed his father's profession. May be so ; may not be.

1579.

In Easter Term Asbies was mortgaged to Edmund Lambert for £40, to revert if repayment be made before Michaelmas 1580.

On 4th July Anne Shakespeare was buried; in the chamberlain's accounts occurs this item: "For the bell and pall for Mr. Shaxper's daughter, 8d.," the highest fee in the list.

On 15th October John Shakespeare and his wife convey their interest in Snitterfield to Robert Webbe. Agnes Arden's will is dated in this year.

1580.

On 3d May, Edmund, son of John Shakespeare, was baptized.

On or before 29th September, the money in discharge of the Asbies mortgage was tendered and refused unless other moneys due were also paid.

1581.

On 19th January the goods of Agnes Arden, deceased, were appraised.

On 1st September Richard Hathaway of Shottery made his will.

1582.

On 28th November the marriage bond between William Shagspere and Anne Hathway was given, under condition that neither party had been precontracted to another person, and that the said William Shagspere should not proceed to solemnization with the said Anne Hathway without consent of her friends. They were to be married with one asking of the banns. The bondsmen were Fulk Sandells and John Richardson,—the seal is R. H., which may be Richard Hathaway's.

1583.

On May 26th Susanna their daughter was baptized. It is assumed that a precontract existed between the parents which, according to the custom of the time, "was not legally recognised, but it invalidated a subsequent union of either of the parties with any one else" (Halliwell, *Outlines*, p. 45). The reader must form his own opinion. Taking into consideration the low morality of the time in such matters, the fact that Anne Hathaway was twenty-six, and Shakespeare eighteen in 1582, the practice still not unknown in rural districts of cohabitation under conditional promise of marriage, should the probable birth of a child make it necessary or prudent, the fact that from 1587 to 1597 we have no evidence that Shakespeare even saw his wife, and the palpable indications in the *Sonnets* that during this interval he was intriguing with another woman—for my own part I cannot help adopting De Quincey's view that he was entrapped into some such conditional promise by this lady and kept his promise honourably. Compare on the precontract question the plays of *The Miseries of Enforced Marriage* by Wilkins, which is founded on the contemporary history of the same Calverley who is the murderer in *The Yorkshire Tragedy*, with Shakespeare's own views in 1604 in *Measure for Measure;* his opinions in *Twelfth Night*, ii. 4 (early part, c. 1592), and *Midsummer Night's Dream*, i. 1, on wives that are older than their husbands : and, by way of showing that his plays do discover sometimes his personal feelings, Valentine's resignation of Silvia in *The Two Gentlemen of Verona*, with the story involved in the *Sonnets* of Shakespeare's own transfer of his illicit love.

1585.

February 2. Hamnet and Judith, Shakspeare's twin children, were baptized at Stratford-on-Avon. By April 26th he had certainly attained his majority, and his apprenticeship had probably expired.

1585–7.

Three or four years after his union with Anne Hathaway, he had, says Rowe, "by a misfortune common enough to young fellows, fallen into ill company, and, amongst them, some, that made a frequent practice of deer stealing, engaged him with them more than once in robbing a park, that belonged to Sir Thomas Lucy of Charlecote, near Stratford; for this he was prosecuted by that gentleman, as he thought, somewhat too severely, and in order to revenge that ill usage made a ballad upon him, and though this, probably the first essay of his poetry, be lost, yet it is said to have been so very bitter that it redoubled the prosecution against him to that degree that he was obliged to leave his business and family in Warwickshire for some time, and shelter himself in London." Whether this tradition be well founded or no, we are compelled by subsequent events to place the date of Shakespeare's leaving Stratford in or about 1587; and whether there be any truth in the story traced to Davenant or not, that he held horses at the play-house door, while their owners were witnessing performances inside, it is certain that he was very soon connected with the stage, first as actor, then as dramatic writer. It becomes therefore of importance to ascertain if possible the specific company with which he originally joined.

In the latter part of 1585 there were two regular theatres existing in London, the Theater and the Curtain. It clearly appears from a report by Recorder Fleetwood preserved in the Lansdown MSS. that at Whitsuntide 1584 these were occupied by the Queen's players and those of Lord Arundel. It is not clear that a third company, that of Lord Hunsdon, acted at the Theater: although Mr. J. O. H. Phillipps (whom I most usually refer to under his former and better known name of Halliwell) assures us that it is so. It is true that the "owner of the Theater," whom he takes to be a temporary occupier of that building, but whom I regard as the ground landlord, Giles Alleyn, is called a servant of Lord Hunsdon's, and that a company of actors, called Lord Hunsdon's men, acted at Court 27th December 1582; but it does not follow that these men were occupiers of the Theater. In fact the only companies anyhow known to us as in London in 1585 are the two already mentioned. It is by no means likely *à priori*, nor would it agree with the passages hereafter to be referred to in the writings of Greene and Nash, that Shakespeare should immediately on his appearance in London obtain employment in either. But there was a third company not noticed in Collier's *Annals of the Stage*, into which he may easily have obtained admittance. When the Queen's company was formed in 8th March 1582–3, by the selection of twelve players from the companies of the two Dudleys, Earls of Leicester and Warwick, there must have been sufficient men left unemployed to form another company. These were probably still retained by the Earl of Leicester: for in a letter from Sir Philip Sidney, dated Utrecht, 24th March 1575–6, mention is made of "Will, the Earl of Leicester's jesting player," who had gone with the Earl to the Netherlands in December 1575. Thomas Heywood, in his *Apology for Actors*, 1612, tells us that "The

King of Denmark, father to him that now reigneth, entertained into his service a company of English comedians, commended unto him by the honourable Earl of Leicester." This King of Denmark, Frederick II., died in 1588, and the exact date of the transaction is fixed by documents dated October 1586, in which we find that five of these actors had been transferred from the service of Frederick II. of Denmark to that of Christian I., Duke of Saxony. I am far from wishing to adopt the conjecture of Mr. Bruce that "jesting Will" was Shakespeare; but when among the names of these five actors—Thomas King, Thomas Stephen, George Bryan, Thomas Pope, Robert Persie—we find two, Pope and Bryan, that are identical with those of two actors in the very first list extant of the first company with which we can positively connect Shakespeare as an actor; when we find this same company acting at Stratford in 1587, at the very time that Shakespeare's disappearance from all known connection with that town for nine years commences; when we find among a list of plays that had been acted by the English in Germany *Hester and Ahasuerus, Titus Andronicus [and Vespasian]*, both of which we shall trace to Shakespeare's company; when we also find a version of the Corambis *Hamlet* existing early in the same country—then I think we are justified in saying that there is great likelihood of this company having been the one in which Shakespeare found his first employment. If so, he accompanied it in all its fortunes, and never (as we shall see) forsook it for another.

1586.

Meanwhile in London the plague had prevailed to such an extent that the theatres were shut up during 1586. It was not then during this year that Shakespeare held horses at stage-doors, or obtained employment in London theatres. But at the end of the year Lord Leicester's players returned to England, and in January 1586–87 are mentioned together with the Queen's, the Admiral's, and the Earl of Oxford's, in a letter to Walsingham from a spy of his, which is preserved in the Harleian MSS.

1587.

This same company, the Earl of Leicester's men, visited Stratford-on-Avon in 1587. I have not been able to trace their previous presence there since 1576, although other companies paid frequent visits to this town. It is singular that in this year, the only one in which this company visited Stratford during the twelve years intervening between the birth and death of Hamnet Shakespeare, we find also the only record of the poet's presence in the place of his nativity. I give this in the words of Mr. Halliwell. "In 1578 his parents had borrowed the sum of £40 on the security of his mother's estate of Asbies, from their connexion, Edmund Lambert of Barton-on-the-Heath. The loan remaining unpaid, and the mortgage dying in March 1587, his son and heir John was naturally desirous of having the matter settled. John Shakespeare being at that time in prison for debt, and obviously unable to furnish the money, it was arranged shortly afterwards that Lambert should, on cancelling the mortgage and paying also the sum of £20, receive from the Shakespeares an absolute title to the estate. His offer would perhaps not have been made had it not been ascertained that the eldest son William had a contingent interest, derived no doubt from a settlement, and that his assent was essential to the security of a conveyance. The proposed arrangement was not completed, but" the poet's sanction to it is recorded. I believe that immediately after this, in 1587, Shakespeare left Stratford either with or in order to join Lord Leicester's company.

1588.

The Earl of Leicester died on 4th September 1588. Previously to this date the company of players acting under his patronage had played in London, probably at the Cross-Keys in Bishopsgate Street, and more frequently had travelled in the country. At the death of Dudley, they had of course to seek for a new patron, and no doubt found one in Ferdinando, Lord Strange, whose company (containing as we shall see some of the actors already known as Leicester's men) are first traceable in 1589. An earlier company bearing the title of Lord Strange's men, c. 1582, seem to have been merely acrobats or posture-mongers. But before entering on the history of this company under its new name, of which we *know* Shakespeare to have been a member, we must note some particulars regarding other dramatists, especially Marlowe, Greene, and Nash, which indirectly concern Shakespeare, and have hitherto been wrongly interpreted.

In 1587, when the Admiral's men re-opened after the plague, they produced, in what succession we need not here determine, Greene's *Orlando* and *Alphonsus of Arragon*, Peele's *Battle of Alcazar*, and Marlowe's *Tamberlaine*. Those plays are enumerated in Peele's *Farewell*, 1589, as—

"Mahomet's pow, and mighty Tamberlaine,
  King Charlemagne, Tom Stukeley, and the rest."

"Mahomet's pow" is the head of Mahomet in *Alphonsus;* King Charlemagne was probably a character in the complete play of *Orlando*, of which only a mutilated copy has come down to us; Tom Stukeley is the hero of *The Battle of Alcazar*; and "the rest" most likely indicate Lodge's *Marius and Sylla* and Marlowe's *Faustus*. Greene and Peele wrote no more for this company, but in 1587 removed to the Queen's men, who had been travelling in the country. On 29th March 1588 Greene's *Perimedes the Blacksmith* was entered on the Stationers' Registers. In the introduction Greene attacks Marlowe and Lodge, who had remained with the Admiral's men, in a passage worth quoting: "I keep my old course still to palter up something in prose, using mine old posy still, *omne tulit punctum;* although lately two gentlemen poets made two madmen of Rome beat it out of their paper bucklers, and had it in derision, for that I could not make my verses jet upon the stage in tragical buskins, every word filling the mouth like the fa-burden of Bow-bell, daring God out of heaven with that atheist Tamberlaine or blaspheming with the mad priest of the sun. But let me rather openly pocket up the ass at Diogenes' hand than wantonly set out such impious instances of intolerable poetry. Such mad and scoffing poets that have poetical spirits as bred of Merlin's race, if there be any in England that set the end of scholarism in an English blank verse, I think either it is the humour of a novice that tickles them with self-love, or too much frequenting the hot-house (to use the German proverb) hath sweat out all the greatest part of their wits." For the fuller understanding of this satire it may be noted that no "priest of the sun" is known in an early play except in *The Looking-glass for London and England* by Lodge and Greene, which is certainly of later date than *Perimedes*, yet may indicate Lodge's liking for that character; that Diogenes is the name assumed by Lodge in his *Catharos*, 1591, and that Marlowe's name was written Merlin as often as Marlowe. There can be no doubt as to the persons aimed at, nor of the effect of the satire, for both of them left off writing for the Admiral's men; and Marlowe during the next two years produced *The Jew of Malta*, which can be traced to the Queen's company, and together with Greene, Lodge, and Peele produced the plays of *The Troublesome Reign of King John*, and *The First Part of York and Lancaster* on which *2 Henry VI.* is founded. The internal evidence for the authorship of these last-mentioned plays is very strong: they were, however, published anonymously.

1589.

Before the entry of Greene's *Menaphon* on the Stationers' Registers on 23d August 1589, *Hamlet* and *The Taming of a Shrew* must have been represented by Pembroke's men, and Marlowe must have left the Queen's company. As *Menaphon* is accessible in Professor Arber's reprint to the general reader, it will be sufficient to refer to it here without quoting passages in full. That Greene refers so satirically to Marlowe as to prevent our supposing that at this date they could be writing jointly for the same theatre, is clear from a hitherto unnoticed passage in p. 54: "Whosoever descanted of that love told you a *Canterbury* tale; some *prophetical* fullmouth, that, as he were a *Cobler's* eldest son, would by the last tell where another's shoe wrings." Marlowe or *Merlin* was a shoemaker's son of Canterbury. That Doron in the story is meant for the author of *The Taming of a Shrew* was shown by Mr. R. Simpson by comparing Doron's speech in p. 74: "White as the hairs that grow on Father Boreas' chin," and the passage in Nash's introduction, p. 5, about mechanical mates, servile imitators of vainglorious tragedians, who think themselves "more than initiated in poet's immortality if they but once get Boreas by the beard," with the words of the play itself: "whiter than icy hair that grows on Boreas' chin." Mr. Simpson was, however, entirely wrong in identifying Doron with Shakespeare, and did not notice that Doron's entire speech parodies one of Menaphon's in p. 31, just as *The Taming of a Shrew* parodies Marlowe's plays, or "the mechanical mates" alluded to by Nash imitate the "idiot art-masters" in the "swelling bombast of a bragging blank verse," or the "spacious volubility of a drumming decasyllabon." The name Menaphon is taken from Marlowe's *Tamberlaine*. In these passages Greene and Nash satirise Kyd, then writing for Pembroke's company. In another paragraph, p. 9, Nash speaks of "a sort of shifting companions" that "leave the trade of *Noverint* whereto they were born," who get their aphorisms from translations of Seneca and can "afford you whole *Hamlets* of tragical speeches." This passage is familiar to all students of Shakespeare; and yet no one has, I think, pointed out that Nash identifies these "famished followers" of Seneca with the "Kidde in Æsop, who, enamoured with the Fox's newfangles, forsook all hopes of life to leap into a new occupation." This pun in a tractate containing similar allusions to the names Greene, Lyly, and Merlin is equivalent to a direct attribution of the authorship of *Hamlet* as produced in 1589 to Kyd, and is also a refutation of those who have seen in the whole passage an allusion to Shakespeare.

Very shortly after Greene's *Menaphon* Nash issued his *Anatomy of Absurdities*, which had been entered on the Stationers' Registers 19th September 1588, and which contains much of the same satirical matter as his address in *Menaphon*.

We have now to pass from the private quarrel of Greene and Nash, as representing the Queen's men at the Theater, with Marlowe and Kyd, the writers for Pembroke's company, to a much more important controversy in which many of the same dramatists were concerned. Between October 1588 and October 1589 the Martinists published their Puritan controversial tracts; in opposition to them various writings had appeared, whose authors were Cooper, formerly schoolmaster, afterwards Bishop; Lyly the Euphuist; Nash the satirist; and Elderton " the bibbing fool " ballad-maker. They had also been ridiculed on the stage, in April 1589, at the Theater, most likely by Greene; at the Paul's school probably by Lyly; and either in ballad or interlude by Antony Munday, even at that early date a dramatic writer. As the anti-Martinist plays were on the side of the clergy and of secular authority they were not interfered with. But in November 1589, in consequence of certain players in London handling "matters of Divinity and State without judgment or decorum"—in other words, having the impertinence to suppose that there could be two sides to a question, Mr. Tylney, the Master of the Revels, suddenly becomes awake to the danger of allowing such discussions on public stages, and writes to Lord Burleigh that he "utterly mislikes all plays within the city." Lord Burleigh sends a letter to the Lord Mayor to "stay" them. The Theater and Curtain, where the Queen's men and Pembroke's were playing, were *without the city*, so that the anti-Martinist plays were not interfered with; the Paul's boys were for the nonce not regarded as a company of players: so that the Mayor could only "hear of" the Admiral's men, who on admonishment dutifully forbore playing, and Lord Strange's, who departed contemptuously, "went to the Cross-Keys and played that afternoon to the great offence of the better sort, that knew they were prohibited." The Mayor then "committed two of the players to one of the compters." These players, however, gained their end, for all plays on either side of the controversy were forthwith suppressed, and commissioners were appointed to examine and licence all plays thenceforth " in and about " the city played by any players " whose servants soever they be."

It is pleasing to find Shakespeare's company acting in so spirited a manner in defence of free thought and free speech: it would be more pleasing to be able to identity him personally as the chief leader in movement. And this I believe he was. The play of *Love's Labour's Lost*, in spite of great alteration in 1597, is undoubtedly in the main the earliest example left us of Shakespeare's work: and the characters in the underplot agree so singularly even in the play as we have it with the anti-Martinist writers in their personal peculiarities that I have little doubt that this play was the one performed in November 1589. If the absence of matter of State be objected, I reply that it would be easy for malice to represent the loss of Love's labour in the main plot as a satire on the love's labour in vain of Alençon for Elizabeth. We must also remember that it is most likely that for some years at the beginning of his career Shakespeare wrote in conjunction with other men, and that in those plays that were revived by him at a later date their work was replaced by his own. In the case of the present play, as the revision was for a Court performance, we may be sure that great care would be taken to expunge all offensive matter: the only ground for surprise is that enough indications remain to enable us to identify the characters at all.

1590.

Love's Labour's Lost would no doubt be closely followed by *Love's Labour's Won*, which play I for other reasons attribute to this year.

We must now again refer to Greene. His *Farewell to Folly* had been entered on the Stationers' Registers, 11th June 1587, but was not published till after his *Mourning Garment*, the entry of which dates 2d November 1590. In the introduction, which was certainly written at the time of publication, although the body of the work had been lying by for some three years and more, Greene distinctly alludes to *Fair Em* and accuses its author of "simple abusing of Scripture," because "two lovers on the stage arguing one another of unkindness, his mistress runs over him with this canonical sentence 'a man's conscience is a thousand witnesses'; and her knight again excuseth himself with that saying of the Apostle, 'Love covereth the multitude of sins.'" The exact words in the play are "Love that covers multitude of sins" and "thy conscience is a thousand witnesses." Greene, says Mr. R. Simpson, who first drew attention to this allusion to *Fair Em* in a paper unfortunately spoiled by an absurd attempt to identify Mullidor,* of "great head and little wit," with Shakespeare, has parallel plots to those of *Fair Em* in his *Tully's Love* (1589) and *Never Too Late* (before 2d November 1590). To me the connexion seems closer between this satire, by Greene the profligate parson, based on Scriptural grounds, of a play written for Lord Strange's company, and the persecution they had just endured for venturing to present a play in favour of the Martinists. And as if to emphasise his intention in this direction, Greene says in his Dedication of his tract, "I cannot *Martinize*." That *Fair Em* was the production of R. Wilson will I think be evident to those who will read it with careful remembrance.

The *Comedy of Errors* was also probably acted this year in its original form.

* A dor, dorne, or drone is the lazy male bee that makes no honey: hence Doron, the dorne (pronounce dor'un). There was a myth that dors or drones were produced by mules, hence Muli-dor (see Minshew *drone*). But a drone is also the drone of a bagpipe, or the bagpipe itself, which was called chevrau (see Cotgrave, *chevrau*) or cheveril: and *chevrau* is Kyd. It is evident from Greene's tracts that Doron was meant for the writer of *The Taming of a Shrew*, and Mulidor for the same author—there cannot be a doubt of the identity of the characters. Nash's address identifies *The Taming of a Shrew* writer with Kyd.

1591.

In this year were most likely produced two plays, not in the shape in which they have come down to us, but as originally written by Shakespeare and some coadjutor, viz., *The Two Gentlemen of Verona* and *Romeo and Juliet*. The question of the dates of these and all other plays of Shakespeare will be separately argued further on. It may be just worth while to note that the "pleasant Willy" of Spenser, who has been so carelessly identified with Shakespeare, with Kemp, and with Tarleton (!) is certainly Lyly. The line "doth rather choose to sit in idle cell" (*Tears of the Muses*) identifies him with "slumbering Euphues in his cell at Silexedra" (*Menaphon*). Compare "Euphues' golden legacy found after his death in his cell at Silexedra" (title of Lodge's *Rosalynde*).

1591–2.

In the Christmas Records of this year, the Queen's company made their final appearance at Court on December 26th. Lord Strange's men performed at Whitehall on December 27th, 28th, January 1st, 9th, February 6th, 8th. The import of this fact has not been fully appreciated. The

ANNALS.

exceptionally large number of performances of Lord Strange's men show a singular amount of Court favour, and go far to prove that Elizabeth did not sanction their persecution at the hands of Burleigh two years before. They henceforth, under various changes of name and constitution, until the closing of the theatres in 1642, retain the chief position in the performances at Court. This date, 1592, is in the history of this company of players, and therefore in that of Shakespeare, their chief poet and one of their best actors, of the very greatest importance.

The old plays of *King John*, on which Shakespeare's was founded, were published this year, as having been acted by the Queen's company—an additional indication of an important change in their internal constitution.

1592.

This year was scarcely less eventful than the preceding for the company to which Shakespeare belonged. On 19th February Henslowe opened the Rose theatre on Bankside for performances by Lord Strange's men under the management of the celebrated actor, Edward Alleyn. Whether (and if at all, for how long) Alleyn had been previously connected with the company, we are not directly informed; but as he gave up playing for Worcester's men, c. January 1588-9, the exact time when the players of the late Earl of Leicester found a new patron in Lord Strange, that is the probable date of his joining them. This possession of a settled place for performance gave his company additional influence and status. At first they played old plays, among which may be mentioned Kyd's *Jeronymo* and *Spanish Tragedy*, Greene's *Orlando* and *Friar Bacon*, Greene and Lodge's *Looking-glass*, Marlowe's *Jew of Malta*, and Peele's *Battle of Alcazar*. This last-named play, may, like Greene's *Orlando*, have been originally sold to the Queen's men, and to the Admiral's afterwards; but whether this be so or not, we have the singular fact to explain that four plays, three by Greene and one by Marlowe, all belonging to the Queen's men, are now found in action by Lord Strange's. Combining this with their sudden disappearance from the Court Revels, it would seem that some grave displeasure had been excited against them, and that they had become disorganised. In fact, although they, or a part of them, lingered on in some vague connecsion with Sussex' players, they now practically disappear from theatrical history. Of new plays Lord Strange's men produced on March 3d, *Henry*

VI., which is by the reference to it in Nash's *Piers Penniless* (entered 8th August 1592) identified with the play now known as *The First Part of Henry VI.* It was acted fourteen times to crowded houses (Nash says to 10,000 spectators), and was the success of the season. I have no doubt that this play was written by Marlowe, with the aid of Peele, Lodge, and Greene, before 1590, and that the episode of Talbot's death added in 1592 is from the hand of Shakespeare himself. In this last opinion it is especially pleasing to me to find myself supported by the critical judgment of Mr. Swinburne. On 11th April the play of *Titus and Vespasian* was first acted. Had it not been for the existence of a German version (given in full in Cohn's *Shakespeare in Germany*) we should not have been aware that this play was identical in story with that known as *Titus Andronicus.* It is unfortunately lost—a loss the more to be regretted since it has led to the supposition of the extant play having proceeded from the hand of Shakespeare. On 10th June *A Knack to Know a Knave* was performed for the first time. Mr. R. Simpson without the slightest ground conjectured that this was the play that Greene says he "lastly writ" with "young Juvenal." The most successful new plays in this season were *Henry VI.* and *Titus and*

Vespasian (performed seven times in two months); of old plays *the Spanish Tragedy* (performed thirteen times), *The Battle of Alcazar* (eleven performances), and *The Jew of Malta* (ten performances).

On June 22 the last performance took place before the closing of the theatres on account of the plague.

On August 8 *Piers Penniless* was entered S. R., which contains Nash's reference to *1 Henry VI*.

On September 3 Greene died.

On September 20 his *Groatsworth of Wit* was entered in the Stationers' Registers. This pamphlet was edited by Chettle, and contains the often quoted address to Marlowe, "young Juvenal," and Peele. In the portion where Greene speaks to all three of them, he says: "Trust them not, for there is an upstart crow, beautified with our feathers, that, *with his Tiger's heart wrapt in a player's hide*, supposes he is as well able to bombast out a blank verse as the best of you, and being an absolute *Johannes Factotum*, is in his own conceit the only shake-scene in our country." Mr. R. Simpson showed that "beautified with our feathers" meant acting plays written by us, but "bombast out a blank verse" undoubtedly refers to Shakespeare as a writer also. The line "O tiger's heart wrapt in a woman's hide" occurs in *Richard Duke of York* (commonly but injudiciously referred to as *The True Tragedy*), a play written for Pembroke's men, probably in 1590, on which *3 Henry VI.* was founded. It is almost certainly by Marlowe, the best of the three whom Greene addresses. In December Chettle issued his *Kindheart's Dream*, in which he apologises for the offence given to Marlowe in the *Groatsworth of Wit*, " because myself have seen his demeanour no less civil than he excellent in the quality he professes ; besides divers of worship have reported his uprightness of dealing, which argues his honesty, and his facetious grace in writing, which approves his art." To Peele he makes no apology, nor indeed was any required. Shakespeare was not one of those who took offence ; they are expressly stated to have been two of the three authors addressed by Greene, the third (Lodge) not being in England.

There were three plays performed at Hampton Court this Christmas, on December 26, 31, January 1, by Lord Strange's men, in spite of the plague.

I think the latter part of 1592 the most likely time for the writing of some scenes in *All's Well that Ends Well* and *Twelfth Night* that show marks of early date.

1593.

On January 5 Lord Strange's company, who had reopened at the Rose, 29th December 1592, produced a new play called *The Jealous Comedy;* this I take to have been *The Merry Wives of Windsor* in its earliest form.

On January 30 they produced Marlowe's *Guise* or *Massacre of Paris*, which has reached us in an unusually mutilated condition.

On February 1 they performed for the last time this year in Southwark; the Rose as well as other theatres being closed because of the plague.

On April 18 *Venus and Adonis* was entered by Richard Field for publication. Shakespeare's choice of a publisher was no doubt influenced by private connection. R. Field was a son of Henry Field, tanner, of Stratford-on-Avon, who died in 1592. The inventory of his goods attached to his will had been taken by Shakespeare's father on 21st August in that year. *Venus and Adonis* was licensed by the Archbishop of Canterbury (Whitgift) (at whose palace near Croydon Nash's play, *Summer's Last Will*, was performed in the autumn of 1592), and was dedicated to Henry Wriothesley, Earl of Southampton. Shakespeare calls it "The first heir of my invention," which may mean his first published work; but more probably means the first production in which he was sole author, his previous plays having been written in conjunction with others; and he vows "to take advantage of all idle hours till I have honoured you with some graver labour." He had probably then planned if not begun his *Rape of Lucrece*.

On May 6 a precept was issued by the Lords of the Privy Council authorising Lord Strange's players, "Edward Allen, William Kempe, Thomas Pope, John Heminges, Augustine Philipes, and George Brian" to play "where the infection is not, so it be not within seven miles of London or of the Court, that they may be in the better readiness hereafter for her Majesty's service." This list of names is by no means a complete one of the company of players; but probably does consist of all the *shareholders* therein. Shakespeare was not a shareholder yet. Alleyn is described as servant to the Admiral as well as to Lord Strange. Accordingly they travelled and acted in the country—in July at Bristol, afterwards at Shrewsbury. Meanwhile on June 1 Marlowe was killed, leaving unpublished his poem, *Hero and Leander*, his play *Dido*, and in my opinion other plays; of which more hereafter.

On 25th September Henry Earl of Derby died, and Ferdinand Lord Strange succeeded to his honours. His company of players are consequently sometimes called the Earl of Derby's for the next six months. There were no performances at Court at Christmas on account of the plague.

1594.

On 23d January *Titus Andronicus* was acted as a new play by Sussex' men at the Rose. This company gave up playing there on 6th February. On 26th February the *Andronicus* play was entered on S. R. Langbaine, who professes to have seen this edition, says it was acted by the players of "Pembroke, Derby, and Essex." Essex is clearly a mistake for Sussex, for in the 1600 edition the companies are given as "Sussex, Pembroke, and Derby." Halliwell's careless statement that Lord Strange's players transferred their services to Lord Hunsdon in 1594, has led me and others into grave difficulty on this matter. The fact is that Lord Derby's players became servants to the Chamberlain between 16th April, when Lord Derby died, and 3d June, when they played at Newington Butts under the latter appellation. There was strictly no Lord Strange's company after 25th September 1593, and no other Derby's company till 1599. The old name Strange, however, does sometimes occur instead of

Derby. Hence it seemed that the transfer to Derby's company must have taken place in 1600. Indeed so little was the fact known even in 1600, that Shakespeare's company enjoyed the title of Derby's men for six months, that although that name is given on the first page, on the title the same men reappear as the Lord Chamberlain's. Why Pembroke's men should have acquired the play on 6th February, and possibly parted with it by the 26th, does not appear, nor is there any parallel instance known: there must have been some great changes in their constitution at this time. But in any case Shakespeare did not write the play; Mr. Halliwell's theory that he left Lord Strange's men, who in 1593 enjoyed the highest position of any then existing, and after having been a member successively of two of the obscurest companies, returned to his former position within a few months, is utterly untenable. There is no vestige of evidence that Shakespeare ever wrote for any company but one.

On 12th March *York and Lancaster* (*2 Henry VI.*) was entered on S. R.

From 1st to 8th April Sussex' men and the Queen's acted at the Rose, among other plays, the old *Leir* (April 8), on which Shakespeare's *Lear* was founded. Both these companies henceforth vanish from stage history.

On April 16 Lord Derby died.

On May 2 *The Taming of a Shrew* was entered on S. R.

On May 9 *The Rape of Lucrece* was entered. The difference in tone between the dedication of this poem to Lord Southampton and that of *Venus and Adonis* distinctly points to a personal intercourse having taken place in the interval. Hence the date of Shakespeare's first interview with his patron may be assigned as between April 1593 and May 1594.

On May 14 *The Famous Victories of Henry V.* and *Leir* were entered on S. R.

On May 14 also the Admiral's company, of which nothing is heard since 1591, began to act at the Rose, having acted at Newington for three days only. Alleyn, Henslow's son-in-law, had left the management of Shakespeare's company on the death of Lord Derby, and now joined the Admiral's men.

Between * June 3 and June 13 the Chamberlain's men played at Newington Butts alternately with the Admiral's: among the Chamberlain's plays we notice on June 3, 10, *Hester and Ahasuerus*, which exists in a German version of which a translation ought to be published; June 5, 12, *Andronicus;*

---

* These dates are so given by Henslow: they should be June 5 and June 15.

June 9, *Hamlet;* June 11, *The Taming of a Shrew.*
The intermediate days were occupied by the
Admiral's men: who on the 15th [17th] went to
the Rose, and the Chamberlain's men no doubt
to the Theater, the Burbadges' own house. The
Chamberlain's company at this date included
W. Shakespeare, R. Burbadge, J. Hemings, A.
Phillips, W. Kempe, T. Pope, G. Bryan, all of
whom, with the possible exception of Burbadge,
had been members of Lord Strange's company;
together with H. Condell, W. Sly, R. Cowley, N.
Tooley, J. Duke, R. Pallant, and T. Goodall, who
had previously been in all probability members
of the Queen's company. C. Beeston must have
joined them soon afterwards. The names of
Richard Hoope, William Ferney, William Blackway, and Ralph Raye occur in Henslow's *Diary*
as Chamberlain's men c. January 1595. The
Queen's men came in on the reconstitution of that
company in 1591–2. See on this matter further
on under the head of *The Seven Deadly Sins.*

On June 19 the old play of *Richard III.* (with
Shore's wife in it) was entered on S. R., a pretty
sure indication, which tallies with other external
evidence, that the play attributed to Shakespeare
was produced about this time. No one can read the
four plays composing the Henry 6th series without

feeling that, however various their authorship, they form a connected whole in general plan. Margaret is the central figure, who hovers like a Greek Chorus over the terrible Destiny that involves King and people in its meshes. But Margaret is not Shakespeare's creation; she is Marlowe's. Shakespeare had no share in the plays on the contention of York and Lancaster, and but a slight one in *1 Henry VI.* Marlowe had a chief hand in *1 Henry VI.* and *York and Lancaster;* probably wrote the whole of *Richard Duke of York*, and laid, in my opinion, the foundation and erected part of the building of *Richard III.* At his death he seems to have left unacted or unpublished his poem of *Hero and Leander,* finished afterwards by Chapman; *Dido,* partly by Nash, and produced (when?) by the Chapel children; *Andronicus* acted (under Peele's auspices?) by the Sussex men, and *Richard III.*, completed by Shakespeare, and acted by the Chamberlain's company as we have it in the Quarto. All these plays were produced or published in 1594. About the same time an earlier play of Marlowe's, originally acted c. 1589, was altered and revised by Shakespeare. The date and authorship of the Shakespearian part of *Edward III.*, viz., from "Enter King Edward" in the last scene of act i. to the end of act ii., are proved by the allusion to the poem of *Lucrece;* the repetition of lines from the *Sonnets:* "Their scarlet ornaments," "Lilies that foster smell far worse than weeds," and many smaller coincidences with undoubted Shakespearian plays : while the original date and authorship of the play as a whole will appear from the following quotations. In the Address prefixed to Greene's *Menaphon*, in a passage in which Nash has been satirising Kyd and another as void of scholarship and unable to read Seneca in the original, he suddenly attacks Marlowe, whom he has previously held up as the object of their imitation, and asks what can they have of him ? in Nash's own words : "What can be hoped of those that thrust Elysium into Hell, and have not learned, so long as they have lived in the spheres, the just measure of the Horizon without an hexameter?" Marlowe in *Faustus** has "confound Hell in Elysium," and, in *Edward III, horízon* is pronounced *hórizon*. This, however, might occur in other plays; but in Greene's *Never Too Late* we find Tully addressing the player Roscius, who certainly represents R. Wilson, in these words : "Why, Roscius, are thou proud with Æsop's crow,

---

* Simpson. But rather in 1 *Tamburlane* v. 2 : "Hell and Elysium swarm with ghosts of men," and similarly a few lines before " where shaking ghosts," &c.

being pranked with the glory of others' feathers? Of thyself thou canst say nothing: and if the Cobbler hath taught thee to say *Ave Cæsar*, disdain not thy tutor because thou pratest in a King's chamber." Unless another play can be produced with "Ave Cæsar" in it, this must be held to allude to *Edward III.*, in which play Wilson must have acted the Prince of Wales (act i. 1. 164). The "cobbler" alludes to Marlowe as a shoemaker's son.

On July 20, *Locrine*, an old play written, says Mr. Simpson, by G. Tylney in 1586, but in which Peele had certainly a principal hand, was entered on S. R. It was issued as "newly set forth, overseen and corrected by W. S." I see no reason to believe that this was Shakespeare. Of course he had no hand in writing the play; and in any case Peele did not probably sanction the publication.

To this year we must assign the production of the earliest of Shakespeare's *Sonnets*. That these (or rather that portion of them which are continuous, 1–126) were addressed to Lord Southampton was proved by Drake. The identity of language between the Dedication of *Lucrece* and Sonnet 26, the exact agreement of them with all we know of the careers of Shakespeare and his patron during the next four years, and the utter absence of evidence of his connection with any other patron, are conclusive on that point. They begin (1–17) with entreaties to marry, which date about 6th October 1594, when Southampton attained his majority, and before he had met Elizabeth Vernon, and end (117) in a time when "peace proclaiming olives of endless age," after the treaty of Vervins, 2d May 1598: and before the Earl's marriage at the end of that year. They involve a story of some frail lady who had transferred her favours to the young lord from the older player (40–42). Far too much has been written on this matter from a moral point of view. The fact remains, and all we can say is: Remember these Sonnets were written "among private friends," and not for publication. The lady has not hitherto been identified, but is, I think, identifiable. On September 3d was entered on S. R., *Wyllobie his Avisa*. Dr. Ingleby has shown in his *Shakespeare Allusion-books* that the W. S. in this poem is William Shakespeare, and that Hadrian Dorrell, the reputed editor, is a fictitious character. He has, however, missed the key to this anonymity; viz., that the book was known to be a personal satirical libel. P[eter] C[olse], according to the author of *Avisa*, "misconstrued" the poem; and so necessitated the further figment in the 1605 edition that the supposed author, A. Willobie, was dead; in this edition the mythical H. D. says: "If you ask me for the persons, I am altogether ignorant of them, and have set them down only as I find them named or disciphered in my author. For the truth of this action, if you enquire, I will more fully deliver my opinion hereafter." But independently of this evidence from the book itself we find in S. R. (Arber, iii. 678) that when the works of Marston, Davies, &c., were burnt in the Hall, 4th June 1599, other books were "stayed;" viz., *Caltha Poetarum*, Hall's *Satires*, and "*Willobie's Adviso* to be called in." This marks the book as of the same character as its companions; viz., libellous, calumnious, personally abusive. The characters in the poems were evidently representations of real living persons. The heroine of the poem is Avīsa, or Avīsa (sometimes written A vis A), that is, Avice or Avice A. This name was not uncommon (see Camden's *Remaines*, p. 93). She lived in the west of England, "where Austin pitched his monkish tent," in a house "where hangs the badge of England's saint." The place is more fully described thus:—

"At east of this a castle stands
By ancient shepherds built of old,

And lately was in shepherds' hands,
  Though now by brothers bought and sold :
At west side springs a crystal well :
There doth this chaste Avisa dwell."

And again :—

"In sea-bred soil on Tempe downs,
  Whose silver spring from Neptune's well
With mirth salutes the neighbouring towns."

These descriptions suit the vale of Evesham, the castle being that of Bengworth and the well that of Abberton. Austin's oak was traditionally placed in this part by some, though others put it in Gloucestershire. Avisa's parents are mentioned as "of meanest trade." They were, I take it, innkeepers, and the inn had the sign of St. George. The other characters are D. B., a Frenchman, with motto *Dudum Beatus;* Didymus H., an Anglo-German, with motto *Dum Habui;* H. W., *Italo Hispalensis*, and W[illiam] S[hakespeare]. The story is that Avisa, the chaste, who "makes up the mess" of four with Lucrece, Susanna, and Penelope, has been married at twenty, tempted by a Nobleman, a Cavaliero, a Frenchman, an Anglo-German, &c., without result, and is consequently England's *rara avis*, who matches those of Greece, Palestine, and Rome. The mottoes of the foreigners, however, point to a different conclusion, and so does this passage: "If any one, therefore, by this should take occasion to surmise that the author meant to note any woman, *whose name sounds something like that name*, it is too childish and too absurd, and not beseeming any deep judgment, considering there are many things which *cannot be applied to any woman*." In plain language, Mr. Dorrell believes no woman to be chaste. H. W., at first sight of Avisa, is infected with a fantastical fit, and bewrays his disease to his familiar friend, W. S., who, *not long before*, had tried the courtesy of the like passion, and was now newly recovered [in 1594]. Having been laughed at himself he determined to see whether it would sort to a happier end for the *new actor* than it did for the *old player*. Doubtless W. S. is Shakespeare, and Avisa is represented ironically as a *trader* who had made a Frenchman long happy (*dudum beatus*), been possessed by an Anglo-German (*dum habui*), had then passed to Shakespeare, and finally to H. W. Such was the slanderous story published in 1594; how far true, whether at all true, I care not to inquire; but that it is the same story as that of the Sonnets, that H. W. is Henry Wriothesley, and that the black woman of the Sonnets is identical with Avisa, I regard as indubitable. Of course the Thomas

Willoby, *Frater Henrici Willoughby nuper defuncti*, of the 1605 edition is a mere device to blind the licensers for the press. Similar devices have often been used, but I know of none so impudently charming as the "author's conclusion" as to the man who is *nuper defunctus*. "H. W. was now again stricken so dead that he hath not yet any further essayed, nor I think ever will, and whether he be alive or dead I know not, and therefore I leave him."

On December 26th and 28th the Chamberlain's servants performed before the Queen at Greenwich, apparently in the daytime. Kempe, Shakespeare, and Burbadge were paid for these performances on the following March. It is singular that the performance of "A comedy of *Errors* like unto Plautus his *Menæchmi*" should have also been performed apparently by the same company at Gray's Inn, also on December 26th. This seems to be the first mention of Shakespeare's play, the true title of which is simply *Errors:* but whether it was written in 1590 or 1593-4, there is no evidence that is absolutely decisive. The allusion to France fighting against her heir, v. ii. 2. 125, would be equally applicable at any date from July 1589, when Henri III. was killed, to February 1594, when Henri IV. was consecrated.

1595.

That the date of *Midsummer Night's Dream* should be fixed in the winter of 1594–5 was long since seen by Malone, the allusions to the remarkable weather of 1594 being too marked to be put aside contemptuously. It has also been attempted to assign other dates on account of the play's being manifestly written for some marriage solemnity. It is not needful to alter the date for that reason. Either the marriage of W. Stanley, Earl of Derby, at Greenwich, on 24th January, 1594–5, or that of Lord Russel, Earl of Bedford, to Lucy Harrington (before 5th February, S. R.), would suit very well in point of time. The former is the more probable; because it took place at Greenwich, where we know the Chamberlain's men to have performed in the previous month, and because these actors had mostly been servants to the Earl of Derby's brother in the early part of the previous year.

There is little, if any doubt, that Shakespeare produced *Richard II.* and *The Two Gentlemen of Verona*, as we now have it, in this year. *A larum for London*, or *The Siege of Antwerp*, by (?) Lodge, was acted about this time.

The play of *Richard Duke of York* was printed

in 1595; and on 1st December *Edward III.* was entered on S. R.

The performances of the Chamberlain's men, 1594–5, at Court, were on December 26, 27, 28; January 5; February 22. Payment was made to Hemings and Bryan.

1596.

Early in this year the play of *Sir T. More* was produced by the Chamberlain's company. The name of T. Goodale, who was one of their actors, occurs in the MS. It appears from the notes of E. Tylney, then Master of the Revels, that much revision had to be made in its form in consequence of its reproducing, under a thin disguise, a narrative of the Apprentice Riots of June 1595. The imprisonment of the Earl of Hertford in October of the same year was too closely paralleled by that of Sir T. More in the play to be agreeable to the Government. Another point objected to was satirical allusion to Frenchmen. The date hitherto assigned to this play is "1590 or earlier" (Dyce), which is palpably wrong.

Soon after Shakespeare's *King John* was acted. It contains, in my opinion, an allusion to the expedition to Cadiz in June (i. 2. 66–75).

On July 23d Henry Carey died, and the "Chamberlain's players" became the men of his son, George Carey L. Hunsdon.

In the same month, or earlier, *Romeo and Juliet* was revived in a greatly altered and improved form. All work by the second hand was cut out and replaced by Shakespeare's own writing. It was not, however, acted at this date at the Curtain, but at the Theater. Lodge's allusion in his *Wit's Misery*, 1596, to *Hamlet*, as acted in that house, is inconsistent with any other supposition. On August 5 a ballad on *Romeo and Juliet* was entered on S. R. This is taken by Mr. Halliwell as evidence that the play was then on the stage. On August 27 ballads are also mentioned on *Macdobeth* and *The Taming of a Shrew*. That on Macbeth could not have been on the play as we now have it, but that a play on this subject, perhaps an earlier form of the extant one, was then acted, is very probable.

On August 11 Hamnet Shakespeare was buried at Stratford: his father undoubtedly was present. This is the first visit to Stratford on his part since 1587 so far as any evidence exists.

Shakespeare returned to his lodgings "near the Bear Garden" in Southwark (Alleyn MS. *teste* Malone) before October 20, where a draft of a grant of arms was made to John Shakespeare, no doubt at his son's expense.

In November, a petition was presented by the inhabitants of Blackfriars against the transformation into a theatre of a large house bought by J. Burbadge on the preceding February 4. The petition was ineffectual.

Shakespeare's play *The Merchant of Venice*, sometimes called *The Jew of Venice*, is generally assigned to this year. I prefer 1597.

On December 29, Henry Shakespeare, the poet's uncle, was buried at Snitterfield; and his wife Margaret on 9th February 1596–7.

The Court performances of Lord Hunsdon's men at Whitehall were six in number, two at Christmas, and others on 1st, 5th January; 6th, 8th February 1596–7.

1597.

Before March 5 a surreptitious edition of *Romeo and Juliet* was published, but not entered on S. R. This consists of an imperfect and abridged copy of the revised play, with lacunæ filled up by portions of the original version of 1591. See hereafter in Section IV.

In Easter term, Shakespeare purchased New Place, a mansion and grounds in Stratford, for £60.

This was freehold, and henceforth his designation is, William Shakespeare of New Place, Stratford, Gentleman. From this time, male heirs failing, his ambition seems to be to found a family in one of the female branches; and Stratford is to be regarded as his residence.

Soon after 5th March, Lord Hunsdon was appointed Chamberlain *vice* W. Brooke, Lord Cobham, deceased, and Lord Hunsdon's men again became the Lord Chamberlain's.

During this year and the next Shakespeare undoubtedly produced *1* and *2 Henry IV*. The name given to the "fat knight" was originally Sir John Oldcastle. This offended the Cobham family, who were lineally descended from the great Sir John Oldcastle, and through their influence the Queen ordered the name to be altered. The new name was that of Falstaff, unquestionably identical with the Fastolfe of history. Shakespeare had unwittingly adopted the name Oldcastle from the old play of *The Famous Victories of King Henry V*. Mr. Halliwell has pointed out that there must have been another play in which a Sir John Oldcastle was represented : he quotes *Hey for Honesty*, "The rich rubies and incomparable carbuncles of Sir John Oldcastle's nose;" and Howell's *Letters*, ii. 71, "Ale is thought to be much adulterated, and nothing so good as Sir John Oldcastle and Smug the Smith was used to drink." I venture to add that this last quotation fixes the other play. It was Drayton's *Merry Devil of Edmonton*, in which Sir John the priest of Enfield drinks ale with Smug the Smith, and " carries fire in his face eternally." This play was probably produced between *1 Henry IV.* and *2 Henry IV.* The words "tickle your catastrophe" in the latter are more likely to be an allusion to the "gag" in the *Merry Devil* than conversely; similar ridicule of this phrase is introduced in *Sir Giles Goosecap*, which is certainly of later date. It seems strange that Sir John Oldcastle should have been used as the name of a priest; but the play has been so greatly abridged (all the part of the story in which Smug replaces St. George as the sign of the inn, for instance, having been cut out) that it would be mere guess-work to try to restore its original form, and without such restoration we cannot judge of the reasons for so singular an impersonation. Of course it was attempted to remove all trace of Oldcastle's name; but just as the prefix *Old.* to one of the speeches in Shakespeare's play bears evidence to Oldcastle having been his original fat knight, so it is possible that in a hitherto unexplained passage there may be a trace of Oldcastle as Drayton's original ale-drinking priest. In scene 9 the words italicised in " My *old Jenerts* bank my horse, my *castle*," look very like a corruption of a stage direction written in margin of a proof thus—

Old- J. enters
castle

—he is on the scene directly after, and his entrance is nowhere marked.

T. Lodge, as well as Drayton, was writing about this date for the Chamberlain's men.

On August 29 *Richard II.* was entered on S. R., and on October 20 *Richard III.* These were evidently printed from authentic copies, duly authorised for publication.

About July 1597 the Theater, with regard to extension of the lease of which James Burbadge had been negotiating up to his death in the spring of that year, was finally closed as a place of performance. In October the Chamberlain's men no doubt began to act at the Curtain, which Pembroke's men left at that date to join the Admiral's company at the Rose; some of them, however, probably Cooke, Belt, Sinkler, and Holland, had already in 1594 joined the Chamberlain's, as we shall see. About this date Mr. Halliwell says "Shakespeare's company" were at Rye (in August), at Dover and

Bristol (in September), &c. Pembroke's company were at these places, but he has given no proof that the Chamberlain's were. The "Curtain-plaudities" of Marston's *Scourge of Villany*, entered S. R. 8th September 1598, would certainly seem to show that they acted at the Curtain in 1598. This does not, however, involve the inference that they acted there in 1596, at which time they no doubt performed at the Theater.

About this same time the play of *Wily Beguiled* was acted, which contains distinct parodies of speeches by Shylock and old Capulet, as well as of other scenes in the *Merchant of Venice*, which must have preceded it. It has been alleged by Steevens and others that this play existed in 1596, but no proof has been given of this assertion.

In November John Shakespeare filed a bill against Lambert for the recovery of the Asbies estate. There is no trace of his having proceeded further with this litigation.

At Christmas the Chamberlain's men performed four plays at Whitehall, one of which was *Love's Labour's Lost*. The corrections and augmentations of the play, as we have it, may be confidently ascribed to the preparation for this performance.

1598.

On January 24 Abraham Sturley wrote to Richard Quiney urging him to persuade Shakespeare to make a purchase at Shottery, on the ground that he would thus obtain friends and advancement, and at the same time benefit the Corporation.

On February 25 *1 Henry IV.* was entered on S. R., and on July 22 *The Merchant of Venice.*

In this spring or in 1597 *Much Ado about Nothing* was probably produced. It was probably an alteration of *Love's Labour's Won.*

In September Jonson joined the Chamberlain's men, and produced his *Every Man in his Humour* at the Curtain. This was the Quarto version with the Italian names. Aubrey has been subjected to much unfounded abuse for asserting that Jonson acted at the Curtain. The actors in this play were Shakespeare, Burbadge, Phillips, Hemings, Condell, Pope, Sly, Beeston, Kemp, and Duke. Shakespeare, it will be noted, is first on the list.

On September 7 Meres' *Palladis Tamia* was entered on S. R. Among the abundant and often-quoted praises of Shakespeare in this work the most important for biographical purposes are the enumeration of his plays, the lists of tragic and comic dramatists, and this passage, which I shall have to refer to hereafter. "As the soul of Euphorbus was thought to live in Pythagoras, so the great witty soul of Ovid lives in mellifluous and honey-tongued Shakespeare. Witness his *Venus and Adonis*, his *Lucrece*, his sugared *Sonnets* among his private friends," &c. A careful comparison of the list of dramatists with that of known plays or titles of plays that have come down to us shows that the *Palladis Tamia* could not have been completed for the press till June 1598, and an examination of the list of Shakespeare's plays shows that it consists of those then in the *repertoire* of the Chamberlain's company, that is, of those either newly written or revived between June 1594 and June 1598. These plays are: *Gentlemen of Verona; Errors; Love's Labour's Lost; Love's Labour's Won; Midsummer-Night's Dream; Merchant of Venice*—comedies. *Richard II.; Richard III.; Henry IV.; John; Titus Andronicus; Romeo and Juliet*—tragedies. It is clear that *Richard III.* and a play on Andronicus, which I believe to be the one we have, were attributed to Shakespeare at that time.

On 25th October Richard Quiney wrote from the Bell in Carter Lane to his "loving good friend and countryman Mr. William Shakespeare," who was, according to the subsidy roll discovered by Mr. J.

Hunter, then living in the parish of St. Helen's, Bishopsgate, asking for the loan of £30. On the same day he wrote to his brother-in-law Mr. Sturley at Stratford, that "our countryman Mr. W. Shakespeare would procure us money." The former letter was sent evidently by hand, an affirmative answer obtained, and soon after instructions given by Shakespeare for the procuring the money. We could not otherwise account for the letter being preserved among the documents of the Corporation.

The Famous Victories of Henry V. was reprinted in 1598; as we so often find to be the case with old plays on which other plays have been founded. The complaint about the name Oldcastle no doubt was a special motive for reproducing the old play in this instance.

There were three plays performed at Court by Shakespeare's company in the Christmas festivities.

1599.

In April a play of *Troylus and Cressida*, by Dekker and Chettle, was written; no doubt an opposition play to some revival of Shakespeare's older one on the same subject.

The Chamberlain's men acted *A Warning for Fair Women* about this time. This play appears to me to come from the hand of Lodge.

In this year *The Passionate Pilgrim*, "by W. Shakespeare," was imprinted by Jaggard. It contains two of the *Sonnets*, two other Sonnets from *Love's Labour's Lost*, and one other poem from the same play by Shakespeare. The remaining poems, as far as they are known, are by Barnefield and other inferior authors. There is not a vestige of reason for reprinting this book as Shakespeare's.

In the spring Shakespeare's company left the Curtain and went to act at the Globe. This was a newly erected building on Bankside, made partly of the materials of the old Theater, which had been removed by Burbadge at the beginning of the year. One of the first plays performed in it was Jonson's *Every Man out of his Humour*, the chief actors in which were Burbadge, Hemings, Phillips, Condell, Sly, and Pope. Kempe, Beeston, Duke, and Pallant had left the company, and did not act at the Globe. But Shakespeare's name is also absent in this list, and this fact, coupled with that of the libellous nature of this "comical satire," and Jonson's leaving the Chamberlain's men immediately after it to continue his strictures on Dekker, &c., at Blackfriars with the Children of the Chapel, makes it exceedingly probable that the disagreement which eventuated in the "purge" given by Shakespeare to Jonson mentioned in *The Return to Parnassus* had already arisen. It would lead to too long a digression to do more than touch on this stage quarrel here. I can only say that it lasted till 1601; that Jonson and Chapman on the one side at Blackfriars, and Shakespeare, Marston, and Dekker on the other, at first at the Globe, Rose, and Paul's, afterwards at the Fortune, kept up one continual warfare for more than three years. Not one of their plays during this time is free from personalities and satirical allusions; nor, indeed, are most comedies of Elizabeth's time; it is only because the allusions have grown obscure and uninteresting to us, that we fail to see that the Elizabethan comedy is eminently Aristophanic. It is not till the reign of James that we find the comedy of manners and intrigue at all generally developed.

Another play produced after the opening of the Globe was *Henry V.*, and soon after in this year *As You Like It*.

Somewhere about this time an attempt was made to get a grant to "impale the arms of Shakespeare with those of Arden," *ignotum cum ignotiore*. The grant was not obtained.

At this Christmas the Chamberlain's men gave three performances at Court, viz., on 26th December at Whitehall, on 5th January 1599–1600 and on 4th February at Richmond.

1600.

Shrovetide, February 4. The play performed at Court was probably *The Merry Wives of Windsor*. This play is assigned by tradition to a command of the Queen, who wished to see Falstaff represented in love, and is said to have been written in a fortnight. It was probably an adaptation of the old *Jealous Comedy* of 1592; and is more likely to have come after than before *Henry V.*, in which Shakespeare had failed, according to his implied promise in the Epilogue to *2 Henry IV.*, to continue the story with Falstaff in it. It stands apart altogether from the historical series.

March 6. The Chamberlain's men acted "Oldcastle" before their patron, Lord Hunsdon, and foreign ambassadors at Somerset House. This could not have been Shakespeare's "Falstaff," for the obnoxious name of Oldcastle would certainly not have been revived before such an audience; nor could it have been the *Sir John Oldcastle*, which belonged to another company; it may have been *The Merry Devil of Edmonton*.

About this time Shakespeare, always attentive to pecuniary matters, brought an action against one John Clayton for £7, and obtained a verdict.

The August entries on S. R. are specially interesting. On the 4th a memorandum (not in the regular course of entry) appears to the effect that *As You Like It, Henry V., Every Man in his Humour,* and *Much Ado about Nothing,* were "to be stayed." On the 14th, *Every Man in his Humour* was licensed; on the 23d, *Much Ado about Nothing,* and along with it *2 Henry IV., "with the humours of Sir John Falstaff.* Written by Master Shakespeare." On the 11th the first and second parts of the *History of the Life of Sir John Oldcastle, Lord Cobham, " with his Martyrdom,"* had been licensed. The "staying" is generally supposed to have relation to surreptitious printing; I think it more likely to have been caused by the supposed satirical nature of the plays. *As You Like It* was not printed; *Henry V.* was printed in an incomplete form * without license; while the emphatic mention of Falstaff and the insertion of the author's name to *2 Henry IV.*, not customary at that date, show that the Oldcastle scandal had not yet died out. This is still further proved by the almost simultaneous entries of the two plays written October to December 1599 for the Admiral's men by Monday, Drayton, Wilson, and Hathaway, on Sir John Oldcastle. Only one has reached us, which is plainly satirical of *Henry V.* It was, however,

Henry V. was transferred to T. Pavier on 14th August.

in one of the editions printed in 1600 ascribed to William Shakespeare. Drayton, who was the chief author concerned in its production, had left the Chamberlain's men in 1597, and been writing for the Admiral's ever since. It is noticeable that after 1597 we find the favourable notices of Lodge and Shakespeare which had been inserted in previous editions expunged from his writings, notably the lines on Lucrece in the legend of *Matilda*. Drayton had probably quarrelled with both his coadjutors. With the entry here on Oldcastle's "martyrdom" compare the Epilogue to *2 Henry IV*. This was not the play acted before Hunsdon on March 6, which was probably *The Merry Devil*.

On 8th October *Midsummer-Night's Dream* was entered on S. R.; on 28th October *The Merchant of Venice*. Curiously enough, two rival issues of each of these plays was made this year, although only one publisher made an entry in each case. On 22d July 1598, J. Roberts had entered *The Merchant of Venice*, but was refused permission to print unless he could get the Lord Chamberlain's license, who was the patron of the actors of that play. He apparently did not get it; but in 1600, when J. Heyes does get the license, he arranges with Heyes to print the book for him, but previously prints a slightly differing copy on his own account. He makes with Fisher, the publisher of the other play, a somewhat similar transaction.

There were three Court performances this Christmas by the Chamberlain's men, December 26, January 5, February 24. The payment for these to Hemings and Cowley indicates that the latter was a shareholder in the Globe.

2 and *3 Henry VI.* were probably revised and revived at the Globe about this time.

1601.

In this year *All's Well that Ends Well* and *Hamlet* were produced. The form in which the latter appeared is matter of dispute; but we may safely assert that it lay between the version of the first Quarto and that of the Folio; the variation of the Quarto from this original form being caused by the surreptitious nature of that edition, and that of the Folio by a subsequent revision in 1603. The company of "little eyases" satirised in this play was not of the Paul's children, with whom the Chamberlain's men were on the most friendly terms, but of the Chapel children at the Blackfriars, who were then acting Jonson's "comical satires" against Dekker, Marston, and Shakespeare. Singularly enough, they were tenants of the Burbadges, who were also owners of the Globe.

In the same year 1601, a poem by Shakespeare appeared along with others by Jonson, Marston, and Chapman in R. Chester's *Love's Martyr, or Rosalin's Complaint*. This publication, could we ascertain its exact date, would show the time when the stage controversy ceased and these four writers could amicably appear together. Dekker, however, does not appear among them, and we cannot tell if his *Satiromastix* was acted with Shakespeare's approval or not. It was produced at the Globe by his company as well as by the children of Paul's at some time between 22d May, up till which day Dekker was writing for the Admiral's men, and 11th November, when it was entered on S. R. This bitter satire seems to have been the last open word in the controversy, but by no means the end of its history.

The next fact we have to notice may perhaps explain why, just at this point of Shakespeare's career, we find in 1602 a cessation of production, accompanied by a change of manner in outward form and inward thought when writing was resumed in 1603. In March 1601, in the Essex trials, Meyrick was indicted "for having procured the outdated tragedy of *Richard II.* to be publicly acted at his own charge for the entertainment of the conspirators" (Camden). From Bacon's speech (*State*

Trials) it appears that Phillips was the manager who arranged this performance. This identifies the company as the Chamberlain's, and therefore the play as Shakespeare's. It may seem strange that a play, duly licensed and published in 1597, could give offence in 1601; but the published play did not contain the deposition scene, iv. 1, the acted play of 1601 certainly did. This point is again brought forward in Southampton's trial: he calmly asked the Attorney-General, "What he thought in his conscience they designed to do with the Queen?" "The same," replied he, "that Henry of Lancaster did with Richard II." The examples of Richard II. and Edward II. were again quoted by the assistant judges against Southampton, while Essex in his defence urged the example of the Duke of Guise in his favour. From all which it is clear that the subjects chosen for historical plays by Marlowe and Shakespeare were unpopular at Court, but approved of by the Essex faction, and that at last the company incurred the serious displeasure of the Queen. Accordingly, they did not perform at Court at Christmas 1601–2;* and we find them travelling in Scotland instead—L. Fletcher with his company of players being traceable at Aberdeen in October.

* Mr. Halliwell (*Outlines*, p. 128, 2d edition) says they performed four plays at Whitehall, but quotes no authority.

ANNALS. 145

Here the actors would hear of the Gowry conspiracy instead of Essex', of which we shall find the result hereafter. Before leaving London, however, or in the next year after their return, they acted *The Life and Death of Lord Cromwell*, Earl of Essex, a play in which the rise and fall of Robert Devereux, the late Earl, was pretty closely paralleled. This was entered on S. R., 11th August 1602, " as lately acted."

On September 8 John Shakespeare, the poet's father, was buried at Stratford.

1602.

On 18th January *The Merry Wives of Windsor* was entered on S. R. : a surreptitious issue. On 2d February, *Twelfth Night* was performed at the Readers' Feast at the (?) Middle Temple, " much like *The Comedy of Errors* or the *Menechmi* in Plautus, but most like and near to that in Italian, called *Inganni*" (Manningham's Diary).

On 19th April *1* and *2 Henry VI.* (evidently the Quarto plays on which *2* and *3 Henry VI.* were founded) were assigned by Millington to Pavier, *salvo jure cujuscumque*, S. R. This entry is important. It shows that the remodelling of the old Quarto plays under the new name of *Henry VI.* instead of *The Contention of York and Lancaster* had taken place; it indicates a doubt or fear as to

K

whether the copyright might be disputed by some publisher, authorised by the Chamberlain's men to produce the amended version.

In May, Shakespeare bought for £320, from the Combes, 107 acres of arable land in Old Stratford. The indenture was sealed and delivered in his absence to his brother Gilbert.

On July 26 the surreptitious *Hamlet* was entered on S. R., and on August 11 *The Life and Death of the Lord Cromwell.*

On 28th September, at a Court Baron of the Manor of Rowington, Walter Getley transferred to Shakespeare a cottage and garden in Chapel Lane, about a quarter of an acre with forty feet frontage, possession being reserved for the lady of the manor till suit and service had been personally done for the same.

Two plays were performed by the Chamberlain's men at Court this Christmas, one at Whitehall 26th December, one at Richmond 2d February.

1603.

February 7. *Troylus and Cressida*, as performed probably in 1602 by the Chamberlain's men, not the play by Dekker and Chettle, was entered on S. R.

The *Taming of the Shrew* as we have it was probably produced in March.

March 24. THE QUEEN DIED.

On 19th May a license was granted to L. Fletcher, W. Shakespeare, R. Burbadge, A. Phillips, J. Hemings, H. Condell, W. Sly, R. Armin, R. Cowley, to perform stage plays "within their now usual house called the Globe," or in any part of the kingdom. They are henceforth nominated the King's Players. The functions of Fletcher are not exactly known : he did not act, and was probably a sort of general manager; the other eight were probably shareholders, among whom it will be noted that Shakespeare and Burbadge stand first. In the list of actors in Jonson's *Sejanus*, Cowley and Armin are omitted, A. Cook and J. Lowin appearing instead. This play got Jonson into trouble. He was accused before the Council for " Popery and treason " in it. When he published it next year he no doubt omitted the most objectionable passages, and put forth an excuse that a second hand had good share in it. This was his usual way of getting out of a difficulty of this kind. Even as the play stands there is abundant room for malice to interpret the quarrel between Sejanus and Drusus as that between Essex and Blount; and to see in Sejanus' poisoning propensities allusions to the Earl of Leicester. Whalley's curious notion that Jonson in his argument alluded to the Powder plot, ignores the fact that the play was entered on 2d November 1604 in S. R. It is Raleigh's plot that is intended.

The London Prodigal, and Wilkins' *Miseries of Enforced Marriage*, were written and perhaps acted (at the Globe?) this year.

The edition of *Hamlet* entered in the preceding year was issued in the autumn.

On December 2 the King's players performed at the Earl of Pembroke's at Wilton, and at Hampton Court before the King on December 26, 27, 28, January 1 [? December 29]; before the Prince, December 30, January 1; before the King at Whitehall, February 2, 18; nine plays in all. A much larger number of plays were acted at Christmas festivities at Court in James's reign than in Elizabeth's. Perhaps the Queen only cared for new plays. We know that James frequently ordered a second performance of any one that specially pleased him, and often had old plays revived.

On 8th February 1604, there occurs an entry in the Revels accounts which explains the small number of public theatrical performances, and the cessation of work of the principal author for the King's men in 1603. To R. Burbadge was given £30, " for the maintenance and relief of himself and the rest of his company, being prohibited to present any plays publicly in or near London by reason of great peril that might grow through the extraordinary concourse and assembly of people to a new increase of the plague, till it shall please God to settle the city in a more perfect health." From July 1603 till March 1604 the theatres were probably closed. Hence my doubt as to whether *The London Prodigal* and *The Miseries of Enforced Marriage* were performed in London till 1604. The King's company were most likely travelling in the provinces till the winter; but were disappointed at not being allowed to reopen at Christmas when the plague had abated.

1604.

The King's men, like those of other companies, had an allowance for cloaks, &c., to appear at the entry of King James on 15th March.

The second Quarto of *Hamlet* was published in this year—"Newly imprinted and enlarged to almost as much again as it was, according to the new and perfect copy." This version was probably that performed at Court in the Christmas festivities 1603–4. We cannot suppose that among the nine plays then exhibited *Hamlet* would not be included. Of course on such occasions plays were always more or less rewritten. In this instance the remodelling is twofold; the Quarto version for the Court, 1603–4, the Folio for the public, of the same date. That the Folio does not merely reproduce the 1601 play, as it was acted in London, " in the Universities of Cambridge and Oxford" (perhaps in going to or returning from Scotland in 1601), " and elsewhere," is clear for many reasons, one of which concerns us here. In the well-known passage in ii. 2 relating to the Children's company, an " inhibition " and " innovation " are mentioned in the 1604 Quarto of which there is no note in that of 1603. The only time at which we know of any contemporary inhibition and innovation was in, January–February 1604. The inhibition on account of the plague, which was going on till nearly 8th February, I have already noticed; the innovation was either the political conspiracy of Raleigh or the attempt at reformation in religion by the Puritans. The Children of the Chapel, who under Evans, Burbadge's lessee, had satirised Shakespeare and other players in their performances at Blackfriars, were reappointed at this time to act in that same theatre under E. Kirkham, A. Hawkins, T. Kendall, and R. Payne, with the new appellation of Children of the Revels. The date of the warrant is 30th January 1604. The King's men acted at Court

2d February, and if *Hamlet* was then performed the passage in ii. 2 may have brought their grievance under the King's notice, and resulted in the gift of £30 by way of compensation. I do not insist on this, however, as it is omitted in the Quarto. No doubt they had expected to get rid of the children at Blackfriars at the end of seven years from the date of the original lease, 4th February 1596. At the end of another seven years they did so, but only by purchasing the remainder of the lease.

In this summer Marston's *Malcontent* was obtained in some indirect manner from these Blackfriars children, perhaps from one of the children actors who "left playing" at the time of the new license, and was played at the Globe, with an Induction by Webster introducing Sinkler, Sly, Burbadge, Condell, and Lowin on the stage. This was a retaliation for the children having in like fashion previously appropriated *Jeronymo* (*The Spanish Tragedy*), which belonged to the Chamberlain's men. The curious thing about the transaction is that the *Malcontent* was originally produced in 1601, containing satirical allusions to *Hamlet;* and that in 1604 both plays, revised, were acted on the same stage, by the same actors.

On 2d November *Sejanus* was entered on S. R.
On 18th December a letter from Chamberlain to

Winwood contains the following notice. " The tragedy of *Gowry*, with all action and actors, hath been twice represented by the King's players, with exceeding concourse of all sorts of people: but whether the matter or manner be not well handled, or that it be thought unfit that princes should be played on the stage in their lifetime, I hear that some great councillors are much displeased with it, and so 'tis thought it shall be forbidden." Shakespeare's work during this year is shown by the transcript of the Revels Accounts obtained by Malone. The King's men acted at Whitehall on November 1 *The Moor of Venice;* November 4, *The Merry Wives of Windsor;* December 28, *Measure for Measure*, and *Errors;* ["Between January 1 and January 5" in the forged copy of this entry still extant]* *Love's Labour's Lost;* January 7, *Henry V.;* January 8, *Every One out of his Humour;* February 2, *Every One in his Humour;* February 10, *The Merchant of Venice;* February 11, *The Spanish Maz;* February 12, *The Merchant of Venice* again. I have given the full list as in the forged copy, but Malone is our safe guarantee for all the Shakespeare plays. It appears then that in this year Shakespeare must have written

* This performance was at Southampton's house before Queen Anne.

Measure for Measure and *Othello*, and, as we have already seen, produced a revision of *Hamlet*. How much of this work was performed in 1603 we cannot tell; but it is not likely that *Othello* was written till 1604. The only definite dates in this year relate to other matters.

In May Shakespeare entered an action at Stratford against one Philip Rogers for £1 15s. 10d., balance of account for malt.

In August the King had a special order issued that every member of the company should attend at Somerset House when the Spanish ambassador came to England (Halliwell, *Outlines*, p. 136). The Christmas Court performances have been noted above.

1605.

On 8th May, the old play on *Leir* was entered on S. R.

On 4th May Phillips made his will, which was proved on the 13th. In it he leaves 30s. each to Shakespeare and Condell, and 20s. each to Fletcher, Armin, Cowley, Cook, and Tooley, all his fellows; to Beeston, "his servant," 30s.; to Gilburne, his "late apprentice," 40s. and clothes; to James Sandes, "his apprentice," 40s. and musical instruments; to Hemings, Burbadge, and Sly, overseers and executors, a bowl of silver of £5 apiece.

On 3d July a ballad on the *Yorkshire Tragedy* was entered on S. R.; the play which has been erroneously attributed to Shakespeare was no doubt acted about the same time.

The London Prodigal was published, but not entered on S. R., this same year, with the name of William Shakespeare on the title-page.

Jonson's *Fox* was acted by the King's men; the chief actors were the same as those of *Sejanus* in 1603, except Phillips, who died in May, and Shakespeare, a most noteworthy exception.

On 24th July, William Shakespeare, *of* Stratford-upon-Avon, bought of Ralph Huband an unexpired term of thirty-one years of a ninety-two years' lease of a moiety of the tithes of Stratford, Old Stratford, Bishopton, and Welcombe for £440, subject to a rent payable to the corporation of £17, and £5 to John Barker. This, at the rate of interest then prevalent, was a dear purchase. In 1598 his "purchasing these tithes" had been mooted at Stratford.

As to Shakespeare's dramatic work during this year I have no doubt that *Lear* was on the stage in May, when the old play was published. I cannot otherwise account for the description of the latter in S. R. as a *tragical* history. Until Shakespeare's play this story had always been treated as a comedy.

Macbeth was probably produced in the winter, or in the following year. When James I. was at Oxford in August, he had been addressed in Latin by the three witches in this story, at an entertainment given by the University. No doubt James would be pleased by their prophecies, and desirous that they should be promulgated in the vulgar tongue. No more likely date can be found for the holograph letter which he is said to have addressed to Shakespeare. It may possibly be that that letter was a command to write this play. But, putting conjecture aside, Oldys says that Sheffield, Duke of Buckingham, told Lintot that he had a letter from the King to the dramatist.

On October 9, Shakespeare's company performed before the Mayor and Corporation of Oxford. It may have been on this occasion that Shakespeare made the acquaintance of the Davenants, and stopped for the first time at the Crown, the license for which inn had only been taken out by Davenant in the preceding year. Enough has been written by others as to the scandal about Mrs. Davenant, and the tradition that William Davenant the poet, the godson of Shakespeare, was really his son. No foundation beyond a Joe Miller joke has been discovered for this report.

At Court, ten plays were acted in the Christmas

season by the King's men; among them the revived *Mucedorus*, which, as we have seen, was an apology for Jonson's satire in *Volpone*.

1606.

In this year, Shakespeare's portion of *Timon of Athens*, and that part of *Cymbeline* which is founded on so-called British history, were probably written.

A play called *The Puritan* (*Widow*), evidently by Middleton, was acted by the Paul's boys this year, in which we find direct allusion to *Richard III.* and *Macbeth*, both of which were probably on the stage. The same scene contains a palpable parody of the action of the scene in *Pericles* in which Thaisa is recovered to life. That play must then have also been on the stage. It does not follow that it was the play as we have it. It may have been, and I believe was, Wilkins' play before Shakespeare's improvement had been introduced.

During July or August, the King's men had performed three plays before the King of Denmark and his Majesty—two at Greenwich, one at Hampton Court; and at Christmas they performed at Court nine plays: on December 26, 29; January 4, 6, 8; February 2, 5, 15, 27. That on 26th December was *Lear*, as we have it in the Quarto version. The Folio is that used on the stage of the same date.

1607.

Anthony and Cleopatra must have been acted about this time, as well as Cyril Tourneur's *Revenger's Tragedy*.

On 25th June Susanna, Shakespeare's eldest daughter, married Dr. John Hall, an eminent physician at Stratford.

On 6th August Middleton's *Puritan Widow* was entered on S. R., and imprinted as by W. S.

Twine's *Pattern of Painful Adventures*, on which Wilkins' version of *Pericles* was founded, was reprinted in this year.

On 22d October Drayton's *Merry Devil of Edmonton* was entered on S. R. The entry on 5th April under the same title, in which the authorship is ascribed to T[homas] B[rewer], refers to the prose story, not the play.

On 26th November *King Lear* was entered on S. R.

On December 31 Shakespeare's brother Edmund was buried at St. Saviour's, Southwark, aged twenty-eight, "a player," "with a forenoon knell of the great bell."

There were thirteen Court performances by the King's men: on December 26, 27, 28; January 2, 6 (two plays), 7, 9, 17 (two plays), 26; February 2, 6.

1608.

On February 21 Elizabeth Hall, Shakespeare's granddaughter, was baptized at Stratford.

The Yorkshire Tragedy was entered on S. R. May 20, as by William Shakespeare. The authorship of this play has not been yet ascertained.

On May 20 *Anthony and Cleopatra*, and *Pericles* (not as in the Quarto version with the three last acts by Shakespeare), were entered on S. R. Wilkins' prose version of the play was printed this same year. I take the order of events regarding this play to have been as follows. Wilkins wrote a play on Pericles in 1606, which was parodied in Middleton's *Puritan* that same year; in 1607 Twine's *Pattern of Painful Adventures* was reprinted; in the same year Wilkins left the King's company and joined the Queen's; in May 1608 the play was entered for publication, but not published; it may have been "stayed" by the Chamberlain's company; in the same year Wilkins issued surreptitiously (it was not entered on S. R.) his "*true* history of the play as it was lately presented by the poet Gower." Such a proceeding as this, a printing of a prose narrative founded on an unprinted play and by the same author, is unparalleled in the history of Shakespearean drama. It must be remembered that Wilkins was not even connected with the King's company at the time. Meanwhile Shakespeare had rewritten Acts iii.–v. In this new shape the play was acted in 1608, and was, as we know from an allusion in *Pimlico, or Run Redcap* (entered S. R. 15th April 1609), very popular. An edition of the play thus altered was issued in 1609, not by Blount, who made the entry in May 1608, but by Gosson, as the "late much-admired play . . . with the true relation of the whole history . . . as also the *no less* strange and worthy accidents in the birth and life of his daughter Marina," that is, of the part written by Shakespeare. This edition is very hurriedly and carelessly got up.

In August Shakespeare commenced an action against Addenbroke.

On September 9 Shakespeare's mother was buried at Stratford. Shakespeare's company had been shortly before travelling on the southern coast (Halliwell, who suppresses the exact date as usual). It is always dangerous to read personal feeling in a dramatist's work; but the coincidences in date of his *King John* and Hamnet's death, of his *Coriolanus* and his mother's death, justify, I think, my opinion that his wife's grief is apotheosised in Constance, and his mother's character in Volumnia. This is confirmed by the great change that takes place in his work at this time; his next four plays are devoted to subjects of family reunion after separation.

On 16th October he was godfather to William Walker at Stratford.

In this autumn *Coriolanus* was probably produced.

The Court Christmas performances by the King's men were twelve, on unknown dates.

1609.

On January 28 *Troylus and Cressida* was entered on S. R., and published from a surreptitious copy, with a preface, stating that it had been "never staled with the stage." This preface was withdrawn before the close of the year, probably at the instance of the King's company. It has been, however, the cause of misleading many modern critics (myself included), as to the date of the production of the play. In the new issue the title states that it is printed "as it was acted by the King's Majesty's servants."

On February 15, a verdict for £6 and £1, 4s. costs was given in favour of Shakespeare against John Addenbroke for debt, and execution issued. This suit began in August 1608; the precept for a jury is dated 21st December, when an adjournment of the trial probably took place. After the final judgment Addenbroke was *non inventus*, and on 7th June 1609, Shakespeare proceeded against his bail, one Horneby. All these proceedings were conducted not personally, but through his solicitor and cousin Thomas Greene.

On 20th May the Sonnets were entered on S. R., and published with dedication to Mr. W. H., who, in my opinion, was some one connected with Lord Southampton, who had obtained a copy from him or his, and possibly may have given Shakespeare the hint to write them in the first instance, at the time (1594) when his friends were anxious for him to marry. Such a person was Sir William Hervey, the third husband of Southampton's mother: she died in 1607, and I conjecture that the delay in publishing the Sonnets was due to the fact that she wished them to remain in MS. at any rate during her lifetime. The copy used may have been found among her papers.

On 20th May 1608 had been entered *Pericles*, and *Antony and Cleopatra*, which were not published by Blount, who made the entry. *Pericles*, however, was printed surreptitiously in 1609 for another firm as we have it in the Quarto. This play was probably then continued on the stage, as we find another edition required by 1611.

Cymbeline was probably produced in the autumn. This year being a plague year there was little dramatic activity; even Jonson did not produce his *Epicene* for the King's men, but had it acted by the Chapel (or Revels) children. For the same reason there were no stage performances at Court at Christmas.

1610.

On 4th January a patent was granted to R. Daborne, P. Rossiter, J. Tarbook, R. Jones, and R. Browne, to set up a new Children's company in Whitefriars. Their success was no doubt the cause that determined the Burbadges to take the Blackfriars into their own hands.* Accordingly they arranged to purchase at Lady Day the remainder of Evans' lease of the Blackfriars (they had already taken the boys, "now growing up to be men," Underwood,† Ostler, &c., to "strengthen the King's service"), and to place men players

* Mr. Halliwell (*Outlines*, p. 150) gives December 1609 as the date of this change. This is certainly not in accordance with other facts which I shall adduce in the following pages; he gives no authority for his statement.

† Cuthbert Burbadge in 1635 adds Field by a slip of memory.

—Hemings, Condell, Shakespeare, &c., therein. Before the end of the year we accordingly find the boys alluded to acting as members of the King's company in Jonson's *Alchemist.* The chief players were Burbadge, Hemings, Lowin, Ostler, Condell, Underwood, Cooke, Tooley, Armin, and Egglestone. Of these Tooley and Cooke had been boy actors in the Chamberlain's company, Underwood and Ostler in the Revels children. Shakespeare's name does not occur; nor do I find any evidence except Mr. Halliwell's unsupported assertion (*Outlines*, p. 111), that he continued to act at this date. It is noticeable that there are ten actors mentioned; this is very unusual in these play lists, and suggests that the number of sharers may have been increased from eight to ten. There are certainly about this time allusions to ten shares scattered about in contemporary plays. If this be the case, Shakespeare would no longer be a shareholder: the whole question of his shares is involved in difficulty, and this conjecture is only thrown out to call attention to any allusions in writings of this date that may throw light on the matter.

The King's men performed fifteen plays at Court this Christmas.

In this year, in my opinion, Shakespeare having produced *The Winter's Tale* and *The Tempest*, retired from theatrical work. Malone's hypothesis that Sir W. Herbert's mention of Sir G. Buck's "allowing" the former play implies a date subsequent to August 1610, is worthless; Buck had the "allowing" of plays in his hands from 1607 onwards. There is direct evidence that the Blackfriars Theatre was occupied even after 1611 by other companies. Field's *Amends for Ladies* was acted there by the Prince's and the Lady Elizabeth's men; and Charles could not be called Prince till after the death of Henry, 6th November 1612. The production of Field's play was probably in the spring 1613. By careful comparison of the dry documents concerning shareholders in 1635, with those of the Blackfriars property in 1596, we ascertain that J. Burbadge bought that property 4th February 1596; that in November the establishment of a theatre there was petitioned against, but carried out soon after; that a lease of twenty-one years was granted to Evans, either at Christmas 1596 or Lady Day 1597, most probably the latter; that at the end of thirteen years the Burbadges bought the remaining eight years of the lease, probably at Lady Day 1610, and took possession of the building;—but that they *at the same time* took the boys into the King's company or set up Hemings, Shakespeare, &c., in the Blackfriars is mere rhetoric of Cuthbert's. Underwood and Ostler had both left the Revels children before the performance of Jonson's *Epicene* in 1609, and Field did not join the King's men till 1618–19.

In June Shakespeare purchased twenty acres of pasture land from the Combes.

At Christmas the King's men performed fifteen plays at Court.

1611.

In this year unusual efforts seem to have been made by the King's company to secure authors of repute to write for their playhouse. Jonson's *Catiline* was acted by nearly the same cast as *The Alchemist*, the only change being that Robinson appears in the list instead of Armin. The second *Maiden's Tragedy* was produced in October, most likely written by Tourneur, having been preceded by the first *Maid's Tragedy* by Beaumont and Fletcher, who also in this year brought out their *Philaster* and *King and no King:* in all we have five new plays of the first rank, acted by a company that hitherto appears to have almost entirely depended on about two plays from Shakespeare, and occasionally a third by some other hand, as sufficient novelty to attract a year's full houses. It is this *quasi* monopoly in writing for his company that explains Shakespeare's accumulation of property; and it is to me incredible that *Macbeth, The Winter's Tale, Cymbeline,* and *The Tempest* should all have been produced in this year. Yet this seems to be the belief of practical critics who believe only what can be supported by what they term "positive evidence," the evidence in this case being that Forman, the astrological charlatan, entered in his note-book that he had seen acted *Cymbeline, Macbeth,* 20th April 1610 [1611]; *Richard II.,* 30th April 1611; *Winter's Tale,* May 15. This evidence has, however, value of another kind, for it shows that a large number of revivals took place in this year; indeed, coupling this with the fact that at this Christmas and the next the unprecedented number of fifty plays were performed by the King's men at Court, it is likely that *all* Shakespeare's plays were revived immediately after his retirement from the stage. We cannot trace fifty plays to the possession of his company at this date without including them.

On September 11 Shakespeare's name occurs in the margin of a folio page of donors (including all the principal inhabitants of Stratford) to a subscription list " towards the charge of prosecuting the bill in Parliament for the better repair of the highways." This appears to confirm the view that Shakespeare was at this time residing in Stratford.

On December 16 the play of *Lord Cromwell* was entered on S. R., and published as by W. S.

The plays at Court were twenty-two: on October 31; November 1, 5; December 26; January 5, February 23, before the King; on November 9, 19; December 16, 31; January 7, 15; February 19, 20, 28; April 3, 16, before Prince Henry and Charles, Duke of York; on February 9, 20 (*sic*), before the Prince; on March 28, April 26, before the Lady Elizabeth.

1612.

On February 3 the burial of Gilbert Shakespeare " adolescens " was entered in the Stratford Register. I agree with Mr. French that this was most likely Shakespeare's brother.

In this year a suit was commenced " Lane Greene, and Shakespeare compl$^{ts.}$ " on the ground that they had to pay too large a proportion of the reserved rent of the tithes purchased in 1605. It appears from the draft of the bill filed before Lord Ellesmere that Shakespeare's income from this source was £60.

The plays produced by the King's men were *The Woman's Prize, Cardenno* (*i.e., Cardenes, or*

Love's Pilgrimage), and *The Captain*, by Fletcher and his coadjutors, and the *Duchess of Malfi* by Webster, who also published *The White Devil*, with the remarkable allusion to the "right happy and copious industry" of Shakespeare, Dekker, and Heywood. Curiously enough, this is often referred to even now as a eulogy on Webster's part; it is really damning with faint praise the poet to whom he hoped to be the successor as provider of plays to the King's company.

The Passionate Pilgrim reached a third edition, and was reissued as "certain amorous Sonnets between Venus and Adonis," by W. Shakespeare; "whereunto is added two love epistles" between Paris and Helen. These were stolen from Heywood's *Troja Britannica* of 1609. In his *Apology for Actors* (1612), he complains of the injury done him, as it might lead to unjust suspicion of piracy on his part, and adds, "As I must acknowledge my lines not worthy his patronage under whom he hath published them, so the author I know much offended with M. Jaggard that altogether unknown to him presumed to make so bold with his name." In consequence, no doubt, of this remonstrance, Jaggard had to substitute a new title-page, from which Shakespeare's name was entirely omitted. He had allowed his name to be used in the titles of *The London Prodigal* in 1605, of *The Yorkshire Tragedy* in 1608, of *The Passionate Pilgrim* of 1609, and even of *Sir John Oldcastle* in 1600 without murmuring; but directly the interests of another demand justice at his hands he takes prompt action, and compels the piratical publisher to withdraw his name altogether.

The King's men at the Christmas festivities, &c., presented at Court fourteen plays before the King and fourteen before the Prince, the Lady Elizabeth, and the Prince Palatine. Among the plays so represented were *Philaster, The Knot of Fools, Much Ado about Nothing, The Maid's Tragedy, The Merry Devil of Edmonton, The Tempest, A King and no King, The Twins' Tragedy, The Winter's Tale, Sir John Falstaff* (*The Merry Wives of Windsor*), *The Moor of Venice, The Nobleman, Cesar's Tragedy, Love lies a bleeding* (*Philaster* repeated), before the Prince, Lady Elizabeth, and the Palatine; *A Bad Beginning makes a Good Ending* (? *All's Well that Ends Well*; but entered S. R. 1660 as Ford's, and destroyed in MS. by Warburton's servant; Ford's revision must, of course, have been later than 1623), *The Captain, The Alchemist, Cardenno, The Hotspur* (*1 Henry IV.*), *Benedicte and Betteris* (*Much Ado about Nothing*), before the King. See Stanhope's Accounts (Halliwell, *Outlines*, p. 597, third edition, and *Revels Accounts*, p. xxiii.) Of these twenty Shakespeare contributes nine, Fletcher (with Beaumont) six, Jonson one, Tourneur one, Drayton (?) one, and two have not been identified.

1613.

On 4th February Richard Shakespeare, the poet's only surviving brother, was buried at Stratford.

On 10th March Shakespeare purchased in Blackfriars a house with yard and haberdasher's shop for £140, subject to a mortgage of £60. This property had greatly increased in value since 1604, when it was sold for £100, probably in consequence of the immediate vicinity of the theatre, which drew large custom for feathers and other articles of attire to Blackfriars. Shakespeare leased it to John Robinson, who had by this time seen the absurdity in a business point of view of his opposition to the establishment of the theatre in 1596. One of the trustees for the legal estate (the mortgage remaining unredeemed till 1613) was John Heming, unquestionably Shakespeare's friend the actor.

On 8th June the King's men played at Court before the Duke of Savoy's ambassadors.

On 29th June the Globe Theatre was burnt down, " while Burbadge's company were acting the play of *Henry VIII.*, and there shooting off certain chambers by way of triumph " (T. Lorkin's letter). Sir H. Wotton says it was "a new play called *All is True*, representing some principal pieces of the reign of Henry VIII." It was of course Shakespeare's play in its original form. A Fool must have acted in it, for in the old ballad about this fire, "the reprobates prayed for the fool and Henry Condy" (Condell), who were apparently the last actors who escaped.

It has been conjectured that at this time Shakespeare retired from the stage, having sold his shares in the Globe and Blackfriars in order to purchase the house above mentioned. There is no particle of evidence that he had not saved the £80 then paid from his usual economies, or that if he had wished to sell his shares he could have done so. It is true that shares in the later Globe (rebuilt 1613–14) were so sold; but all the evidence as to the theatre in which Shakespeare was concerned points the other way. It appears from the 1635 documents that Hemings, Shakespeare, &c., had their shares without paying any consideration, and that all the shares held by Pope, Kempe, Bryan, Shakespeare, Sly, and Cowley had reverted by 1614 into the hands of the surviving shareholders, the Burbadges, Hemings, and Condell. If we examine the wills of these men, we find that Pope indeed, in

1603, leaves all his estate or interest in the Globe, "which I have or ought to have," to Mary Clark and Thomas Bromley; but that Phillips in 1605, and Cooke in 1614, make no mention of any shares. It seems most likely that this will of Pope's raised the question as to whether these shares were held during office as actor or absolutely. There can be little doubt that the former was the case, as is only reasonable where the shares, as in the first Globe, were given "without consideration." Purchased shares, like those in the latter Globe, are in a different position. At any rate, the shares left to Bromley and Clark in fact reverted to the surviving shareholders. Sly's will in 1608, which is in similar terms to Pope's, leaves his shares to Robert Brown, who, like Clark and Bromley, disappears from all future history of these shares. Moreover, there is no mention of any shares belonging to Cowley, Beeston, or Kempe: yet there can be no doubt that Kempe was till 1599 a shareholder.

On 15th July, in the Ecclesiastical Court at Worcester, the case of Dr. John Hall *v.* John Lane, for slandering his wife, was heard, and the defendant excommunicated on the 27th.

There were sixteen plays performed at Court by the King's men this year, on November 4, 16; January 10; February 4, 8, 10, 18; and nine others.

1614.

Fletcher, Webster, and Beaumont had all left the King's men, and now, 31st October, Jonson leaves them too, and produces his *Bartholomew Fair* at the Hope, with abundant sneers at Shakespeare's plays, especially the *Tempest* and *Winter's Tale*. He does not allude to *Henry VIII*. Fletcher was now, as well as Jonson, a writer for the Princess Elizabeth's players.

In July John Combe left Shakespeare £5 as a legacy.

In the autumn an attempt was made by W. Combe, the squire of Welcombe, to inclose a large portion of the neighbouring common fields; this attempt was opposed by the Corporation, but supported by Mr. Manwaring and Shakespeare. The latter clearly acted simply with a view to his own personal interest. His name as an ancient freeholder occurs in a list, 5th September, as having claim for compensation if the inclosure took place. On 18th October, Replingham, Combe's agent, covenanted to give him full compensation for injury by "any inclosure or decay of tillage:" on 16th November he went to London: on 17th November his "cousin," T. Greene, town clerk of Stratford and at the same time his own solicitor, called to see him: he said the inclosures were to be less than had been represented, that nothing would be done till April, and that he and Mr. Hall thought nothing would be done at all. On 23d December letters to Mr. Manwaring and Shakespeare were written, with "almost all the company's hands" to them, and a private letter in addition by Greene to "my cousin," with copies of all the acts of the Corporation, and notes of the inconveniences that would result from the inclosure. The inclosure was not made, and Shakespeare did not get his compensation.

1616.

On 25th January the first draft of Shakespeare's will was drawn up. On 10th February his daughter Judith was married without a license to T. Quiney, vintner of Stratford; they were summoned in consequence to the Ecclesiastical Court of Worcester a few weeks after. On 25th March the will was executed, and on 25th April "Will. Shakspere, gent." was entered in the burial register at Stratford. He died just before completing his fifty-fourth year; but it is usually supposed on the 23d, his birthday.

SECTION IV.

THE CHRONOLOGICAL SUCCESSION OF SHAKESPEARE'S PLAYS.

IT is of the greatest importance, in investigating the chronological succession of an author's works, that we should start from a definite and certain date. The neglect of this point, especially in so difficult an instance as the present, involves us too often in thorny discussions at the very onset. Such an epoch is presented us at once by the publication of Shakespeare's earliest poem. I begin therefore at this point.

Venus and Adonis was entered on S. R. 18th April 1593 by Richard Field, printer, son of Henry Field, tanner, of Stratford-on-Avon, who parted with his copyright to Mr. Harrison, senior, 25th June 1594. There were editions in 1593, 1594 (R. Field); 1596 (R. Field for J. Harrison); 1599 and 1602, *bis* (W. Leake); 1617 (W. Barrett); and 1620 (J. Parker). Harrison had assigned his copyright to Leake 25th June 1596. It was transferred to W. Barrett 16th February 1616–17; and again to J. Parker 8th March 1620. This was "the first heir of my invention," which means—the first production in which I have had no co-labourer. Compare Ford's expression "the first-fruits of my leisure" applied to *'Tis pity she's* &c., although he had certainly at that time written plays in connection with Dekker and others.

Lucrece. Entered on 9th May 1594 in S. R. by Mr. Harrison, senior. Editions 1594 (R. Field for J. Harrison); 1598 (P. S. for J. Harrison); 1600 (J. H. for J. Harrison); 1607 (N. O. for J. Harrison; 1616 (T. G. for R. Jackson). This poem is a pendant to the former; the one exhibiting woman's chastity, the other her lust. Such opposition of subject in successive productions is very characteristic of Shakespeare.

A Lover's Complaint, published with the *Sonnets* 1609, written probably 1593–4, between the *Venus* and *Lucrece*.

Sonnets, entered on S. R. 20th May 1609 for T. Thorpe. I have on pp. 25, 120 already stated my opinion that these were written during 1594–8.

Titus Andronicus was a new play in 1594, acted for the first time by Sussex' men at the Rose on 23d January.

Richard III. was no doubt acted this same

year by the Chamberlain's men; just before the old play which had been acted by the Queen's players was published (S. R. 19th June 1594). A *Richard* is alluded to in John Weever's *Epigrams*, published 1599, when the author was twenty-three, but written when he was not twenty; they must therefore date at latest in 1596 (not 1595 as usually stated). Weever mentions *Venus and Adonis*, *Lucrece*, *Romeo*, and *Richard* as the issue of honey-tongued Shakespeare. We shall see that *Romeo*, as referred to here, was acted in 1595-6, and I believe the *Richard* referred to is the *Richard II.* of 1595. *Edward III.* I have shown in p. 118 to be an alteration of an old play of Marlowe's written in 1590, revived in 1594 about the autumn, after *Lucrece* was published. It will be most convenient to defer the consideration of authorship of the preceding plays till I have to treat of *Henry VI.*; the dates of editions of all the plays will be exhibited in tabular form further on, which will save much repetition and interruption of argument. We now come to an unquestionable date; and it is from this, the first recorded date in connection with an undoubted play, that I wish the reader to regard our investigation of play dates as beginning.

1594.

December 28. Shakespeare's only farcical comedy of *Errors* was acted at Gray's Inn at night: the same players had acted before the Queen at Greenwich on that day, very likely in the same comedy. In April 1595 the English agent in Edinburgh wrote to Burghley, how ill King James took it that the comedians in London should scorn the king and people of Scotland in their plays. The barrenness of Scotland is mentioned in iii. 2. Neither would James approve of a play in which witchcraft and exorcising is so constantly ridiculed. The opening scene is very like in method to that of *Midsummer-Night's Dream;* and the reiterated allusions by either Dromio to being transformed to an ass (ii. 2. 201; iii. 1. 15; iv. 4. 28; iii. 2. 77) remind us so strongly of that play as almost to infer contemporaneity of production; especially as in iii. 1. 47 the same quibble, an *ass* and *ace*, occurs as in *Midsummer-Night's Dream*, v. 1. 317. Now in 1593, in his *Pierce's Supererogation*, and in 1592 in his *Four Letters*, Gabriel Harvey had rung the changes on *an ass* and *a Nash* even to wearisomeness; just as Shakespeare in this play puns on *an ell* and *a Nell* (iii. 2. 112). This may seem very forced; but I must remind the reader, that *s* and *sh* were not distinguished in pronunciation except by pedants at the end of the sixteenth century. It seems then most likely that in dwelling on this transformation, Shakespeare meant to recall to his audience the dyslogistic name inflicted on his old enemy Nash by Gabriel Harvey. All this points to a production of the play in 1594, by the Chamberlain's men; but there are also indications of its having been altered from an earlier version. In the stage directions there are traces of the name Juliana * for Luciana: in the text Dowsabel occurs instead of Nell, and in v. 1, the prefix *Fat.* (Father) has been clearly replaced by *Mar.* (Merchant) in a revision; note especially v. 1. 195, where both prefixes have by a common printer's error been inserted at once. The older form, again, had Antipholus Sereptus for A. of Syracuse, and Erotes or Erratis for A. of Ephesus; and it had twenty-five years of separation between the parents for thirty-three in the later version. This last difference occurs in i. 1, which is throughout written in a more mechanical and antique style of metre than the rest of the play; and, indeed seems to be one of the earliest specimens left us of Shakespeare's attempts to bombast out a blank verse. There is

* This name occurs in *Apollonius and Sylla*, of which more hereafter.

also the name Menaphon (v. 1. 368), which is likely to have been adopted from Greene's *Menaphon* (1589), who again took it from Marlowe's *Tamberlaine* (1587-8). The Adam "that goes in the calf-skin," surely alludes to the Adam in the *Looking-glass for London* (1590), whose "calf-skin jests" were even after seven years an object of ridicule to the playwrights. For all these reasons I believe that a version of this play was acted c. 1590, perhaps in the winter of that year. It does not follow that that version was entirely by Shakespeare, as the present play is; he may have replaced a coadjutor's work of 1590 by his own of 1594. The plot, with its time-unity, is not likely to be of his arranging. As to the pun on the war made by France against her heir (iii. 2. 126), which is usually relied on for the date of production, it merely gives as limits August 1589, when the war of succession began, and 27th February 1594, when Henri IV. was crowned. It does, however, enable us to say positively that the first performance of the play was before the formation of the Chamberlain's company, who only revived it, no doubt in an amended shape, on 28th December 1594, most likely for the sake of the Court performance. The original plot was probably suggested by Plautus' *Menæchmi* and *Amphitryo;* and perhaps more directly by the

History of Error performed by the Chapel children in 1576, which, by the bye, has nothing to do with the *Ferrar* of the Earl of Sussex' men in 1582. But we cannot assume in these early plays that Shakespeare was the plotter. It is certain, however, that he did afterwards adopt the likeness of twins in *Twelfth Night* as a means of introducing "errors" on the stage.

1595.

January 26 was the date of the marriage of William Stanley, Earl of Derby, at Greenwich. Such events were usually celebrated with the accompaniment of plays or interludes, masques written specially for the occasion not having yet become fashionable. The company of players employed at these nuptials would certainly be the Chamberlain's, who had, so lately as the year before, been in the employ of the Earl's brother Ferdinand. No play known to us is so fit for the purpose as *Midsummer-Night's Dream*, which in its present form is certainly of this date. About the same time Edward Russel, Earl of Bedford, married Lucy Harrington. Both marriages may have been enlivened by this performance. This is rendered more probable by the identity of the Oberon story with that of Drayton's *Nymphidia*, whose special patroness at this time was the newly married Countess of Bedford. That poem contains an allusion to Don Quixote, which could not well have been written till 1612, and certainly not till 1605; but Drayton is known to have constantly altered his poems by way of addition and omission, and no date of original production can in his case be fixed by allusions of this kind. The date of the play here given is again confirmed by the description of the weather in ii. 2. In 1594, and in that year only, is there on record such an inversion of the seasons as is there spoken of. Chute's *Cephalus and Procris* was entered on S. R., 28th September 1593; Marlowe's *Hero and Leander*, 22d October 1593; Marlowe and Nash's *Dido* was printed in 1594. All these stories are alluded to in the play. The date of the Court performance must be in the winter of 1594-5. But the traces of the play having been altered from a version for the stage are numerous. There is a double ending. Robin's final speech is palpably a stage epilogue, while what precedes from "*Enter Puck*" to "break of day— *Exeunt*" is very appropriate for a marriage entertainment, but scarcely suited to the stage. In Acts iv. and v., again, we find in the speech-prefixes *Duke, Duchess, Clown* for *Theseus, Hippolita, Bottom*: such variations are nearly always marks of alteration, the unnamed characters being anterior in date. In the prose scenes speeches are several times assigned to wrong speakers, another common mark of alteration. In the Fairies the character of Moth (Mote) has been excised in the text, though he still remains among the *dramatis personæ*. It is not, I think, possible to say which parts of the play were added for the Court performance; but a careful examination has convinced me that wherever *Robin* occurs in the stage-directions or speech-prefixes scarcely any, if any, alteration has been made; *Puck*, on the contrary, indicates change. The date of the stage play may, I think, be put in the winter of 1592; and if so it was acted, not at the Rose, but where Lord Strange's company were travelling. For the allusion in v. 1. 52, "The thrice three Muses mourning for the death of Learning, late deceased in beggary," to Spenser's *Tears of the Muses* (1591), or Greene's death, 3d September 1592, could not, in either interpretation, be much later than the autumn of 1592; and the lines in ii. 1. 156—

> "I am a spirit of no common rate;
> The summer still doth tend upon my state,
> And I do love thee "—

are so closely like those in Nash's *Summer's Last Will*, where Summer says—

> "Died I had indeed unto the earth,
> But that Eliza, England's beauteous Queen,
> *On whom all seasons prosperously attend,*
> Forbad the execution of my fate
> Until her joyful progress was expired"—

that I think they are alluded to by Shakespeare. The singularly fine summer of 1592 is attributed to the influence of Elizabeth, the Fairy Queen. Nash's play was performed at the Archbishop's palace at Croydon in Michaelmas term of the same year by a "number of hammer-handed clowns (for so it pleaseth them in modesty to name themselves);" but I believe the company originally satirised in Shakespeare's play was the Earl of Sussex', Bottom, the chief clown, being intended for Robert Greene. Thus much for date of production. For the title of the play, compare the conclusion of *The Taming of a Shrew* and Peele's *Old Wife's Tale*, the latter of which is performed in a dream, and the former is supposed by Sly to be so; the interpretation that it means a play performed at midsummer is quite inconsistent with iv. 1. 190, &c., and other passages. The names of the personages are interesting, because they show us what books Shakespeare was reading at this time: from North's *Plutarch*, Life of Theseus, the first in the book, he got Periginia (Perigouna), Aegles, Ariadne, Antiope, and Hippolita; from

Chaucer's *Knight's Tale*, also the first in the printed editions, which he afterwards dramatised, Philostrate; from Greene's *James IV*. Oberon. This last name, with Titania's, also occurs in the Queen's *Entertainment* at Lord Hertford's, 1591. The time-analysis of this play has probably been disturbed by omissions in producing the Court version. I. 1. 128-251 ought to form, and probably did, in the original play, a separate scene; it certainly does not take place in the palace. To the same cause must be attributed the confusion as to the moon's age; cf. i. 1. 209 with the opening lines: the new moon was an afterthought, and evidently derived from a form of the story in which the first day of the month and the new moon were coincident after the Greek time-reckoning. It is worth notice that not only is the title of Preston's *Cambyses* parodied in the Pyramus interlude, but his pension of sixpence a day is ridiculed in iv. 2. Nor must we quite pass over the fact, which confirms the 1595 date, that on 30th August 1594, at the baptism of Prince Henry (of Scotland), the tame lion which was to have been brought in in the triumph was replaced by a Moor, "because his presence might have brought some fear." The play is nearly as much an error play (iii. 2. 368) as the *Errors* itself, and, like it, has no known immediate source for the plot. The Pyramus interlude is clearly based on C. Robinson's *Handfull of Pleasant Delights* (1584); and some of the fairy story may have been suggested by Montemayor's *Diana*. The line ii. 2. 104, is from Peele's *Edward I.* (near end), "how nature strove in them to show her art," and I think the man who dares not come in the moon because it is in snuff may allude to the offence given at Court by Lyly's *Endymion* in 1588. An absolute downward limit of date is given by a line imitated in *Doctor Doddypol*, a play alluded to in 1596 by Nash, and spoiled in the imitation—

> "Hanging on every leaf an orient pearl,
> Which shook together by the silken wind
> Of their loose mantles made a silver chime."

This solidification of the dewdrops does not occur in the Shakespeare parallel, ii. 1. 15. Mr. Halliwell's fancy that Spenser's line in *Fairy Queen*, vi.—"Through hills and dales, through bushes and through briers" must have been imitated by Shakespeare in ii. 1. 2, is very flimsy; hill and dale, bush and brier, are commonplaces of the time. Nor is there any proof that this song could not have been transmitted to Ireland in 1593 or 1594.

1595.

Richard II. cannot be definitely dated by external evidence, but all competent critics agree that it is the earliest of Shakespeare's historical plays; the question of authorship, &c., of *Richard III.* being reserved for the present. It is a tragedy like Marlowe's *Edward II.*, not a "life and death" history. The *Civil Wars* of Daniel, from which Shakespeare seems to have derived a few hints, was entered on S. R. 11th October 1594. The play probably was produced after this date, and before the publication of the Pope's bull in 1596, inciting the Queen's subjects to depose her. In consequence of this bull the abdication scene was omitted in representation, and in the editions during Elizabeth's lifetime. In like manner, Hayward was imprisoned for publishing in 1599 his *History of the First Year of Henry IV.*, which is simply the story of Richard's abdication. The omitted scene was restored in 1608 under James I. as "new additions." Such *new* additions on title-pages are often restorations of omitted passages. The Folio copy omits a few other speeches, the play having been evidently found too long in representation; but it contains the abdication scene. This being the first play of Shakespeare's that passed the press was carelessly corrected, whence much apparently unShakespearian and halting metre, which is easily set right. The source of the plot is Holinshed's *Chronicle;* "the earlier play on *Richard II.* lately printed" (says Mr. Stokes in 1878) "I have not seen; but it concludes with the murder of the Duke of Gloster." The play seen at the Globe by Forman in 1611 began with the rebellion of Wat Tyler. It was not Shakespeare's. There is no prose in this play, in *John*, or the *Comedy of Errors;* a sign of early work.

1595.

The Two Gentlemen of Verona is a striking instance of the difficulties in which we are involved if we attempt to assign a single date for the production of every play, and neglect the fact that alterations were and are continually made by authors in their works. Drake and Chalmers date this play in 1595; Gervinus, Delius, and Stokes 1591. Malone at different times adopted both dates. I believe that all these opinions are reconcilable, that the play was produced in 1591, with work by a second hand in it, which was cut out and replaced by Shakespeare's own in 1595. For a date after 1593 is distinctly indicated in the play as we have it by the allusions to *Hero and Leander* in i. 1. 21, iii. 1. 119; and to the pestilence in ii. 1. 20;

a still closer approximation is shown to the *Merchant of Venice*, by the mistake of Padua for Milan in ii. 5. 2. If Shakespeare had not, at the time when he finally produced the *Two Gentlemen*, begun his study for the Venetian story, whence this name? It only occurs there, once in *Much Ado*, and in the non-Shakespearian parts of *The Taming of the Shrew*. In like manner the mistake of Verona for Milan in iii. 4. 81, v. 4. 129, indicates that he had been preparing *Romeo and Juliet*. That our play lies between the *Errors* and the *Dream* on one hand and *The Merchant* on the other, becomes pretty clear by comparing the development of character in the Dromios, Launce and Speed, Lancelot Gobbo; in Lucetta and Nerissa; in Demetrius and Lysander, Valentine and Proteus. Nor are marks of the twofold date wanting. In the first two acts we find Valentine at the Emperor's court, no Duke mentioned; in the last three at the Duke's, no Emperor mentioned. The turning-point is in ii. 4, where, though "Emperor" occurs in the text, "Duke" is used in the stage directions. In i. 1. 32, "If haply won perhaps a hapless gain; if lost, why then a grievous labour won," there is surely an allusion to *Love's Labour's Won*, and *Love's Labour's Lost;* we shall see hereafter that in 1591 these were quite recent plays.

The Eglamour of Verona mentioned in i. 2. 9 is not the Eglamour of Milan who appears in iv. 3, v. 1. Style and metre require an early date for i. ii. 1–3 and parts of iii. 1; but in any argument of an internal nature, Johnson's weighty remark should be remembered—" From *mere* inequality, in works of imagination, nothing can with exactness be inferred." The immediate origin of the plot is unknown; parts of the story are identical with those of *The Shepherdess Filismena* in Montemayor's *Diana*, translated in MS. by Young, c. 1583, and of Bandello's *Apollonius and Sylla* in Rich's *Farewell to Military Profession* (1581). *Felix and Philiomena* had been dramatised and acted at Court by the Queen's players, 1584–5. That the revision of *The Two Gentlemen* was hurriedly performed is clear from the unusually large number of *Exits* and *Entrances* that are not marked. This hurry accounts, in some degree, for the weakness of the play, which induces so many critics to insist on an early date for it as a whole. Yet the special blemish they discover, v. 4. 83, the yielding up of Silvia by Valentine, is paralleled in the *Dream*, where (iii. 2. 163) Lysander says, "With all my heart, in Hermia's love I yield you up my part:" and that Shakespeare felt the unreality of this part of the plot is clear from *Two Gentlemen*, v. 4. 25, which to

me seems a manifest reminiscence of his last play,
" How like a dream is this I see and hear!" (cf.
Midsummer-Night's Dream, iv. 1. 190, "It seems
to me that yet we sleep, we dream"). He had
been reading Chaucer, as we know, and from him
had adopted this method of presenting stories in a
dream. A slighter reminiscence of Chaucer's *Knight's
Tale* occurs in the mention of Theseus, iv. 4. 173.

1595-6.

Romeo and Juliet was surreptitiously printed by
J. Danter in 1597; "as it hath been often with
great applause played (publicly), by the Rt. Hon.
the L. of Hunsdon, his servants." This edition
must have been printed in 1596 (old reckoning),
for the players would have been called the Chamberlain's servants except during the tenure of that
office by W. Brooke, Lord Cobham, from 23d July
1596 to 5th March 1597. That it was on the
stage as well as *Richard II.* in 1595-6, appears
from Weever's *Epigrams*. A correct edition of
Romeo appeared in 1599. The relation of these
two versions of the play presents a difficult problem. The 1599 Quarto Q_2 is unquestionably the
play of 1595-6, as acted by the then Chamberlain's
players at the Theater; for it does not follow, as
Mr. Halliwell supposes, that because they continued

to act it when called Lord Hunsdon's players, they had not ever acted it before. Such reasoning would compel us to assign all plays published as "acted by the King's players" to a date subsequent to 1602—*Hamlet*, for example, and *Troylus and Cressida*. Nor does it follow that because it was acted at the Curtain, where Marston mentions it in his *Scourge of Villany* (S. R. 8th September 1598), that it was *produced* at that same theatre. Mr. P. A. Daniel has shown, in his Parallel Text Edition, that the 1597 Quarto Q_1 is a shortened version of the play, no doubt for stage purposes (compare the Quartos in i. 1; i. 3; iii. 1). He has also with great ingenuity conclusively proved that Q_2 is a revised copy made on a text in many places identical with Q_1 (see i. 1. 122; i. 4. 62; ii. 3. 1–4; iii. 2. 85; iii. 3. 38–45; iii. 5. 177–181; iv. 1. 95–98, 110; v. 3. 102, 107). But his conclusion that Q_1 is partly made up from notes taken during the performance, is not borne out by any evidence. There are no "mistakes of the ear" in this play, nor is this conclusion consistent with his own theory that Q_2 was a revision made on the text of Q_1. I owe what I believe to be the real solution to a hint from my son, a boy of thirteen. When a play was written and licensed, at least three copies would be made of it. One, with the Master of the Revels' endorsement (which I will call R), would be kept in the archives of the theatre intact; one would be made for the manager (M), which would have occasional notes of stage direction, &c., inserted; and one, an acting copy, for the prompter (P), usually much abridged from the original and always altered: this would contain stage directions, &c., in full, but in the unaltered passages would be identical with M. Now Q_1 shows evident signs of being printed from a shortened copy P; Q_2 is manifestly a revision of a full copy M. The genealogy of the Quartos then stands thus :—

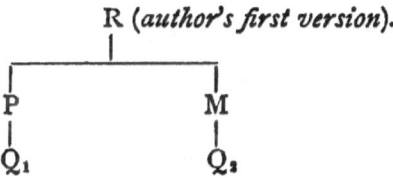

Q_2 is, according to this theory, a revised version made on a *complete* copy of an early version of the play, while Q_1 is printed from the prompter's copy of the same early version. When the revision took place this copy would be thrown aside as worthless; and any dishonest *employé* of the theatre could sell it to an equally dishonest publisher, who would publish it as the play now acted. If this solution be correct, and it is the only one yet proposed that meets all the difficulties of the case, Q_1 is specially interesting as being the earliest extant play (as acted) in which Shakespeare had a share. For it is clear that some passages in it, especially ii. 6, the laments in iv. 5, and Paris' dirge in v. 3, are not only unlike the corresponding passages in Q_2, but unlike anything we have from Shakespeare's hand. The date of the early form of the play was 1591, eleven years after the earthquake of 1580 (i. 3. 23, 30). As confirmatory of the conclusion that Q_2 was revised from an early play note that in i. 1 the servants are nameless in Q_1, but have names in the stage directions in Q_2; that in i. 3 the servant is called clown in Q_1; that in iii. 5 in Q_2, where the prefixes vary between *Lady* and *Mother*, it is in the unaltered parts that *Mother* is used as in Q_1, but *Lady* always where enough alteration has taken place to require a completely fresh transcript; that in v. 3 there is a double entry marked for the Capulets (a sure sign); that in ii. 3. 1–4, v. 3. 108–111, duplicate versions occur. On the other hand, the printing of the Nurse's speeches in italics in both Quartos is conclusive for identity of origin in that scene. Other points worth noting are that "Queen Mab, what's she?" i. 4. 55 in Q_1 are omitted in Q_2: Mab had become well known in 1595, probably through Drayton's *Nymphidia*.

SUCCESSION OF HIS PLAYS.

In ii. 2. 144, "I am afraid all this is but a dream," reminds us of similar passages in *Errors*, ii. 2. 184; *Two Gentlemen*, v. 4. 26; and *Dream*, iv. 1. 199, &c. W. Kempe acted the part of Peter (see entry in iv. 5); Balthazar is proparoxyton in v. 1. The line in iii. 2, 75, "O serpent heart hid with a flowering face" (where Q_1 has "serpent's hate"), is very like the often-quoted "O tiger's heart wrapt in a woman's hide" (*3 Henry VI.* i. 4. 137). The play is founded on Arthur Brooke's poem, *The Tragical History of Romeus and Juliet, containing a rare example of true constancy*. Constancy in love is its main subject. He took the Italian form of the name Romeo, and the time of Juliet's sleep forty-two hours ("forty at least" in the novel) from *Rhomeo and Julietta* in Painter's *Palace of Pleasure*. Much unnecessary writing has been expended on this forty-two hours; the plot requires forty-eight. Daniel, in his *Rosamund* (S. R. February 1591-2), and the author of *Doctor Doddypol* (c. October 1594), have passages very like some in this play. A ballad founded on the play was entered S. R. 15th August 1596. On the mention of "the first and second cause" in ii. 4. 26 and (in Q_1 only) in iii. 1, some critics base the conclusion that this play must be subsequent to Saviolo's *Book of Honour*, &c. (S. R. 19th November 1594). I believe that the book referred to is *The Book of Honor and Arms, wherein is discussed the* CAUSES *of quarrel,* &c. (S. R. 13th December 1589). The same expression occurs in *Love's Labour's Lost,* i. 2. 184; in any case it probably belongs to the revised version of this last named play. The alteration in ii. 4 from "to-morrow morning" to "this afternoon," shows that in the revision Shakespeare attended to details in the time of action.

1596.

King John was founded on the old play acted by the Queen's men, called *The Troublesome Reign of King John.* The lines ii. 1. 455–460 are imitated in *Captain Stukeley* by Dekker and others, acted at the Rose, 11th December 1596; iii. 1. 176–179 refer manifestly to the Pope's bull in 1596, inciting the English to depose Elizabeth; Chatillon's speech ii. 1. 71–75 is most applicable to the great fleet sent against Spain in the same year; Constance's lamentations have been reasonably referred to the death of Hamnet Shakespeare (buried 11th August); the *Iron Age* is alluded to in iv. 1. 60, and never elsewhere in Shakespeare. Now, Heywood's play of that name was on the stage from June 23 to July 16 under the title of *Troy.* The summer of 1596 is thus undoubtedly the date of Shakespeare's play.

There are some indications of the play having been shortened; Act ii. in the Folio has only seventy-four lines, and Essex has a part of only three lines, although in the older *John* he appears in five scenes. I think he was meant to be entirely cut out c. 1601 after Essex' execution, and these three lines should be given to Salisbury. The rival play of *Stukeley* was shortened in the same way; a whole act was expunged before its publication in 1605. In i. 2 (Folio) the Citizen on the walls is called Hubert; this indicates that the same actor represented both characters.

1596–7.

The Merchant of Venice, or *Jew of Venice*, was no doubt founded on an old play called *The Jew of Venice*, by Dekker. It seems, from the title of the German version of this play, that the Jew's name was Joseph. The name Fauconbridge in i. 2 (where Portia's suitors are enumerated, compare *Two Gentlemen*, i. 2) points to a date soon after *John;* and the "merry devil" of ii. 3. 2, a phrase never elsewhere used in Shakespeare, indicates contemporaneity with *The Merry Devil of Edmonton* produced in the winter of 1596. Again, the manifest imitations of this play in *Wily Beguiled,* which I show elsewhere to date in the summer of 1597, give a posterior limit, which must be decisive. This play has no sign whatever of having been altered; the Clarendon Press guesses, founded on the discrepancy of the number of suitors (iv. for vi.) are as worthless as Mr. Hales' proof, referred to by Mr. Halliwell (*Outlines*, p. 251), of the date of *Wily Beguiled*. The conclusive evidence of imitation in this play is the conjunction of the "In such a night" lines in scene 16, with the "My money, my daughter" iterations of Gripe in scene 8 of the same play. On 22d July 1598, J. Roberts entered *The Merchant or Jew of Venice* on S. R., but had to get the Lord Chamberlain's license before printing. On 28th October 1600, he consented to the entry of the play for T. Hayes; nevertheless, he issued copies of his own imprint independently.

1597.

The First Part of Henry IV. was entered on S. R. 25th February 1598; a genuine and authorised imprint. The publication of this play was hurried in order to refute the charge of attacking the Cobham family in the person of Sir John Oldcastle, the original name of the character afterwards called Falstaff (cf. "my old lad of the castle," i. 2. 48). Moreover, in i. 2. 182, we find in the text the names Harvey and Russel instead of Peto and Bardolph.

SUCCESSION OF HIS PLAYS. 199

The name Russel for Bardolph again occurs in a stage direction in *2 Henry IV*. ii. 2. These were evidently originally the names of the characters, and were changed at the same time as that of Oldcastle: Russel was the family name of the Bedford Earls, and Harvey that of the third husband of Lord Southampton's mother. The new names were picked up from the second part; in which Lord Bardolph and Peto (a distinct personage from the "humourist" of Part I.) were serious characters. The play was produced in the spring; the only mentions of June in Shakespeare's plays are in ii. 4. 397 (*sun* F.); iii. 2. 75; and *Anthony*, iii. 10. 14. In ii. 4. 425, Preston's *Cambyses* is ridiculed (cf. *Dream*). There is an imitation of iii. 2. 52 in *Lust's Dominion* (the *Spanish Moor's Tragedy*, by Dekker, Haughton, and Day, February 1600, absurdly quoted by Stokes as Marlowe's). For the "abuses of the time" i. 2. 174; iv. 3. 81; see under *Sir T. More*, 1596. This play, as well as *2 Henry IV*. and *Henry V.*, is founded on *The Famous Victories of Henry V.*, an old play produced by the Queen's company; from which the name Oldcastle was taken.

1597-8.

The Second Part of Henry IV. was entered on S. R. 23d August 1600. This Quarto is much abridged in i. 3, ii. 3, iv. 1, iv. 4, and a whole scene, iii. 1, is omitted. It abounds in oaths apparently foisted in by the players, and is apparently printed from a prompter's copy. The omissions arise, I think, from expurgations made by the Master of the Revels. Plays in which rebellion was the subject were especially disagreeable at Court. In the Epilogue there is evidence of alteration, the words "if my tongue . . . good-night," having been inserted after the first production of the play, as is clear from their succeeding in Q. the clause about praying for the Queen, which must have been final in either version. The newly inserted words contain the allusion to Oldcastle, and show that in this play, as well as the former, that was the original appellation of Falstaff. This is confirmed by the appearance of *Old.* in a speech prefix in i. 2. 137; and Russel in a stage direction in ii. 2. Mr. Halliwell's notion that Russel and Harvey were names of actors, has not the slightest foundation, nor are such actors known. Note also that in iii. 2. 29, Falstaff is mentioned as having been page to the Duke of Norfolk, which was historically true of Oldcastle (compare the "serving the good Duke of Norfolk" in *The Merry Devil.* The date of that play is 1597.) The early part i. 1, or. ii. 4, was written before the entry of *1 Henry IV.* on S. R., 25th February 1598, in which Falstaff is mentioned. "Sincklo" occurs in a stage direction in v. 1; he is not known in connection with Shakespeare's company till this play was acted; he was previously a member of Pembroke's troop, and acted in *3 Henry VI.* when it belonged to them along with Humfrey [Jeffes], and Gabriel [Singer]. These two last named, and others, joined the Admiral's company at the Rose in October 1597, when Pembroke's men broke and went into the country. Sinkler, Beeston, Duke, and Pallant, stayed with the Chamberlain's men from c. 1594 till they left the Curtain in 1599, and then Kemp, Duke, Beeston, and Pallant set up a new company under the patronage of the Earl of Derby. Not one of these can be shown to have acted for the Chamberlain's, except between these dates, and that they left in discontent is probable from their being all omitted in the list of the 1623 Folio. Sinkler remained in Shakespeare's company till 1604. Pistol, in his first appearance in ii. 4, does not for a while talk in iambics. Mrs. Quickly (i. 2. 269) appears to be called Ursula (Nell in *Henry V.*) For the changes in the names of this and other characters in the series of Falstaff plays, see hereafter in the table given on p. 212.

1597.

Love's Labour's Lost was published in 1598, "as it was presented before her Highness this last Christmas." This was undoubtedly the earliest of Shakespeare's plays that has come down to us, and was only retouched somewhat hurriedly for this Court performance. The date of original production cannot well be put later than 1589. The characters are in several instances confused. In ii. 1 Boyet occurs in place of Berowne in the prefixes, and Rosaline for Katharine in the text. In iv. 2, and v. 1, there is still greater muddling of Holofernes and Nathaniel; now one, now the other appears, first as Curate, then as Pedant; in iv. 2, Berowne is called "one of the strange Queen's Lords," and *Queen* for *Princess* occurs in the prefixes through the greater part of the play. It is pretty clear that this lady ambassador was in the 1589 play called Queen. In ii. 1, the lines 21–114 were almost certainly added in 1597. They begin with a prefix *Prin.* inserted in the middle of one of the Queen's (Princess's) speeches; and in them only throughout the play is the prefix *Nav.* (Navarre) used for *King.* In iv. 3, the speech of Berowne (l. 290–365) must be mostly assigned to 1597; the repetition of the lines, "From women's

SUCCESSION OF HIS PLAYS.

eyes . . . Promethean fire" is an unmistakable indication of revision (see the similar instances in *Romeo*). A like instance of substitution of a long version for a short one, occurs in v. 1. 847–879, which are manifestly the 1597 substitute for v. 1. 827–832; again, v. 2. 575–590 could not have conveyed any amusement in the conceit of " Ajax " till after the publication of Harrington's *Metamorphosis of Ajax* in 1596. The mention of " first and second cause," &c., in i. 2. 171–192, may imply that this was another of the additions. But it is in iv. 2 that the greatest changes have been made. It is clear from v. 1. 125, that Sir Holofernes was originally the Curate. Modern editors either omit Holofernes or substitute Nathaniel; Sir Holofernes is also the Curate in iv. 2. 67–156— "This is a gift . . . colorable colours." In the rest of this scene Sir Nathaniel is the Curate, and Master Holofernes the Pedant. This latter is the 1597 version. I am not aware that this singular change of character has been noted, or any reason assigned for it, except my conjecture, that it was intended to disguise a personal satire which, however pertinent in 1589, had become obsolete in 1597. For a full discussion of all these changes made in 1597, see my article on *Shakespeare and Puritanism* in *Anglia*, vol. 7.

1597-8.

Much Ado about Nothing is more likely than any other play to be identical with *Love's Labour's Won*. The internal evidence has been set forth by Mr. Brae; but there are points of external evidence also, that have been overlooked. It is very frequent, in old plays, to find days of the week and month mentioned; and when this is the case, they nearly always correspond to the almanac of the year in which the play was written. Now, in this play alone in Shakespeare is there such a mark of time; comparing i. 1. 285, and ii. 1. 375, we find that the 6th July came on a Monday; this suits the years 1590 and 1601, but none between; an indication that the original play was written in 1590. Unlike *Love's Labour's Lost*, it was almost recomposed at its reproduction, and this day-of-the-week mention is, I think, a relic of the original plot, and probably due, not to Shakespeare, but to some coadjutor. Again, Meres' list in his *Palladis Tamia* consists of the following plays:—*Gentlemen of Verona* (1595), *Errors* (1594), *Love's Labour's Lost* (1597), *Love's Labour's Won* (?), *Midsummer-Night's Dream* (1594-5), *Merchant of Venice* (1596-7), *Richard II.* (1595), *Richard III.* (1594), *Henry IV.* (1597), *King John* (1596), *Titus Andronicus* (1594),

Romeo and Juliet (1595–6). The dates I have appended to these may in some instance be slightly erroneous; but I think no one will deny that the plays mentioned by Meres must have constituted the Shakespeare repertoire of the Chamberlain's men, and have been played by them between the dates of their constitution as a company in 1594, and the publication of Meres' book in 1598. But there is absolutely no other comedy of Shakespeare's that can be assigned to such a date. *All's Well that Ends Well* was certainly not played by his company so early. Again, Cowley and Kempe played the constables in this play; but Kempe had left the company by the summer of 1599. There is no argument against this conclusion yet produced. The main subject of the play had been dramatised before in *Ariodante and Geneuora*, acted at Court by the Merchant Tailors' boys in 1582–3. The old German play of Jacob Ayrer, *The Beautiful Phœnicia* (c. 1595, Cohn) also contains points of similarity with Shakespeare's play that are not found in the Bandello novel which Belleforest translated in 1594. Pedro and Leonato are the only names which Shakespeare retains from the novel; which Ayrer follows in this respect. When the title was altered is doubtful: the play was known as *Benedick and Beatrice* in 1613.

1599.

Henry V. was acted, with the choruses as we have them in the Folio, between 15th April and 28th September, while Essex was in Ireland; see chorus to Act v. That this was the final revision of the play, I am by no means convinced. The scene with the Scotch and Irish captains, iii. 2. 69 to end, I take to be an insertion for the Court performance, Christmas 1605, to please King James, who had been so annoyed that year by depreciation of the Scots on the stage. That the Quarto copy is printed from an abridged version made for acting purposes, is palpable. By omitting i. 1, and substituting one Bishop for two in i. 2 (two being retained in the stage direction) Ely is disposed of; by simple omission and transference of a speech in iv. 3 to Warwick, Westmoreland disappears; in a similar way Bedford gives place to Clarence; in iv. 3. 69 Salisbury is replaced by Gloster, and was evidently meant to be in l. 5-9 of the same scene; in iv. 1 Erpingham remains in the stage direction, but has been cut out in the text. That the version from which the Quarto was abridged was the 1599 copy, is a separate question to which I am inclined to say no. I rather hold that it was an earlier one without choruses, and following the Chronicle his-

SUCCESSION OF HIS PLAYS.

torians much more closely. I cannot otherwise account for the substitution of Gebon for Rambures in iii. 7, and iv. 5; and of Bourbon for Britany in iii. 5, and for Dolphin in iii. 7, iv. 5. Mr. Daniel's theory is that the Quarto was later than the Folio version, that is to say, that Shakespeare wrote a play historically incorrect, that his errors were corrected in a stage version before 1600, *i.e.*, while he was still himself an actor; that the errors were afterwards restored, and have kept the stage ever since. I cannot think this. I believe that the Quarto is (as we have seen in other instances) a shortened version of a play written early in 1598 for the Curtain Theatre, and that the Folio (except such alterations as were made after James's accession) is a version enlarged and improved for the Globe Theatre later in the same year. With regard to this series of Falstaff plays, the following table may be of interest.

	NAMES OF "IRREGULAR HUMOURISTS" IN—						
Famous Victories.	*1 Hen. IV.* (original version).	*1 Hen. IV.* (altered version).	*2 Hen. IV.* (i. 1 to ii. 4 altered).	*2 Hen. IV.* (ii. 4 to end unaltered).	*Hen. V.* (both versions).	*Merry Wives.*
Gadshill.	Gadshill.	Gadshill.					
Ned.	Ned Poins.	Poins.	Poins.				
Tom.	Harvey.	Peto.	Peto.				
	Russell.	Bardolph.	Bardolph.	Bardolph.	Bardolph.	Bardolph.
Oldcastle.	Oldcastle.	Falstaff.	Falstaff.	Falstaff.	F. in text.	Falstaff.
	? Hostess.	Quickly.	Quickly.	Quickly.	Quickly.	Quickly.
				Doll.	Doll.	
				Pistol.	Pistol.	Pistol.
					Nym.	Nym.
				Shallow.		Shallow.

According to my hypothesis, the original names Oldcastle, Ned Poins, Gadshill, &c., were chiefly taken from *The Famous Victories of Henry V.;* all these disappear from the series by ii. 4 of *2 Henry IV.:* the later names, Bardolph, Falstaff, Nym, Pistol, Shallow, persist to the end of the series, but did not occur in the original forms of *1* and *2 Henry IV.* The name Falstaff was no doubt taken from *1 Henry VI.*, in which Shakespeare had been writing on March 1592, and which we know from the Epilogue to *Henry V.* to have been revived by 1598 at latest.

1599.

As You Like It was "stayed" on the 4th August 1600, and was written after "Diana in the fountain" (iv. 1. 154) was set up in Cheapside in 1598 (Stow). In iii. 5. 83 a line is quoted from *Hero and Leander*, published in 1598; the only instance in which Shakespeare directly refers to a contemporary poet. The date may, I think, be still more exactly fixed from i. 2. 94, "the little wit that fools have was silenced," which alludes probably to the burning of satirical books by public authority 1st June 1599. Every indication points to the latter part of 1599 as the date of production. This play is a rival to the *Robin Hood* plays acted at the Rose in 1598;

SUCCESSION OF HIS PLAYS.

Jaques, "the traveller," seems to have been the origin of Jonson's Amorphus in *Cynthia's Revels*, and Touchstone of Cos the whetstone in the same play; compare i. 2. 56. The female characters differed considerably in height, as in *Much Ado* and *The Dream*. The remarks of Touchstone on quarrels and lies in v. 4 should be compared with *Love's Labour's Lost*, i. 2 to end; *Romeo and Juliet*, ii. 4. 26, &c. The comparison of the world to a stage in ii. 7 suggests a date subsequent to the building of the Globe, with its motto of *Totus mundus agit histrionem;* and the introduction of a fool proper, in place of a comic clown such as is found in all the anterior comedies, confirms this: the "fools" only occur in plays subsequent to Kempe's leaving the company. The title is taken from Lodge's address prefixed to his *Rosalynde*, on which the play is founded—"if you like it, so," says Lodge—and it is alluded to in the Epilogue (which, like that to *2 Henry IV.*, is spoken by a female character), and again by Jonson in the Epilogue to *Cynthia's Revels*, which play has much more connection with the present than is usually supposed. There is a tradition that Shakespeare took the part of Adam.

1600.

The Merry Wives of Windsor, as we have it in the Folio, was probably made for the Court performance in February 1600; in i. 4, the "King's English" does not imply that James, not Elizabeth, was on the throne; but that the time of action is under a king, Henry IV. It was written after *Henry V.;* perhaps, according to the old tradition, in obedience to the Queen's command, who wished to see Falstaff in love, Shakespeare not having fulfilled his promise in the Epilogue to *2 Henry IV.* to introduce him in the *Henry V.* play; a failure probably caused by the defection at this date of the actor who had taken this part—Kempe, Beeston, Duke, and Pallant having quitted the King's men between the production of *2 Henry IV.* and that of this play. The title, *The Merry Wives of Windsor,* suggests approximation in subject with *The Merry Devil of Edmonton* (1597), and so does the great likeness in the characteristics in the Hosts of these plays; while the plot of the Anne Page story is identical with that of *Wily Beguiled* (1597), Fenton corresponding to Sophos, Caius to Churms, Simple to Plodall, Evans to R. Goodfellow. It appears from the Quarto edition that Ford's assumed name was originally Brook, not Broome. This was probably altered because Brook was the name of the Lord Cobham, who took offence at the production of Oldcastle on the stage. The song of Marlowe's sung by Evans in iii. 1 was published as Shakespeare's in the *Passionate Pilgrim* in 1599; not necessarily by any means in consequence of its previous introduction in this play. Mr. P. A. Daniel has rightly pointed out that iii. 5 is really composed of two scenes, one between Falstaff and Quickly, the other between Falstaff and Ford; and that the latter ought to begin the fourth Act: he has also shown that in various places the Folio has inconsistencies not explicable without the aid of the Quarto. But all this does not prove any "degradation" of the play at "managerial" hands; it rather indicates hurried and careless production, such as we might expect in a play ordered to be produced in a fortnight, according to the old tradition. Another internal proof of such hurry, both in this play and in *Much Ado about Nothing*, lies in the fact that they are almost entirely in prose; which is not the case in any other play by Shakespeare. And this brings us to the question of the nature of the Quarto version. It has been held to be merely a first sketch of the play: this theory is untenable. Mr. P. A. Daniel holds it to be a stolen version made up by a literary hack from shorthand notes obtained at a representation. This hypothesis gives no explanation of the "cousin-Garmombles" of iii. 5, nor does it enable us to understand how no better a representation of the play was issued, nor how whole scenes (that of the fairies for example) appear in quite a different version from the Folio. My own opinion is that the case is parallel to that of *Romeo and Juliet;* that the Quarto is printed from a partly revised prompter's copy of the older version of the play, which became useless when Shakespeare had made his final version. I believe also that this older version was produced soon after the visit of the Count of Mümplegart (Garmombles) to Windsor in August 1592; that it was probably the *Jealous Comedy*, acted as a new play by Shakespeare's company 5th January 1593; that when Shakespeare revived this old play, he accommodated the characters to *Henry IV.* as best he could. Mr. Daniel's argument that *The Merry Wives* was a later play than *Henry V.*, because Nym would otherwise have had no title to special mention in the title-page of the Quarto, has not much weight. This Quarto was printed three years after *Henry V.* was produced, and Nym's reputation from either play was three years old, according to Mr. Daniel himself. Why then should he not be mentioned?

SUCCESSION OF HIS PLAYS. 213

I must add a word on the Fairy scene, v. 5. The fairies are Nan the Queen (in red?), cf. iv. 4. 71; Will Cricket (in grey?); two other boys, Bede and Bean, in green and white; and Evans, Puck Hobgoblin or Robin Goodfellow, in black. The prefixes *Qu.*, *Qui.*, and *Pist.* are mistakes for *Queen* and *Puck*. Pistol and Quickly cannot be actors in this scene, nor in the entrance are they placed with " Evans, Anne Page, Fairies," but at the ends of the second and third lines, as if by afterthought. All the Pistol fairy speeches belong to Evans (Puck). There seems to have arisen some confusion in the final revision, when this scene was probably altered. Further confirmation of the original early date of the play may be found in Falstaff's statement that the Thames shore was "shelvy and shallow" (iii. 5. 15); for in 1592 the Thames was so low as to be fordable at London Bridge, and Falstaff was thrown in the ford at Datchet. But the allusions to "three Doctor Faustuses" and Mephistopheles are not helpful; *Faustus* was on the boards till 1597 at least. One of Henry Julius' plays *derived from English sources*, printed in 1594, *The Adulteress*, contains the same story as *The Merry Wives*. If this was not derived from Shakespeare's play, whence was it? The ground of the English play was probably the story in Tarleton's

News out of Purgatory (1590). Note that the other play by Julius distinctly traceable in origin to the English stage is *Vincentius Ladislaus* (1594), in which the similarities to *Much Ado* (1590), are as marked as in the present instance. We have already seen that Evans acts the part of Robin Goodfellow, and that Will Cricket is another fairy; but these are two characters in *Wily Beguiled*, in which play Robin Goodfellow means Drayton and Will Cricket Kempe. I believe that in Shakespeare's play, Evans and Dr. Caius are satirical representations of Drayton and Lodge. Drayton is introduced as Evan, a Welsh attorney, by Jonson in *For the Honour of Wales*, and Lodge was frequently satirised on the stage as a French doctor. The part of Falstaff was acted in Charles the First's time by Lowin, and there is no reason why he should not have been the original performer of it in this play as revised. He was twenty-four years old in 1600.

1600.

Julius Cæsar is alluded to in Weever's *Mirror of Martyrs* (Sir John Oldcastle), 1601; and the actor of Polonius in *Hamlet* iii. 2. 109 had probably acted the part of Cæsar; at any rate *Cæsar* must be anterior to the Quarto *Hamlet* which was

SUCCESSION OF HIS PLAYS.

produced in 1601. The structure of this play is remarkable; the first three acts and last two have no characters in common except Brutus, Cassius, Antony, and Lucius; there are in fact two plays in one, *Cæsar's Tragedy* and *Cæsar's Revenge*. Contemporary plays by other dramatists were produced in a double pattern: *e.g.*, Marston's *Antonio and Mellida*, in two parts; Chapman's *Bussy d'Ambois*, in two parts; Kyd's old play of *Jeronymo*, in two parts. All these were on the stage at the same time as *Julius Cæsar*. Revenge-plays with ghosts in them were the rage for the next four years. That the present play has been greatly shortened, is shown by the singularly large number of instances in which mute characters are on the stage; which is totally at variance with Shakespeare's usual practice. The large number of incomplete lines in every possible position, even in the middle of speeches, confirms this. That alterations were made we have the positive testimony of Jonson, who in his *Discoveries* tells us that Shakespeare wrote, " Cæsar did never wrong but with just cause " (compare iii. I. 47). That this original reading stood in the acting copies till not long before the 1623 Folio was printed, is clear from the fact that Jonson, in the Induction to his *Staple of News* (1625), alludes to it as a well-known line requiring no explanation

—"Cry you mercy," says Prologue, "you never did wrong but with just cause." This would imply that Shakespeare did not make the alterations himself; a hypothesis confirmed by the spelling of Antony without an *h:* this name occurs in eight of Shakespeare's plays, and in every instance but this invariably is spelled Anthony. Jonson himself is more likely to have been called on to make this revision than any other author connected with the King's company c. 1622. The "*et tu Brute*" about which so much has been written was probably taken from Jonson's *Every Man out of his Humour* (i. 1); it is found in the *Duke of York* (1595) and elsewhere. Nicholson, in his *Acolastus his after wit* (S. R. 8th September 1600), probably took it from Shakespeare's play, "Et tu Brute! wilt thou stab Cæsar too?"

1601.

All's Well that Ends Well manifestly contains passages—i. 1. 230–244; 1. 3. 130–142; ii. 1. 130–214; ii. 3. 80–110, 132–151; iii. 4 letter: v. 3 concluding part—which are of very early date; certainly written not later than 1593. It is not, however, in my opinion, to be identified with *Love's Labour's Won:* the allusions to the present title in iv. 4. 35; v. 1. 24; v. 3. 333, 336, all occur in rhyme passages, and some of them, at least, belong to the earlier date. The play, as we have it, was written after Marston's *Jack Drum's Entertainment* (1600), to which there is a palpable allusion in iii. 6. 41; and before *The Dutch Courtesan* (probably 1602) by the same author, which contains several allusions to its title. The name *Corambus* in iv. 3. 185 suggests the same date, as this is the appellation of Polonius in the Quarto *Hamlet*. The introduction of Violenta, a mute character, in iii. 5, and the substitution of the same name in *Twelfth Night*, i. 5, for Viola, show that this last-named play was the last written of the two, but not much interval could have occurred between them. In confirmation of this approximation of dates, compare the name Capilet, v. 3. 147, 159, with *Twelfth Night*, iii. 4. 315. In plot this play agrees with *Much Ado* in the supposed death of Helen, and the promise of Bertram to marry Maudlin Lafeu; with *Measure for Measure*, in the substitution of Helen for Diana; with *The Gentlemen of Verona*, in Helen's pilgrim disguise, and her meeting with the Hostess. In it and *Twelfth Night* we find a few slight allusions to the Puritans; another confirmation of date. The only other use even of the word Puritan is in the late play *Winter's Tale*, iv. 3. 46. Compare the doubtful *Pericles*, iv. 6. 9.

The way in which the earthquake is mentioned in i. 3. 91, gives a still further confirmation. There was an earthquake in London in 1601. I take the boasting Parolles to be Marston; born under Mars, muddied in Fortune's displeasure, an egregious coward, an accuser of Captain Dumain of being lousy, he in all points agrees with Marston, as figured in the other satirical plays of the time. The charge against Dumain is repeated against Jonson in *Satiromastix;* Marston had left the Admiral's company in 1599, just before the Fortune Theatre was built for them. His cowardice is dilated on in Jonson's *Conversations*, and the allusions to him as *Jack Drum* are frequent in the play. Once we find Tom Drum in v. 2 (from *Tom Drum's Vants* in *Gentle Craft*, 1598), a hint that Thomas Dekker, author of *The Shoemaker's Holiday, or The Gentle Craft* (1600), was aiding and abetting John Marston in his satirical plays. Helen was acted by a short boy (i. 1. 202). The incident of the King's gift to Helen of his ring, only referred to in the last scene, seems to point at the gift of a ring to Essex by Elizabeth in 1596. Essex was executed in 1601, just before this play was acted. The older parts pointed out above were, I think, incorporated from detached scenes written in 1593 during the plague time, and laid by for future use. The plot is from *Giletta of Narbonne* in Painter's *Palace of Pleasure*, a book used by Shakespeare in 1594 for his alteration of *Edward III*. Mr. Stokes says that Eccleston and Gough acted in this play, on the authority of Mr. Halliwell; one of the many *ignes fatui* that have misled this unwary compiler.

1601-2.

Twelfth Night, or What You Will, was first acted 2d February 1602 at one of the Inns of Court (Manningham's *Diary*). Its date lies between Marston's *Malcontent* (1602), (of Malevole in which play Malvolio is clearly a caricature), and *What You Will* (1602) by the same author. This adoption of the name of his play seems to have induced Shakespeare to replace it by the now universally adopted title. The appellation Rudesby (v. 1. 55) is from Chapman's *Sir Giles Goosecap* (1601). Several minor points have been already noticed under the previous play *All's Well*. In this play, as in that, I believe that earlier written scenes have been incorporated. It is only in similar cases that we find such contradictions as that between the three months' sojourn of Viola at the Count's court (v. 1), and the three days' acquaintance with the Duke in i. 4. In ii. 4 there are palpable signs of alteration, and iii. 1. 159-176, v. 1. 133-148 are surely of early date. Moreover, the singular agreement of the plot with the *Comedy of Errors* in the likeness of the twins, and with *The Gentlemen of Verona*, or rather with *Apollonius and Sylla*, whence part of that play was derived, point to a likelihood that the first conceptions of these plays were not far apart in time. I think the early portions were written in 1593, like those of the preceding play. For the change from Duke (i. 1-4) to Count in the rest of the play compare *The Gentlemen of Verona*. I believe that Sir Toby represents Jonson and Malvolio Marston; but that subject requires to be treated in a separate work from its complexity.

1602.

Troylus and Cressida was published surreptitiously in 1609, with an address to the reader stating that it had been "never staled with the stage." This statement was withdrawn in the same year, and a new title-page issued, "as it was acted by the King's Majesty's servants at the Globe." It had in fact been entered in S. R. 1603, February 7, by J. Roberts, and licensed for printing, "when he hath gotten sufficient authority for it"—which he evidently did not get. It could not therefore have been produced later than 1602.

Nor could it, as we have it, have been earlier; the line i. 3. 73, "rank Thersites with his mastic jaws" evidently alluding to Dekker's *Satiro*-MASTIX (1601). I once thought Marston, as *Histriomastix* or *Theriomastix*, was alluded to; but the character of Thersites suits Dekker, not Marston. Jonson describes him in *The Poetaster*, iii. 1, as "one of the most overflowing *rank* wits in Rome; he will slander any man that breathes if he disgust him." In 1602, Jonson, Marston, and Shakespeare had become reconciled; of reconciliation with Dekker, at any time, there is no trace. This play is probably the "purge" given by Shakespeare to Jonson when he put down all those "of the university pen" (*The Return from Parnassus*, iv. 3, acted in the winter 1602-3); Ajax representing Jonson, Achilles Chapman, and Hector Shakespeare: but whether this conjecture be true or no, Dekker is certainly Thersites. All this part of the play (the camp story) splits off from the love story of Troylus and Cressida, which is of much earlier date, c. 1593. The two parts are discrepant in minor points, notably in the existence of a truce (i. 3. 262), "dull and long-continued" fighting having been abundant in i. 2. The parts written in 1602 are i. 3; ii. 1; ii. 2; ii. 3; iii. 3. 34 to end; iv. 5. (except lines 12-53); v. 1; v. 2 (retains much older work; v. 3. 1–97. All this part bears evident marks of the reading of Chapman's *Iliad* i.–vii. (1598); the love story is somewhat from the old Troy book printed by Caxton, but more from Chaucer's *Troilus and Cressid*. At the end of v. 3, in the Folio v. 10. 32–34, are repeated; this shows that the 1602 *acting* copy was meant to end with v. 3, thus making the play a comedy; as it now stands it is usually classed with the tragedies; in the Folio, it is placed unpaged between the Histories and Tragedies, and is not mentioned in the "Catologue" of contents. The prologue and v. 4–10 contain much work that is unlike Shakespeare's, and are probably by some coadjutor whose other lines have been replaced by the 1602 additions. Heywood in his *Iron Age* treated this same subject, and the date of that play is important in this investigation. The *Ages* of Heywood were acted before 1611 (see his Address to the Reader in *The Golden Age;* *The Iron Age* was "publicly acted by two companies on one stage at once," and "at sundry times thronged three several theatres." These were the Rose, the Curtain, and the Bull; Pembroke's men, and the Admiral's, acted together at the Rose, October to November 1597. This must have been the time when the *Iron Age* was performed; but not as a new play. It would otherwise have been entered in

SUCCESSION OF HIS PLAYS.

Henslowe's *Diary* as such. All the *Ages* were then probably old in 1597. In 1595–6 we find them accordingly entered by Henslowe under other names; in 1595, March 5, *The Golden Age*, whose scenes are in Heaven and Olympus, appears as Steleo (Cœlo) and Olempo; he subsequently writes Seleo for Steleo; *The Silver* and *Brazen Ages* on May 7 and May 23, as the first and second parts of *Hercules*. These three plays were produced in succession. The entry of *Galfrido and Bernardo* is a forgery, and a clumsy one, for it necessitates a Sunday performance, which is a thing unknown in Henslowe's *Diary*, if the dates be properly corrected. On 23d June 1596, *Troy* was acted, palpably *The Iron Age;* and on 7th April 1597, *Five Plays in One* may have been the second part of that play. About February 1599, Heywood left the Admiral's men, and joined Lord Derby's; in April, Dekker and Chettle produced their *Troylus and Cressida;* in May their *Agamemnon*, and Dekker his *Orestes' Furies*. I believe that all these were merely enlargements of Heywood's *Iron Age*. Dekker was a "dresser of plays" and a shameless plagiarist; witness the stealing of Day's work, which he afterwards reclaimed in his *Parliament of Bees*. At the same time that Dekker was thus pillaging Heywood, his friend Marston was satirising Heywood as Posthaste in *Histriomastix* for appropriating Shakespeare's *Troylus* (of 1593) and bringing out *The Prodigal Child*, the old *Acolastus* of 1540, as a new play. There can be no doubt that the company satirised in *Histriomastix* is Derby's. It was a "travelling" company, newly set up, with a poet who extemporises his plays (Heywood had a share in 220) and uses

"No new luxury of blandishment,
But plenty of Old England's mother's words."

The allusion to *Troylus*, l. 267–275, in which "he shakes his furious spear," has led some persons to a very absurd identification of Posthaste with Shakespeare. I have noticed before the singular allusion to *The Iron Age* in *John* iv. 1. 60 (1596).

1603.

The Taming of the Shrew is unlike any play hitherto considered; the Shakespearian part of it being evidently confined to the Katharine and Petruchio scenes—ii. 1. 167–326; iii. 2 (except 130–150, 242–254); iv. 1; iv. 3; iv. 5 (except three lines at end); v. 2 (except ten lines at conclusion). The construction of the play shows that it was not composed by Shakespeare in conjunction with another author, but that his additions are replacements of the original author's work; alterations made hurriedly for some occasion when it was not thought worth while to write an entirely new play. Such an occasion was the plague year of 1603, when the theatres were closed and the companies had to travel. We shall see, hereafter, that Shakespeare's other similar alterations of other men's work were made in like circumstances. This date is confirmed by the allusions to other taming plays, of which there were several; the present play, in its altered shape, being probably the latest: ii. 1. 297 refers to *Patient Grissel*, by Dekker, Chettle, and Haughton, December 1599; "curst" in ii. 1. 187, 294, 307; v. 2. 188, to Dekker's *Medicine for a Curst Wife*, July 1602; and iv. 1. 221 to Heywood's *Woman Killed with Kindness*, March 1603. There is nothing but the supposed inferiority of work to imply an earlier date; and this, on examination, will be seen to be merely a subjective inference arising from the reflex action of the less worthy portion with which Shakespeare's is associated. Rudesby in iii. 2. 10 is from *Sir Giles Goosecap* (1601), and Baptista, as a man's name, could hardly have come under Shakespeare's notice, when in his *Hamlet* he made it a woman's. The earlier play thus altered probably dates 1596, when an edition of *The Taming of a Shrew* was

P

reprinted. This last-named play was written for Pembroke's company in 1588-9. Another limit of date is given by the name *Sincklo* in the Induction. Sinklo was an actor with the Chamberlain's men, from 1597 to 1604. *Nicke* in iv. 1. is Nicholas Tooley. The play is not mentioned by Meres in 1598. In the Induction, "The Slys are no rogues: we came in with Richard Conqueror," is, I think, an allusion to the stage history of the time. Sly and Richard the Third (Burbadge) came into Lord Strange's company together in 1591. In the Pembroke play, Don Christophero Sly was probably acted by Christopher Beeston. The Induction, partly revised by Shakespeare, seems to have been clumsily fitted by the players (as, indeed, the whole play is, especially in the non-appearance of "my cousin Ferdinand," iv. 1. 154, whose place seems to be taken by Hortensio): surely Sly ought to have been replaced, as in the 1588 play; and is it possible that Shakespeare even in a farce should have made Sly talk blank verse, sc. 2, l. 60-120? *The Taming of a Shrew*, as acted in June 1594 at Newington Butts, was the old play which had belonged to Pembroke's men, probably by Kyd; but the first version of the play, afterwards altered by Shakespeare, was written, I think, by Lodge, (? aided by Drayton in the Induction). This

Induction was, I think, greatly altered by Shakespeare in 1603.

1603.

Hamlet is extant in three forms—the Folio, which is evidently a stage copy considerably shortened for acting purposes; the 1604 Quarto, which is a very fair transcript of the author's complete copy, with a few omissions; and the 1603 Quarto, imperfect and inaccurate. The date of the perfect play is certainly 1603. In ii. 2. 346, &c., we find that the tragedians of the city—*i.e.*, Shakespeare's company—are "travelling," and that "their inhibition comes of the late innovation." This has been interpreted in various ways, the most absurd being that which regards the establishment of the Revels children in 1604 as the innovation: hardly less so is Malone's notion that the putting down of the Curtain players in 1600 is the inhibition referred to. The Globe company travelled in 1601 in consequence of Essex' attempt at political innovation, and their acting *Richard II.* in connection therewith; they travelled again in 1603, the theatres being shut because of the plague: this latter is the time referred to in the final version, for in the latter part of that year the Puritan party had by millenary petitions at Hampton Court conferences, and so forth, attempted a religious "innovation;" and their anxiety to avoid this charge is evident in their continual protests that it was a reformation, not an innovation, that they wanted (see Fuller, *Church History*, under 1603–4 *passim*). The immediately succeeding passage, l. 351–379, however, which also occurs in the earlier version, distinctly points to 1601. The "berattling of the common stages by the aery of little eyases," the controversy between poet and player, ended in that year; these lines are not contained in the second Quarto. The words "if they should grow themselves to common players," indicate a possible date of writing c. 1610, when Ostler and Underwood, Chapel boys in 1601, had grown up and been taken into the King's men; but the use of the present tense in the preceding paragraph shows that the same Chapel children who had been engaged in the Jonson and Marston quarrel were still on the stage, and that the date of writing is anterior to their replacement by the Revels boys in January 1604. The growing to common players then must be taken generally, not specifically; unless we suppose a still further revision c. 1610, which on other grounds is not unlikely. It may be worth noting that the play of *Dido*, in rivalry of which the player's speech in ii. 2 is recited, belonged to these same Chapel children. In like manner the Pyrgus in Jonson's *Poetaster* recites bits of *The Battle of Alcazar* in rivalry with Dekker's *Captain Stukeley*. But although the date of the perfect play is almost certainly 1603, *Hamlet* had certainly been on the stage some years at that time. Tucca in *Satiromastix* (1601) says, "My name's *Hamlet Revenge*," and he comes on, "his boy after him, with two pictures under his cloak." In Marston's *Malcontent* (1601), "Illo, ho, ho, ho! art thou there, old Trucpenny?" must refer to *Hamlet*. In iii. 2. 42, "Let those that play your clowns speak no more than is set down for them," refers, I think, to extemporising Kempe, who left Shakespeare's company in 1599. Florio's *Montaigne*, which is implicitly referred to throughout the play (see Mr. Feis, *Shakespeare and Montaigne*, 1884), was entered S. R. 4th June 1600. On the title-page of the first Quarto it is said that the play had been acted in the Universities of Oxford and Cambridge and elsewhere; *i.e.*, in the travelling of 1601. It is pretty clear, then, that 1601 was the date of its production. Polonius (iii. 2. 108) had already played Julius Cæsar *in the University*, which could hardly have been before 1601; and *Hamlet* was entered by Roberts 26th July 1602, in S. R., "as it was lately acted." Plays thus produced during "travels," were almost always hurried and careless performances; indeed, this form of *Hamlet* seems to have been an unfinished refashioning of the old play by Kyd, that had so long been performed by the Chamberlain's men. The names Corambis and Montano for Polonius and Reynaldo, and a good deal of Acts iii. and iv., seem to be remnants of this old play. The name Corambus is found in the German version, which probably dates c. 1592. It also occurs in *All's Well*, iv. 3. 185. The first Quarto is in this instance, as in those of *Romeo*, *Henry V.*, and *Merry Wives*, in my opinion, printed from a partly revised prompter's copy of the 1601 play, which became useless when the fuller version was made. In this instance there are traces of alterations having been made on this copy similar to that in *Romeo*, iii. 5. 177. The usual explanation of the peculiar text of imperfect Quartos is, that notes were taken in shorthand at the theatre, which, eked out by the vampings of some playdresser, made up a saleable version, however incorrect. The stronghold of this theory is the soliloquy in iii. 1. 56, &c. The minor errors of "right done" for "write down," i. 2. 222; "invenom'd speech" for "in venom steept," ii. 2. 533; "honor" for "owner," v. 1. 121; and the like, can be easily paralleled in the most authentic copies of printed plays of the

SUCCESSION OF HIS PLAYS.   231

period. But a careful examination of the text of that speech of Hamlet's in the first Quarto, shows that its present meaningless shape arises from the displacement of two lines only, an error which is most unlikely to have occurred in shorthand notes, and is completely subversive of the hack play-writing botcher hypothesis. I append this soliloquy, as I suppose it to have stood in the MS. of the prompter's copy, after the partial 1601 correction:

> "To be, or not to be? Ay, there's the point.
> To die—to sleep—is that all? Ay. All? No.
> To sleep—to dream—ay, marry, there it goes.
> For in that dream of death when we, awake,
> *Are doom'd* before an everlasting Judge,
> The happy smile and the accurst are damn'd.
> But for the joyful hope of this, who'ld bear
> The scorns and flattery of the world, the right
> Scorn'd by the rich, the rich curst of the poor,
> The widow being opprest, the orphan wrong'd,
> The taste of hunger, or a tyrant's reign,
> And thousand more calamities besides,
> When that he may his full *quietus* make
> With a bare bodkin? Who would this endure,
> But for a hope of something after death,
> *The undiscover'd country, from whose bourne*
> *No passenger has e'er return'd?* Ay that
> Puzzles the brain and doth confound the sense;
> Which makes us rather bear the ills we have,
> Than fly to others that we know not of.
> This consciënce makes cowards of us all."

(marginal note: The undiscover'd country from whose sight no passenger ever return'd. Ay, that bourne)

I have put in italics in the text the marginal corrections of "proof" as shown above, inserted in their proper places; a comparison with the first Quarto will show how the printer, not the shorthand man or playdresser, by inserting them in the wrong places, has produced the nonsense that has caused so many groundless hypotheses.

> "When we awake,
> *And borne* before an everlasting Judge,
> *From whence no passenger ever return'd*
> *The undiscover'd country, at whose sight*
> The happy smile," &c.

And farther on :

> " *Ay that* O this conscience," &c.

The erroneous notions with regard to these imperfect Quartos arise, in a great measure, from their being compared with the carefully edited later versions; were they also edited and emended the differences would appear much smaller than they do now. The earlier (1601) form of this play was evidently hurriedly prepared during the journey to Scotland, in which the company visited the universities, at a time when the public taste for revenge-plays had been revived by the reproduction of Kyd's *Jeronymo* (*Spanish Tragedy*) by the

Chapel children, probably at Jonson's suggestion; a new version of Kyd's *Hamlet* naturally followed. Other such plays were: Marston's *Antonio and Mellida* (Paul's, 1599–1600); Shakespeare's *Julius Cæsar* (1600); Chettle and Heywood's *Hoffman, or Revenge for a Father*, also called *Like quits Like* (Admiral's, January 1603): Chapman's *Revenge of Bussy* is of later date. A passage in *Ram Alley* (c. 1609), v. 1, "The custom of thy sin so lulls thy sense," &c., is apparently imitated from iii. 4. 161, &c., a passage not found in the Folio. This would lead to the conjecture that the Folio abridgment was made after 1609; on the other hand, the re-insertion in it of ii. 2. 350–379 points to a date, about 1610, when Underwood and Ostler had "grown to common players," and were admitted among the King's men. It was probably made then by Shakespeare himself. It is indeed most unlikely, that were it not so, its text should have been preferred, by the editors of the Folio, to the fuller one of the Quarto, which lay ready printed to their hands. We have, then, in the forms of this play, an example of Shakespeare's hurried revision of the work of an earlier writer, but it must be remembered in a most mutilated form; of the full working out of his own conception, in the shape fittest for private reading; and finally, of his practical adaptation of it to the requirements of the stage. The date of the printing of the first Quarto, and, therefore, of the revision made in the second, is after 19th May 1603, as the actors are called "King's servants" in the title-page. I. 1. 107–125, which surely allude to the death of Elizabeth, are omitted in the Folio. In iii. 2. 177, iv. 5. 77, alternative readings—

{ "For women fear too much even as they love".
{ "And women's fear and love hold quantity,",

{ "And now behold"
{ "O Gertrard, Gertrard "—

are printed side by side, a sure mark of revision.

1604.

Measure for Measure was written, in my opinion, in rivalry to Marston's *The Fawn*, which was printed March 1606, but produced 1603–4. It was also subsequent to Chettle and Heywood's *Like quits Like*, 14th January 1603; v. 1. 416. All the allusions in it suit 1604. The avoidance of publicity by James I. (i. 1. 68–71; ii. 4. 27–30); the existing war and expected peace (i. 2. 4, 83); the stabbers—four out of ten prisoners—in iv. 3; the stuffed hose, to which Pompey's name is appropriate, all agree in this; peace was concluded in the autumn; the "Act of Stabbing" was passed in this year, the bombasted breeches revived with the new reign. But these are more valuable in showing what reliance can be placed on such allusions than in fixing the date of the play; for it was acted at Court, 26th December 1604. The title was probably taken from a line in *3 Henry VI.*, ii. 6. 55; the plot is like *All's Well* in the substitution of Mariana, *Twelfth Night* in the Duke's love declaration at the end. It is founded on Whetstone's *Promos and Cassandra* (1582). An order was made in 1603, that no new houses should be built in the suburbs of London. Compare i. 2. 104.

1604.

Othello was acted at Court 1st November 1604, being, no doubt, like *Measure for Measure*, 26th December, a new play that year. The *Merry Wives*, 4th November, and *Henry V.*, 7th January, were revised for the same Revels. The *Errors*, 28th December, *Love's Labour's Lost*, between New Year and Twelfth Day, and *The Merchant of Venice*, January 10, 12, were also reproduced. The document in the Record Office containing these details is a modern forgery, but Malone possessed a transcript of the genuine entry in the Revels accounts. It was a bold thing for Shakespeare to have performed before James I. in two plays on unfounded jealousy, at a time when the King was so jealous of the relations of the Queen with Lord Southampton. The 1622 Quarto copy of this play is abridged for stage reasons; by whom we cannot say. The allusion to the "huge eclipse" (v. 2. 99), points to the total eclipse of 2d October 1605. Shakespeare had probably been reading Harvey's *Discoursive Problem concerning Prophesies* (1588), in which he speaks of "a *huge* fearful eclipse of the sun" as to happen on that day. The likeness of this play in small details to *Measure for Measure* indicates close contemporaneity of date, *e.g.*, the name Angelo (i. 3. 16); the word "grange" (i. 1. 106), and "seeming" (iii. 3. 209). This play was again acted at Court in 1613. It was founded on Cinthio's novel *Hecatomithi*, Third Decad, Novel 3. The "men whose heads do grow beneath their shoulders" (i. 3. 145) came from Raleigh's narrative of *The Discovery of Guyana* (1600). He was "resolved" of their credibility. In *The Patient Man*, by Dekker, S. R. 9th November 1604, there is a distinct reference to Othello—

"Thou kill'st her now again,
    And art more savage than a barbarous Moor" (i. 1).

1605.

King Lear was probably on the stage when the old play of *Leir* on which it was founded was published. This latter was entered on S. R. 8th May, as "The Tragical History of King Leir and his three daughters, as it was lately acted," but was published as "The true Chronicle History of King Leir and his three daughters, &c., as it hath been divers and sundry times lately acted." It is not tragical in any sense, and ends happily. Shakespeare was the first person who, in opposition to the chronicles, made a tragedy on this story. There can be no doubt that Stafford, the publisher, meant to pass the old play as Shakespeare's; the last trace we have of it on the stage is in April 1594, when it was acted at the Rose by the Queen's and Sussex' men, who almost immediately afterwards broke up. That Shakespeare's play remained on the stage till the end of 1605 is evident from the words "these *late* eclipses" (i. 2. 112) which clearly refer to the huge eclipse of the sun in October 1605, and the immediately preceding eclipse of the moon in September. The word "late" could not be used, whether in the original text or by subsequent insertion, till October. That Shakespeare had been probably reading

Harvey on the subject I have noticed under the preceding play, to which the present is every way closely allied. Compare, for instance, the characters of Iago and Edmund. The Quarto of 1608, entered S. R. 26th November 1607 as acted at Whitehall St. Stephen's Day, *i.e.*, 26th December 1606, is abridged and slightly altered for Court representation and carelessly printed; the Folio is, on the other hand, somewhat shortened for the public stage. The names of the spirits in iii. 4 are from Harsnett's *Declaration of Egregious Popish Impostures*. The two lines at the end of Act i. and the Merlin's Prophecy (iii. 2. 79–95) are not in Shakespeare's manner; they are mere gag, inserted by the Fool-actor to raise a laugh among the groundlings. The story of Gloster and his sons is probably founded on Sidney's *Arcadia*, ii. 133–138, ed. 1598.

1606.

Macbeth, as we have it, is abridged for the stage in an unusual degree. Nevertheless it contains one scene, iii. 5, and a few lines, iv. i. 39–43, which are not by Shakespeare. The character of Hecate, and the songs in these passages (*Black spirits and white*, and *Come away*), are from Middleton's *Witch*, acted 1621–22. The insertions in *Macbeth* must have

SUCCESSION OF HIS PLAYS. 239

been made in 1622; they were probably merely intended to introduce a little singing and music then popular; and music has ever since been an essential ingredient in the stage representations. Omitting these forty lines, we have ample evidence of the date of the play as Shakespeare left it. In the Porter's speech, ii. 3. 1–23, 26–46, the "expectation of plenty" refers to the abundance of corn in 1606; the allusions to equivocation certainly allude to the trial of Garnet and other Jesuits in the spring of that year: the "stealing out of a French hose" agrees with the short and strait fashion then in vogue, when "the tailors took more than enough for the new fashion sake" (A. Nixon's *Black Year*, 1606); the touching for the King's evil, iv. 3. 140–159, implies that James was on the throne. Camden, in his *Remains* (1605), a book certainly known to Shakespeare, refers to it as a "gift hereditary." The "double balls and treble sceptres" in iv. 1. 119–122, necessitate a time of writing subsequent to 24th October 1604, when the constitution was changed. The applicability of the circumstances of the play to the Gowry conspiracy would be especially pleasing to James, and the predictions of the weyward sisters had already been presented to the King at Oxford in Latin in 1605. Warner added an account of Macbeth to his new edition of

Albion's England in 1606, but the absolute argument against this being a new play when Forman saw it performed 20th April 1610, lies in the distinct allusion in *The Puritan* by Middleton, acted 1606—"instead of a jester, we'll ha' th' ghost in a white sheet sit at upper end o' th' table." This was Shakespeare's first play without a jester, and Banquo's ghost sits in Macbeth's place at the upper end. There is little doubt that Malone was right in assigning the visit of the King of Denmark in July and August 1606 as the occasion for the production of this play at Court. But was this the date of its first production on the stage? All the evidences for it are gathered from ii. 3. 1–23, 26–46; iv. 1. 119–122; iv. 3. 140–159; every one of which passages bears evident marks of being an addition to the original text. The description of Cawdor's death is remarkably like that of the Earl of Essex in Stow (by Howes, p. 793), who minutely describes "his asking the Queen's forgiveness, his confession, repentance, and concern about behaving with propriety on the scaffold." Steevens (ii. 4) reminds us of corresponding passages in *Hamlet* and *Cæsar*, to which plays *Macbeth* is throughout more closely allied than to *Lear* or *Timon*. The references to Antony, i. 3. 84, iii. 1. 57, are just what might be expected from one who had recently read Plutarch's life of Antony for writing *Julius Cæsar*. Shakespeare's company were in Scotland in 1601, and were appointed the King's Servants; Laurence Fletcher being admitted burgess of the guild of the borough of Aberdeen, 22d October 1601. This, I think, is the date of production of *Macbeth* on the stage, 1606 being that of the revised play at Court. But there are traces of a still earlier play. In 1596, August 27, there is, says Mr. Collier, an entry in S. R. (I suppose in that portion relating to fines, &c., which Mr. Arber has not been allowed to reprint) referring to two ballads, one on *Macdobeth*, the other on *The Taming of a Shrew*. Kempe, in his *Dance from London to Norwich* (1600), refers to this ballad as made by "a penny poet whose first making was the miserable stolen story of *Mac-do-el* or *Mac-do-beth* or *Mac* somewhat, for I am sure a *Mac* it was, though I never had the maw to see it;" he bids the writer "leave writing these beastly ballads; make not good wenches prophetesses, for little or no profit." This ballad was in all probability founded on a play, as its companion was; a play probably written some year or two before. That Shakespeare had some connection with this early play, is rendered probable by iv. 1. 94–101, in which Dunsin'ane is accented in the southern manner; in the rest of the play it is always, as in Scotland, Dunsina'ne. This passage, in which Macbeth speaks of himself in the third person, and rhymes in a manner which strongly reminds us of the pre-Shakespearian stage, suggests that the old play of c. 1593-4 was used by Shakespeare in making his 1601 version. I may ask the reader who doubts the remarkable alterations to which this play has been subjected, to examine the following incomplete lines at points where compression by omission seems to have taken place, i. 3. 103; i. 4. 35; ii. 1. 16; ii. 1. 24; ii. 3. 120; iii. 2. 155; iv. 3. 15; and to compare the later alterations by Davenant and others, as given in my article in *Anglia*, vol. vii.

1606-7.

Timon of Athens unquestionably contains much matter from another hand. The Shakespearian part is so like *Lear* in matter, and *Anthony and Cleopatra* in metre, that the conjectural date here assigned to it cannot be far wrong. It was founded on the passage in North's *Plutarch* (Life of *Antony*), and perhaps on the story as told in Painter's *Palace of Pleasure*, with a hint or two from Lucian's *Dialogues* (? at second hand; no translation of that time is known). It would be out of proportion in this work to reproduce my 1868 essay on the authorship, which awaits some slight corrections from recent investigation. It will be found in the New Shakspere Society's *Transactions* for 1874. I can only here point out the parts that are certainly not Shakespeare's, namely, ii. 1; ii. 2. 194–204; iii. 1; iii. 2; iii. 3; iii. 4 (in great part); iii. 5; iii. 6. 116–131; iv. 2; iv. 3. 70–74, 103–106, 464–545; v. i. 157; v. 3. Delius and Elze say the second author was George Wilkins. Perhaps so; but they are certainly wrong in regarding the play as an alteration made by Shakespeare of another man's work. Whether Wilkins completed the unfinished sketch by Shakespeare, or the actors eked it out with matter taken from a previous play by him, I cannot tell: but Shakespeare's part is a whole *totus teres atque rotundus*. There is no trace of his ever working in conjunction with any author after 1594, although in this play, in *The Shrew*, and *Pericles* there is evidence of his writing portions of dramas which were fitted into the work of other men. Wilkins left the King's men in 1607 and wrote for the Queen's. This migration to an inferior company is so unusual as to indicate some rupture on unfriendly terms. Perhaps the insertion of Shakespeare's work in his play offended him. The unShakespearian characters in the play are three Lords—Lucius, Lucullus, and Sempronius; three Servants—Flavius (Steward always in the Shakespeare part), Flaminius, and Servilius; three Strangers; three Creditors—Hortensius, Philotus, and 2d Varro; three Masquers; and the Soldier. I have not here assigned to Wilkins all parts of the play that have been suspected, but only those with regard to which the evidence is definite, with entire exclusion of merely æsthetic opinion.

1607.

Anthony and Cleopatra was entered on S. R. 20th May 1608; and no doubt was written not much more than a year before that date. Wherever we find plays entered but not printed in their author's lifetime, it is pretty safe to conclude that they were then still on the stage: compare, for Shakespeare, the instances of *The Merchant of Venice, Troylus and Cressida*, and *As You Like it.*

1608.

Coriolanus in all probability was produced not long after *Anthony*. There is no external evidence available. Both these Roman plays are founded on North's *Plutarch*.

1608.

Pericles as we now have it was probably on the stage in 1608, when Wilkins published his prose version of "the play, as it was lately presented by the worthy and ancient poet John Gower." He was probably annoyed by the adoption of Shakespeare's version of the Marina story in place of his own. The rest of the play as it stands—*i.e.*, Acts i. ii. and Gower chorus to Act iii.—are by Wilkins, in whose novel the only distinctly traceable piece of Shakespeare's is from iii. 1. 28–31, which is repeated almost verbatim. The play was published in 1609, probably as an answer to Wilkins; whose unaltered play must have been on the stage as early as 1606, seeing that *The Puritan*, acted that year, contains a distinct parody of the scene of Thaisa's recovery. This original form of the play was founded on Gower's *Confessio Amantis* and Twine's novel of *Prince Apollonius*, which was probably, in consequence of the popularity of the play, reprinted in 1607. It was, I think, this Wilkins' play that was entered in S. R. along with *Anthony and Cleopatra* 20th May 1608, and the publication of which was stayed. There is no trace of any transfer of Blount's interest as so entered to Gosson, who published the altered play.

To the popularity of this drama there are many allusions, notably one in *Pimlico, or Run Redcap* (1609).

1609.

Cymbeline was probably produced after the Roman plays and before *Winter's Tale;* and the Iachimo part was doubtless then written. There is, however, (strong internal evidence) that the part derived from Holinshed, viz., the story of Cymbeline and his sons, the tribute, &c., in the last three acts, was written at an earlier time, in 1606 I think, just after *Lear* and *Macbeth*, for which the same chronicler had been used. All this older work will be found in the scenes in which Lucius and Bellarius enter. A marked instance in the change of treatment will be found in the character of Cloten. In the later version he is a mere fool (see i. 3; ii. 1); but in the earlier parts he is by no means deficient in manliness, and the lack of his "counsel" is regretted by the King in iv. 3. Especially should iii. 5 be examined from this point of view, in which the prose part is a subsequent insertion, having some slight discrepancies with the older parts of the scene. *Philaster*, which contains some passages suggested by this play, was written in 1611. The Iachimo story is found in Boccaccio's *Decameron*,

Day 11, Novel 9. The verse of the vision, v. 4. 30–122, is palpably by an inferior hand, and was probably inserted for some Court performance after Shakespeare had left the stage. Of course the stage directions for the dumb show are genuine. This would not have been worth mentioning but for the silly arguments of some who defend the Shakespearian authorship of these lines, and maintain that the play would be maimed without them. Forman saw this play acted c. 1610–11; which gives our only posterior limit of date.

1610.

The Winter's Tale was founded on Greene's *Dorastus and Fawnia;* it was still on the stage when Dr. S. Forman saw it, 15th May 1611; but this gives only a posterior limit. Sir H. Herbert mentions it as an old play allowed by Sir G. Buck. But Buck, although not strictly Master of the Revels till August 1610, had full power to "allow" plays from 1607 onwards. We are, after all, left in great measure to internal evidence. One really helpful fact is that Jonson in *Bartholomew Fair* links it with *The Tempest:* "If there be never a *servant monster* in the Fair who can help it? nor a *nest of antics?* He is loth to make nature afraid in his plays like those that beget *Tales, Tempests,* and such like drolleries." This was written in 1614, and at that date he would of course allude to the *latest* productions of Shakespeare, if to any. This allusion occurs in a play written for a rival company, the Princess Elizabeth's. In his *Conversations* with Drummond, Jonson again refers to this play *apropos* of Bohemia having no sea-coast. I suspect that the Bear was a success in *Mucedorus,* and therefore revived in this play.

1610.

The Tempest was shown by Malone to contain many particulars derived from Jourdan's narrative, 13th October 1610, *A Discovery of the Bermudas, otherwise called the Isle of Devils; by Sir Thomas Gates, Sir George Somers, and Captain Newport, with divers others.* He is not equally successful in showing that Shakespeare used *The True Declaration of the Colony of Virginia,* S. R. 8th November 1610, in which the reference to *The Tempest* as a "Tragical Comedy" seems to me to show that the play was already on the stage. It does not follow that because the October pamphlet was used in the storm scenes, that none of the play was written before that month; but that the date of its first appearance was in October to November 1610, I have little doubt. Gonzalo's description of his ideal republic is from Florio's *Montaigne*. The play as we have it is evidently abridged; one character, the son of Anthonio the Duke of Milan, i. 2. 438, has entirely disappeared, unless the eleven lines assigned to Francisco are the *débris* of his part. The lines forming the Masque in iv. 1 are palpably an addition, probably made by Beaumont for the Court performance before the Prince, the Princess Elizabeth, and the Palatine in 1612–13; or else before the King on 1st November 1612 (*The Winter's Tale* being acted on 5th November). This addition consists only of the heroics, ll. 60–105, 129–138; the mythological personages in the original play having acted in dumb show. In the stage directions (l. 72) of the dumb show "Juno descends;" in the text of the added verse l. 102, she "comes," and Ceres "knows her by her gait." This and the preceding were surely Shakespeare's last plays; compare Prospero's speech, v. 1. 50, &c., and the Epilogue. He began his career with the Chamberlain's company (after his seven years' apprenticeship in conjunction with others, 1587–94), with a Midsummer Dream, he finishes with a Winter's Tale; and so his playwright's work is rounded; twenty-four years, each year an hour in the brief day of work, and then the rounding with a sleep.*

1613.

Henry VIII. as we have it is not the play that was in action at the Globe when that theatre was burned on Tuesday, 29th June 1613. Howes (Stow, *Chronicles*, p. 1003) says, " By negligent discharging of a peal of ordnance, close to the South side thereof the Thatch took fire, and the wind suddenly disperst the flame round about, and in a very short space the whole building was quite consumed and no man hurt; the house being filled with people, to behold the play, viz., of *Henry the Eight.*" A letter from Thomas Lorkin to Sir Thomas Puckering, 30th June 1613, and another from John Chamberlain to Sir Ralph Winwood, 8th July 1613 (Winwood's *Memorials*, iii. 469), give similar accounts. Sir Henry Wotton (*Reliquiæ,* p. 475),

---

* Compare with this Masque, that by Beaumont written for the Inner Temple, 1613.

1. " Thy banks with pioned and twilled brims " (*Tempest*).
    "Bordered with sedges and water flowers" (*Inner Temple Masque*).
    "Naiades with sedged crowns " (*Tempest*).
2. " Blessing . . . and increasing " (*Tempest*).
    " Blessing and increase " (*Inner Temple Masque*).
3. The main part played by Iris in both.
4. The dance of the Naiads in both. Many of the properties could be utilised in both performances.

in a letter of 2d July 1613, says it was at "a new play acted by the King's players at the Bankside, called *All is True*, representing some principal pieces of the reign of Henry the Eighth." The title "All is True" is clearly alluded to in the Prologue, ll. 9, 18, 21; but the same Prologue shows that the extant play was performed as a new one at Blackfriars, for the price of entrance, a "shilling," l. 12, and the address to "the first and happiest hearers of the town," l. 24, are only applicable to the "private house" in Blackfriars; the entrance to the Globe was twopence, and the audience at this "public house" of a much lower class. This play is chiefly by Fletcher and Massinger, Shakespeare's share in it being only i. 2; ii. 3; ii. 4; while Massinger wrote i. 1; iii. 2. 1–193; v. 1. It was not, however, written by these authors in conjunction. Shakespeare appears to have left it unfinished; his part is more like *The Winter's Tale* than any other play, and was probably written just before that comedy in 1609, during the prevalence of the plague. I have before noted the disturbing effect of these plague times, with the concomitant closing of the theatres, &c., on Shakespeare's regular habits of composition. This play is founded on Holinshed's *Chronicle* and Fox's *Christian Martyrs* (1563). It is worth noting that its success called forth new editions of S. Rowley's *When you see me you know me*, and the *Lord Cromwell* of W. S. in this year; both plays on Henry the Eighth's times. On the authorship question see Mr. Spedding's Essay in *The Gentleman's Magazine*, August 1850, Mr. Boyle's Essay and my own letter in the *Athenæum*. That the 1613 play (probably finished by Fletcher, and destroyed in great part in the Globe fire) was not that now extant is certain, for in a contemporary ballad on the burning of the Globe we are told that the "riprobates prayed for the fool," and there is no fool in *Henry VIII*. The extant play was produced by Fletcher and Massinger in 1617.

1625.

The Two Noble Kinsmen was published in 1634, as written by Fletcher and Shakespeare. There is no other evidence that Shakespeare had any hand in it, except the opinions of Lamb, Coleridge, Spalding, Dyce, &c. These, on analysis, simply reiterate the old argument, "It is too good for any one else." Hazlitt and Hallam held, notwithstanding, the opposite opinion. I have myself shown in *The Literary World*, 10th February 1883 (Boston), that the play was first acted in 1625. It was printed from a playhouse MS., with stage directions, such as i. 3: "2 Hearses ready with Palamon and Arcite; the 3 Queens. Theseus and his Lords ready;" and in iii. 5: "Knock for Schoole." But in iv. 2, we find an actor named Curtis taking the part of Messenger. No actor of that name is known except Curtis Greville, who joined the King's men between 1622, when he belonged to the Palsgrave's, and October 1626, when he performed in Massinger's *Roman Actor*. Moreover, the Prologue tells us this was a *new* play performed in a time of losses, and in anticipation of leaving London. The company did leave London in 1624, after their trouble in August about Middleton's *Game of Chess*. On this occasion they travelled in the north, and performed at Skipton three times for £3; and again, in July 1625 they travelled, on account of the plague in London; where they ceased to perform in May, when the deaths from that disease exceeded forty per week. Greville probably joined the King's men on the breaking up of the Palsgrave's, of whom the last notice dates 3d November 1624. This gives Easter 1625 as the likeliest date for the play. But whether in 1624 or 1625 (and it must be one of these years) it was first acted, the advocates of Shakespeare's part-authorship are now reduced to the hypothesis that a play begun by Shakespeare was left unnoticed for some dozen years, although a similarly unfinished play had been finished and acted twelve seasons before, and a collected edition of Shakespeare's works had been issued in the interim, in which had been included every available portion of his writings.* I cannot believe this; nor can I think that if Shakespeare were really concerned in this play it would have been put forth in 1625 with so modest a Prologue. This might have suited while he lived, but nine years after his death, and two years after his collected works had been published, it is incredible. With the highest respect then for the eminent æsthetic critics who hold that Shakespeare did write part of this play, I must withdraw my adhesion, and state my present opinion that there is nothing in it above the reach of Massinger and Fletcher, but that some things in it (ii. 1a; iv. 3) are unworthy of either, and more likely to be by some inferior hand, W. Rowley for instance. The popular instinct has always been on this side; editions containing this play have not been sought after; and had it not been *known* not to have been Shakespeare's, it would surely have been gathered up with the W. S. plays in the Folio of 1663.

* *Pericles* and *Edward III.* are no exceptions to this statement; the copyrights of both belonged to other publishers, and were retained by these after the Folio was issued.

SECTION V.

ON THE MARLOWE GROUP OF PLAYS.

1 HENRY VI. was acted as a new play at the Rose by Lord Strange's men 3d March 1592. It is evidently written by several hands. No successful attempt has yet been made to discriminate these; yet it will be found that on this discrimination depends the elucidation of so many difficult circumstances of Shakespeare's early career, that no apology is required for giving to this play an amount of consideration which it would not deserve on account of its intrinsic merits. It is convenient to commence our investigation by a brief summary of the historical parts contained in the play.

A 1422, August 31. Henry VI. succeeded to the throne at "nine months old."

A 1422, November 7. Henry V. was buried at Westminster (i. 1).

A 1425. Gloster was refused admission to the Tower (i. 3).

A 1425, January 19. The Earl of March died *at Trim*, leaving Richard Plantagenet his heir. [This Edmund Mortimer was not imprisoned in the Tower, as in the play; but his uncle, Sir John Mortimer, was so, who was executed shortly before.] (ii. 5.)

A 1426, March. A Parliament was held *at Leicester* (iii. 1).

B 1427 September to 1428 May. Orleans was besieged (i. 2, 4, 5, 6; ii. 1, 2, 3).

A 1429. The battle of Patay [called *Poitiers*, iv. 1. 19] at which Fastolfe [called Falstaff in the play] fled, and Talbot was taken (i. 1. 103–140; compare iii. 2. 103–108).

A 1429. Charles was crowned at Rheims (i. 1. 92).

A 1429. The French towns revolted (i. 1. 60). For Paris mentioned among them compare v. 2. 2.

E 1430, May. Joan of Arc was taken, and (1431, May) burned (v. 3. 1–44; v. 4. 1–93).

B 1430, December. Henry VI. was crowned at Paris (iii. 4; iv. 1).

C 1435, September. Bedford died *at Paris* (iii. 2), and Burgundy made peace with France (iii. 3).

E 1436. Paris submitted to Charles (v. 2. 2).

E 1443. The match between Henry and Margaret was arranged (v. 3. 45–195; v. 5).

E 1443. A truce was made for eighteen months (v. 4. 94–175).

D 1452. Talbot and his son were killed in battle (iv. 2, 3, 4, 5, 6, 7).

THE MARLOWE GROUP OF PLAYS. 257

The capital letters prefixed to these dates will enable us to follow readily the arrangement of these events in the play. The A. group, comprising i. 1. 3, ii. 5, iii. 1, is manifestly by one writer. The time limits of his scenes are 1422 and 1426: the first scene contains allusions to events of a subsequent date, thrust in for dramatic effect without regard either to historical accuracy or the internal consistency of the play. Specially the battle of Patay, the crowning of Charles, and the revolt of the French towns may be noted. It is hardly requisite to do more than read the opening speech to see that the author of these scenes was Marlowe. It may be noticed, however, that in these scenes, and in these only, we find Gloster (Gloucester elsewhere), Reynold (Reignier or Reigneir elsewhere), and Roän (monosyllabic elsewhere). All these scenes are laid in London.

The B. group, i. 2. 3. 4. 5. 6, ii. 1. 2. 3, iii. 4, iv. 1., contains only events that happened between 1427 and 1430, the scene being laid at Orleans, Auvergne, or Paris. The bit of the battle of Patay iii. 2. 103-108, thrust into the midst of scenes at Rouen in 1435, would probably belong to this group. It seems to be a preparation for iv. 1, stuck for dramatic purposes in a position historically most incongruous. The author of these scenes is

R

not easy to identify: his work is rather colourless, yet minor coincidences with the known work of Robert Greene and Thomas Kyd point to one of them as the writer. In this group only we find the spellings: Joane de Puzel (Pucelle elsewhere), Reigneir (occasionally also Reignier), and Gloucester (Gloster elsewhere, except in one instance, where Glocester is probably a misprint). There can be no doubt that these scenes are all by one author, and that not the writer of group A., but very far inferior.

Group C., iii. 2. 3, is very like Group B. in general handling, but has some marked characteristics: here, and here only, we find Burgonie (Burgundy or Burgundie elsewhere) and Roan monosyllabic; Pucelle (Puzel in Group B.) and Joane (Jone in Group D.) also differentiate it from these groups. The time is 1435, place Rouen. I conjecture the author to have been George Peele.

Group D. v. 2–5 is made up of the Joan of Arc story of 1430–1 and the Margaret match of 1443. This group has Gloucester invariably (Gloster in Group A.), Jone (Joane in B., C.), Reignier (never Reigneir, as B.) The author of these scenes is without doubt Thomas Lodge. His versification is unmistakable, and the phrase "cooling card" occurs in *Marius and Sylla*, the older plays of *John* and

THE MARLOWE GROUP OF PLAYS. 259

Leir (both times in parts by Lodge). It has not been traced in Greene, Peele, or Marlowe.

Before considering Group E., iv. 2–7, which is concerned only with Talbot's last fight near Bourdeaux in 1452, I would draw attention to the fact that it is clear that this episode did not form part of the original play: it is merely connected with it by the two lines, v. 2. 16, 17, which may have been inserted for that purpose; belongs chronologically to the next play, and is so different from, as well as so superior to, its surroundings, that in 1876 I suggested that Shakespeare might have written it. Mr. Swinburne has since sanctioned this opinion by adopting it. This, however, is not evidence; what follows is. The scenes in the Folio are not divided in Acts i., ii.; in the other Acts they are. Acts iii. and iv. 1 coincide with the modern division; but v. 1 of the modern editors is iv. 2 in the Folio; v. 2. 3. 4, are iv. 3 in the Folio, and v. 5 in the Folio is the whole fifth Act. Here then is the play completed without iv. 2–7, *which are not numbered at all.* It is plain that they were written subsequently to the rest of the play and inserted at a revival. They had to be inserted in such a manner as not to break the connection between this play and *2 Henry VI.*, and were put in the most convenient place, regardless of historic sequence. I take it for granted that this play in its original shape was acted before *2 Henry VI.*, the commencement of which was evidently meant to fit on to the end of the preceding play. It is in accordance with the hypothesis here announced (that the play acted 3d March 1592 was new only in these Talbot scenes,) that we find Nash in his *Piers Penniless* (S. R. 8th August 1592) referring only to the Talbot scenes as new. "How it would have joyed brave Talbot, the terror of the French, to think that after he had lain two hundred year in his tomb, he should triumph again on the stage, and have his bones embalmed with the tears of ten thousand spectators at least." It was acted thirteen times at the Rose between March 3 and June 22, that is, at least once a week; was the most popular play of the season, and was probably still in action "about the city" or in the country during the time that the theatres were closed for the plague, from 22d June 1592 till January 1593, when it was again played at the Rose. It was, therefore, in action when Greene's celebrated address "to those gentlemen, his quondam acquaintance, that spend their wits in making plays," was written. This address was published in Greene's *Groatsworth of Wit* after 2d September, when Greene died, and before 8th December, when Chettle's *Kind-Hart's*

THE MARLOWE GROUP OF PLAYS. 261

Dream was entered on S. R., and was probably written about June. It is addressed to Marlowe, Lodge, and Peele. Attempts have been made to show that Nash, not Lodge, was the second playwright of this trio, on the ground that Lodge was too old to be called "young Juvenal" or "sweet boy;" was absent from England; was not a satirist, and had foresworn writing for the theatre. The only important argument is that of Lodge's age. As this is important in other respects, I give here a table of the known birth dates, matriculations, B.A. and M.A. degrees, and first appearances as authors of the University men connected at that time with the stage :—

	Born.	Matriculated.	B.A.	M.A.	Author in
Lyly	1553-4	1571	1573	1575	1579
Peele	1558	1574	1577	1579	1584
Greene	...	...	1578	1583	1580
Lodge	...	1573	1577	...	1580
Marlowe	1564	1581	1583	1587	1587
Nash	1567	1582	1585-6	...	1589

It will be seen from the above table that the degree of B.A. was usually taken at eighteen or nineteen; that Lodge and Greene were probably of about the same age; and if we may judge from Greene's slowness in obtaining his M.A. degree, that he was not speedy in fulfilling the earlier

University requirements. Greene was probably the elder. At any rate, Lodge's age in 1592 was about thirty-three, surely not too old for one of about his own age to call "boy." He was a satirist before 1592. *The Looking-glass for London* is bitter enough for any "young Juvenal." On the other hand, Nash was certainly not the "biting satyrist that lastly with me [Greene] wrote a comedy." He had at the time of Greene's death written no comedy whatever: his first connection with the stage was his *Summer's Last Will*, acted at Archbishop Whitgift's, in November 1592. Lodge, we know, had written with Greene *The Looking-glass*, and there is strong internal evidence of his having a hand in *George-a-Greene* and *James IV*. Nor could the statement that "those puppits that speak from our mouths, those anticks garnished in our colours," had "all been beholding" to you, be with any consistency applied to Nash. Greene was evidently addressing the principal playwrights of the time, and, if my present view is a true one, he seized the opportunity of Shakespeare's having made "new additions" to a play in which all of them had been concerned to endeavour to create an ill-feeling between "the upstart crow beautified with our feathers" and those of the University men, who had hitherto enjoyed a monopoly of writing for the stage, or nearly so. To have omitted Lodge in such an attempt would have been weak; to have included Nash, absurd. The effect of Greene's address was not what he desired. Peele had probably already been a coadjutor of Shakespeare, and Marlowe immediately, and no doubt Lodge later on, joined Shakespeare's company and wrote for them. In Greene's excuse must be considered how galling it must have been to a man in poverty and bad health to see a play which, while he was connected with it, had attracted little notice, suddenly raised to the highest success by the insertion of a few scenes written by a "Johannes factotum," a "Shakescene," who was "able to bombast out a blank verse" without being "*Magister in artibus utriusque universitatis.*" Confirmations of my views as to this play will be found in the succeeding ones. The scene ii. 4 has long been recognised as so far superior to the rest of the play as to be probably due to the hand of Shakespeare at a later date, c. 1597–8.

2 Henry VI.—This play exists in two forms: one in the 1623 Folio, hereafter for convenience called F.; the other in Quarto, entered S. R. 12th March 1594, hereafter called Q. It was published in 1594 as *The First part of the Contention betwixt the two Famous Houses of York and Lancaster.* This Quarto version is a mangled and probably surreptitious copy of the original play, greatly abbreviated for acting. The play as first written will be hereafter called O. But F. and O. are not identical, although in many parts O. was more like F. than Q. It will be convenient to enter on the proof that O. was revised and altered before beginning the discussion of the authorship of either version, which is the most difficult, if not the most important, problem in Shakespearian criticism.

In the Folio of 1623 a list is given of the principal actors in Shakespeare's plays. The method in which this list is arranged has never been pointed out. It is chronological. The first ten names are those of the original *men* actors when the Chamberlain's company was instituted in 1594; the next five were added not later than 1603; the next five (excepting Field, who is inserted here from his early connection with Underwood and Ostler) c. 1610; the final six after 1617. By a comparison of this list with the names of the actors in *The Seven Deadly Sins*, originally acted before 1588, but the extant plot of which dates c. 1594, we shall get the evidence we want. The first seven names in the Folio list are (1.) W. Shakespeare, (2.) R. Burbadge, (3.) J. Hemmings, (4.) A. Phillips,

THE MARLOWE GROUP OF PLAYS. 265

(5.) W. Kempe, (6.) J. Pope, (7.) G. Bryan. The last five of these we know to have been members of Lord Strange's company in 1593. In the 7. *D. S.* we find neither Shakespeare nor Hemmings; but we do find (2.) R. Burbadge, (4.) Mr. Phillips, (5.) Will Foole, (6.) Mr. Pope, (7.) Mr. Bryan. It will be noticed that the prefix Mr. is confined to members of Lord Strange's company. Next in the Folio list come (8.) Henry Condell, (9.) William Sly, (10.) Richard Cowley. These appear in 7. *D. S.* as (8.) Harry, (9.) W. Sly, (10.) R. Cowley. At this point we are struck with the fact that Harry, Will, and Dick are names of three Cade conspirators in Q., and naturally try to see if the other names, Nick, Jack, Robin, Tom, and George, occur in 7. *D. S.* For it is certain that in very early plays up to the end of the sixteenth century it was frequently the case that the actors in plays are designated by their proper christian names. We do find (11.) Nick (*i.e.*, Nicholas Tooley, a boy-actor in 1597, but a man c. 1610 in the Folio of 1623), (12.) John Duke, (13.) Robert Pallant, (14.) Thomas Goodall; but George, *i.e.*, G. Peele, is not there discoverable. I may notice that Duke and Pallant, like Beeston, all three of whom left the Chamberlain's men for the Earl of Derby's in 1599, are excluded from the Folio list. On turning to another play, *Sir Thomas More*, c. 1596, the only other one that can give us similar information on the same scale, I find (8.) Harry, (13.) Robin, (14.) T. Goodall, (15.) Kit (*i.e.*, Christopher Beeston), and two boys, (16.) Ned and (17.) a second Robin, *i.e.*, Robert Gough, who occurs in the Folio list as a man c. 1617. In the 7. *D. S.* these latter correspond to (15.) Kitt, (16.) Ned, (17.) R. Go. In *Sir T. More* there are two other names of this kind, Giles and Rafe. Of Giles nothing more is known, but Rafe Raye is mentioned in Henslowe's *Diary* as a Chamberlain's man in 1594. A further examination of older plays leads to little additional information; but what is to be found all confirms the opinion that I had formed (as will be seen), on other grounds, that *2 Henry VI.* was written for the Queen's men. Thus in plays known to have belonged to that company, I find in *The Famous Victories*, (12.) John, (13.) Robin, (14.) Tom, (16.) Ned and Lawrence; in *Orlando*, (14.) Tom and Rafe (Raye); in *Friar Bacon*, (10.) Dick, (14.) Tom; and in *James IV.*, Andrew. There is no Andrew in our lists, but one occurs in *Much Ado About Nothing*, iv. 2, 1597-8, in place of Kempe: apparently a remnant of the older form of *Love's Labour's Won* before Kempe undertook the part. But our list of the 7. *D. S.* is not yet exhausted: (18.) Sander (a boy-player, but the same as Alexander Cooke, a man in 1603 in the Folio list), (19.) T. Belt, and (20.) Will (another boy), occur in *The Taming of a Shrew*, 1588. Of (21.) Vincent, nothing is known; but (22.) J. Sinkler acted with Gabriel (Spenser) and Humfrey (Jeffes) in *3 Henry VI.*, which belonged to Pembroke's company. Now as the last two, with Antony Jeffes and Robert Shaw, appear in Henslowe's *Diary* for the first time immediately after the partial breaking up of Pembroke's company and their juncture with the Admiral's in October 1597, it is morally certain that Sinkler had gone to the Chamberlain's, and Spenser Shaw and the two Jeffes to the Admiral's, at or before that date. I feel, therefore, justified in concluding that the 7. *D. S.* gives us a nearly complete list of the Chamberlain's actors, formed of Lord Strange's players as a nucleus; such of the Queen's men as joined them in 1591-2, when they obtained many Queen's plays (see p. 108), and such of Pembroke's as joined them in 1594, when they obtained Pembroke's plays (see p. 21). I have omitted only one name, and the absolute coincidence of nearly every one of the rest with the lists obtained from other sources is too remarkable to be the mere effect of accident: in fact, the chances are many millions to one against this being the case. The one name omitted is (23.) John Holland. This name occurs nowhere else to my knowledge, but in the *7. D. S.* plot and *2 Henry VI.*, Act iv. in the Folio, where he replaces Nick of the Quarto. There can be no doubt of this being an actor's name; and its occurrence shows at once that the Cade part of the play was revised, and that the revision was probably made after 1594. Had it been earlier, there would have been two Johns in the company, Duke and Holland, and Duke would not have been called simply Jack.

If the above conclusions are well founded, *2 Henry VI.* was originally written for the Queen's men as a continuation of *1 Henry VI.*, and, like the latter-mentioned play, passed into the hands of Lord Strange's men in 1591–2, but was not, like it, then revised; or it may, like *George a Greene*, have passed to Sussex' men; from them, like *Titus Andronicus*, to Pembroke's; and thence to the Chamberlain's. It is noticeable that although published in Quarto by the same person, Millington, who published *3 Henry VI.* as the *True Tragedy of Richard Duke of York* in 1595, he put no name of acting company on the former play, as he did that of Pembroke's on the latter. This distinctly shows that the original companies for whom these plays were written were not identical, and that

that of *2 Henry VI.* was probably unknown to Millington. As to the authorship of *2 Henry VI.*, it will be well to make F. the basis of investigation, always having in mind the possibility of passages having been inserted by the ultimate reviser. The corruption and omission in Q. caused by the shortening for stage purposes have been so great, that the usual plan of beginning with Q. becomes altogether misleading. The example of *1 Henry VI.* induces me to attach great weight to the chronological arrangement of the historical facts. Henry's marriage in 1445 forms the subject of i. 1, evidently written by Greene originally. The word "alderliefest" in l. 28 should specially be noted: it is used by Greene in his *Mourning Garment*, and "aldertruest" in his *James IV.* Such words are not found in Marlowe, Peele, Lodge, or Shakespeare; yet here one occurs in a passage found in F. but not in Q., plainly indicating omission in Q., not addition in F. The next portion, i. 2–ii. 4, is concerned with the banishment of the Duchess of Gloster, 1441, and the story of Saunder Simcox, 1441, with which is incorporated the accusation of the armourer for high treason, 1446. This part (except i. 3. 45–103) is mainly by George Peele, but much altered in the F. revision. Peele his mark, "sandy plains," occurs in i. 4. 39. The Simcox anecdote, however, ii. 1. 59—153, which is quite unconnected with the rest of the play, is more like Kyd's work than Peele's, and may have been written by him. The exceptional bit, i. 3. 45—103, to the conversation in which no historical date can be assigned, is manifest Marlowe; a preparation for iii. 1–iv. 1, which is beyond question by him. The events in this section are (iii. 1a) the accusation and (iii. 2) murder of Gloster in 1447; (iii. 3) the banishment of Suffolk, 1447; (iii. 3) the death of Winchester in 1447; (iii. 1b) the Irish insurrection in 1449; and, finally, (iv. 1) the death of Suffolk in 1450. These scenes are the salt of the play. The opening lines of iv. 1, the description in iii. 2. 160, &c., the awful pathos of the death of Winchester, are from the same hand as the end of *Doctor Faustus*. The differences of Q. and F. in this portion are mostly due to omissions in Q.: iii. 3, for instance, could not have been left in the state in which Q. has it by the meanest of the authors of the play: it is cut down by some illiterate actor. That revision there has been is, however, plain from the singular circumstance that in iii. 2 Elianor is given for Margaret as the Queen's name. This is probably due to Marlowe's almost simultaneous work on the older *John*, in which Queen Elianor is a prominent character. It would seem that the revisor missed this scene, although correcting Margaret properly in the others. It is no printer's error; for in l. 26 we have "Nell," for which some modern editors euphoniously substitute "Meg." The rest of the play, iv. 2–v. 3, is by one hand, and that hand Lodge's. The notion that Greene wrote it arises from want of discriminating Greene's work from Lodge's in *The Looking-glass for London*, all the better part of which is by Lodge. I fear that those who underrate the powers of this elegant and (in his own line) powerful writer estimate him by his earliest dramatic effort, *Marius and Sylla*. He should be read in his *Glaucus* and *Rosalynde;* and his evident wish to avoid being known as a dramatic writer should be taken into account. That he did continue to write plays for many years, I have no doubt, but the evidence is too extensive to be given here. This part of the play includes Cade's insurrection, 1450, and the battle of St. Albans, 1455.

As regards the date, &c., of revision, see under the next play.

3 Henry VI. is of very different character from the two preceding plays. If read in the F. version, no change of authorship is perceptible; all is consistent; and if the Q. version had not come down to us, no one would have suspected a second author. It is plainly by Marlowe, but the Marlowe of *Edward II.*, not of *Faustus*, later in date than *2 Henry VI*. F. is nearly if not quite identical with the original play. Q. is not, as in the case of the preceding play, an abridgment for the stage made by the actors, but one made for the same purpose, carefully and accurately, apparently by the author himself. The reason for this difference in the treatment of the plays is manifest. *3 Henry VI.* was, as we know from the title-page, acted by Pembroke's men, and F. is printed from a prompter's copy, in which the names of Gabriel [Spenser], Humphrey [Jeffes], and [John] Sinkler appear in the stage directions; and they were actors for that company. There is not a particle of evidence that this stage copy was ever altered in any way after the Chamberlain's company acquired it. A careful examination of such passages as ii. 5, the stronghold of the revision theory, shows too much coincidence between Q. and F. for any likelihood of rewriting having taken place, except by way of abridgment in Q. But in *2 Henry VI.* things are quite different: the Greene and Marlowe parts are merely abridged in Q., and the Peele a good deal revised in F. as well as abridged in Q.; but the Lodge part at the end is absolutely rewritten in

THE MARLOWE GROUP OF PLAYS. 273

the St. Alban's battle, and the very names of the actors are changed in the Cade insurrection. Who could have done this but Shakespeare? Here, and here only, can we find an explanation of the inclusion of these plays in the Folio edition of his works in 1623. In my opinion the history of the plays is this: About 1588–9, Marlowe plotted, and, in conjunction with Kyd (or Greene), Peele, and Lodge, wrote *1 Henry VI.* for the Queen's men. About 1589 the same authors wrote *2 Henry VI.*; in that year I have ascertained that Marlowe left the Queen's men, and in 1590 joined Pembroke's, for whom he alone wrote *3 Henry VI.* In 1591–2 the Queen's men were in distress, and sold, among other plays, *1 Henry VI.* to Lord Strange's men, who produced it in 1592 with Shakespeare's Talbot additions as a new play. In the autumn of that year or in 1593–4, when the companies travelled on account of the plague, they cut down their plays for country representation; among others, *2 Henry VI.* (altered by some illiterate) and *3 Henry VI.* (abridged by Marlowe himself). On this point compare the parallel instances of abridged plays, *Hamlet, Orlando,* and *The Guise.* In May 1593 *2 Henry VI.* passed to the Sussex' men with *Leir*, &c., when the Queen's men broke up; in February 1594 with *Andronicus* to Pembroke's; in April,

s

when Pembroke's company partly dissolved, all three plays were reunited in the hands of the Chamberlain's men; and for them *2 Henry VI.* was, c. 1600, after Lodge had retired, remodelled by Shakespeare, and *3 Henry VI.* corrected—the other authors, Peele, Marlowe, (Kyd?), and Greene, having died before 1598. Meanwhile Millington published *2 Henry VI.* Q. as *York and Lancaster*, and *3 Henry VI.* Q. as *Richard Duke of York*, these abridged copies having become useless to Pembroke's men on the ceasing of the plague and of their travels.

I have not noticed here the many parallel passages from the works of Marlowe and others which confirm the assignment of authorship now advocated. It would be out of all proportion to give them here unless imperfectly: the reader will find some in Dyce's *Marlowe*, and more in my edition of *Edward II.* Nor have I noticed the schoolboy interpretation that explains "their" in *Henry V.*, Epil. l. 13, as referring to *2* and *3 Henry VI.*: "their," *more Shakespeariano*, like "they" in the previous line, refers in form to the "many" of l. 12, but in meaning to the actors of *1 Henry VI.*, in which play, and not in *3 Henry VI.*, the loss of France is treated of. It is also most unlikely that the 1600 edition of *The Duke of York* should have been issued as played by Pembroke's servants if the play had

THE MARLOWE GROUP OF PLAYS. 275

been previously acted by the Chamberlain's. Compare the parallel case of *Andronicus*. Miss Lee's statement, "Greene wrote, Nash tells us," more than four others " for Lord Pembroke's company," is absolutely without foundation. Nash says "the company" (*Apology*, 1593), and evidently alludes to the Queen's men, for whom *Orlando, Bacon, Selimus*, and *The Looking-glass* were written. In fact, Greene's only known connection with any other company was his fraudulent selling of *Orlando* a second time to the Admiral's. Marlowe, and he alone, is *known* as a writer for Pembroke's: Kyd may have been, however, and in my opinion was, a contributor to their stage.

Richard III. is closely connected with *3 Henry VI.*, and written with direct reference to it. In i. 2. 158, iv. 2. 98, iv. 4. 275, scenes in that play are plainly alluded to. Nor is it possible, if the two plays be read in immediate sequence, to avoid the feeling that they have a common authorship. On the other hand, a closer analysis shows that in *Richard* the Latin quotations, classical allusions, and peculiar animal similes which are characteristic of *Henry* have entirely disappeared. There are also discrepancies, such as Gray's fighting for the Lancastrians, i. 3. 130, whereas in *3 Henry VI.*, iii.

2. 2, he is represented as a Yorkist, which shows a different hand in the two plays. *Richard III.* has always been regarded as entirely Shakespeare's, and its likeness to *3 Henry VI.* has more than anything else kept alive the untenable belief that this last-named play was also, in part or wholly, written by our greatest dramatist. Yet the unlikeness of *Richard III.* to the other historical plays of Shakespeare, and the impracticability of finding a definite position for it, metrically or æsthetically, in any chronological arrangement, have made themselves felt. Even cautious Mr. Halliwell says, "There are slight traces of an older play to be observed, passages which belong to an inferior hand;" and again, "To the circumstance of an anterior work having been used do we owe some of its weakness and excessively turbulent character" (*Outlines*, 94). A careful examination of the editions will be found to confirm and extend this conclusion. The 1597 Quarto (Q_1), which is evidently an abridged version made for the stage, and which no doubt was the version acted during nearly all Elizabeth's reign, differs from the Folio in a way not to be paralleled in any other Shakespearian play. Minute alterations have been made in almost every speech, in a fashion which could not have been customary with him who uttered his thoughts so easily as scarcely to make

THE MARLOWE GROUP OF PLAYS. 277

a blot (*i.e.* alteration) in his papers. The question of anteriority of the Q. and F. versions has been hotly debated on æsthetic grounds; but the mere expurgation of oaths and metrical emendations in F. are enough to show that it is the later version, probably made c. 1602; while the fact that it was preferred by the editors of the 1623 Folio shows that they considered it the authentic copy of Shakespeare's work. In other instances, *Macbeth*, *The Tempest*, &c., they have indeed given us abridged editions; but there is neither proof nor likelihood that any other were accessible. We do not know what original copies were destroyed in the Globe fire of 1613, and should be thankful for such versions as we have, which were probably the acting versions used at Blackfriars. But in this case the editors had at hand the Quartos, and unless they thought the Folio more authentic, I cannot see why they preferred it. Furthermore, the F. version appears to have been defective in some places; for v. 3. 50, end of play, and iii. 1. 17–165, are certainly printed from Q_3 (1602). This has been controverted, but on very insufficient grounds. Now directly we compare the Folio and Quarto versions, we meet with evidence that alteration and correction have been largely used in both of them. For instance, Derby is found as a character in the play in i. 1, ii. 1, 2, iv. 5, v. 5, in both versions; in iii. 1. 2, iv. 1, v. 2, he is called Stanley. This shows correction by a second hand. In iv. 1, while Stanley has been inserted in the text, Derby remains in the prefixes; v. 3 is only partially corrected, and both names occur. The names were not used indifferently, for in iv. 2, 4, we find Stanley in F. but Derby in Q. This shows a progressive correction in which Q. precedes F. It may be noticed that Darby is the original author's spelling. In like manner, *Gloster*, the original prefix, has in i. 1, 2, 3, ii. 1. 2, iii. 4, 5, 7, been replaced in F. by *Richard*, but in iii. 1, in the part printed from Q_3, and there only, *Gloster* remains. So again Margaret is indicated in the older version by *Qu. Mar.*, *Qu. M.*, &c., but never *Mar.*, as in F. iv. 4. In F. i. 3 we find by side of *Mar.* a remainder of the older form in *Q. M.* This is not an exhaustive statement, but sufficient I think to show that alterations were made, as I suggest. There can be little doubt that in this, as in *John*, Shakespeare derived his plot and part of his text from an anterior play, the difference in the two cases being that in *Richard III.* he adopted much more of his predecessor's text. I believe that the anterior play was Marlowe's, partly written for Lord Strange's company in 1593, but

THE MARLOWE GROUP OF PLAYS. 279

left unfinished at Marlowe's death, and completed and altered by Shakespeare in 1594. It was no doubt on the stage when, on 19th June 1594, the older play on *Richard III.*, "with the conjunction of the two Houses of Lancaster and York," was entered S. R. That was acted by the Queen's players. The unhistorical but grandly classical conception of Margaret, the Cassandra prophetess, the Helen-Ate of the House of Lancaster, which binds the whole tetralogy into one work, is evidently due to Marlowe, and the consummate skill with which he has fused the heterogeneous contributions of his coadjutors in the two earlier *Henry VI.* plays is no less worthy of admiration. I do not think it possible to separate Marlowe's work from Shakespeare's in this play—it is worked in with too cunning a hand; but wherever we find *Darby, Qu. M., Glo.*, &c., we may be sure that some of his handiwork is left. Could any critic, if the older *John* were destroyed, tell us which lines had been adopted in the later play? Nor can I enter, unless in a special monograph, on the relations of the Quartos to each other. The question is of no importance, and I need only say that the usual corruptions take place from Q_1 to Q_5, and that in Q_6 (1622) many readings are found agreeing with F.

which are not in the other Quartos. The same phenomenon is observed in the 1619 edition of *The Whole Contention*, and far too much has been made of it. It merely indicates correction by attendance at the theatre and picking up a few words during the action. The only Quartos deserving special notice are Q_1, as containing Shakespeare's first "additions," and Q_3, as having been used in printing part of F. I do not think the allusion in Weever's *Epigrams*, written 1595-6, is to this play. It may be so.

Titus Andronicus.—That this play is not by Shakespeare is pretty certain from internal evidence. The Latin quotations, classical allusions, use of *pour* as prefix in iv. 1, manner of versification, and above all the introduction of rape as a subject for the stage, would be sufficient to disprove his authorship. Fortunately we know that it was produced by the Earl of Sussex' men, 23d January 1594, and Shakespeare belonged then to Derby's (Lord Strange's). It was afterwards, on the breaking up of that company, acted by Pembroke's and Derby's before 16th April, when Lord Derby died. Enlargement in the Folio or abridgment in the Quarto, 1600 (we have no copy extant of the first edition, entered S. R. February 1594), appears in iii. 2, found in F., not in Q., and there is a distinct continuity between Acts i. and ii.; at the end of Act i. we have "*manet* Moore," not *Exeunt* simply. Whether this play got into the Folio by some confusion with *Titus and Vespasian*, played by Lord Strange's men 11th April 1592, which was, as we know from a German version extant, written on the same subject, and in which Shakespeare may have had some share, we cannot tell; but it was certainly played and revised (there was another edition in 1611), while the other play has perished. That it was written by Marlowe I incline to think. What other mind but the author of *The Jew of Malta* could have conceived Aaron the Moor? Mr. Dyce has warned us against attributing too many plays to the short career of Marlowe, but he did not consider that Marlowe probably wrote two plays a year from 1587–1593, and that we have only at present seven acknowledged as his. Those now attributed to him, in whole or part, by me will raise the number to a baker's dozen; but in some of these, as the older *John* and *1* and *2 Henry VI.*, his share was comparatively slight. Nevertheless, I think the opinion that Kyd wrote this play of *Andronicus* worth the examination, although, with such evidence as has yet been adduced, Marlowe has certainly the better claim. Shakespeare probably never touched this play unless by inserting iii. 2, which is possible.

Edward III. The Shakespearian part of this play, i. 3, ii. 1. 2 (beginning at "What, are the stealing foxes"), which contains lines from the then unpublished *Sonnets*, ii. 1. 10, 450, and an allusion to the recently published *Lucreece*, ii. 2. 194, was clearly acted in 1594, after 9th May, when *Lucreece* was entered on S. R. *Edward III.* was entered 1st December 1595. This love-story part is from Painter's *Palace of Pleasure*. The original play is by Marlowe, and was acted in 1590 and is thus alluded to in Greene's *Never too Late*, c. December in that year: "Why, Roscius, art thou proud with Æsop's crow, being prankt with the glory of others' feathers? Of thyself thou canst say nothing; and if the Cobler hath taught thee to say *Ave Cæsar*, disdain not thy tutor because thou pratest in a king's chamber." *Ave Cæsar* occurs in i. 1. 164, but not in any other play of this date have I been able to find it. There are many similarities between the Marlowe part of this play and *Henry VI.* As the Roscius in Greene's pamphlet was the player who had interpreted the puppets for seven years, who induced Greene to write for the stage, and had himself written *The Moral of Man's Wit* and *The Dialogue of Dives*, there can be no doubt that Robert Wilson is Roscius, and that he was an actor in *Edward III.* in 1590. It was acted by Pembroke's company, and must have been acquired by Lord Strange's men with the other Pembroke plays in 1594.

SECTION VI.

ON THE PLAYS BY OTHER AUTHORS ACTED BY SHAKESPEARE'S COMPANY.

DURING Shakespeare's career, 1589–1611, we only know of some two dozen plays having been produced by his "fellows," in addition to the three dozen included in his works; and of these, about two-fifths are anonymous, and have been at some time or other ascribed, in whole or part, to the great master. It is evident that he had the management of the playwriting for his house pretty nearly in his own hands, and that his method was the polar opposite to that of which we know most, viz., Henslowe's. While the latter employed twelve poets in a year, who produced for the Admiral's men a new play every fortnight or so, the Chamberlain's company depended almost entirely on two poets at a time, and produced not more than four new plays a year. Hence the explanation of the vastly higher character of the Globe plays as compared with the Fortune: hence also the explanation of the small pay and needy condition of the latter, and their jealousy of the rapid advancement in wealth and position of Shakespeare, who had virtually a monopoly of play-providing for his company. It would be out of place to discuss at length the plays written for it by Jonson, Dekker, &c., but fuller notice of the anonymous plays is due to the reader. They have, strange to say, never yet been treated as a complete group; and yet surely as much may be learned by considering Shakespeare's theatrical surroundings, the plays in which he acted, and which he probably had more or less suggested, supervised, or revised, as by elaborately working out the debtor and creditor details of his malt-bills. I will treat of these plays in nearly chronological order.

1590.

Fair Em is the earliest play we certainly know of as acted by Lord Strange's company. It is alluded to by Greene in his address prefixed to his *Farewell to Folly*. He quotes as abusing of Scripture, "A man's conscience is a thousand witnesses," and "Love covereth the multitude of sins," and says these words were used by "two lovers on the stage arguing one another of unkindness." Greene's tract was written and entered S. R. 1st June 1587, but not published till 1591, when the address which mentions his *Mourning Garment* (S. R. November 2, 1590) was added. *Fair Em* dates, therefore, late in 1590. It was probably written by R. Wilson, and is certainly not a romantic, but a satirical play; else why should Greene have been offended at it?

In Sc. 14 of *The Three Ladies of London*, produced before 1584, Wilson uses the expression, "I, Conscience, am a thousand witnesses," and in his *Three Lords and Three Ladies of London*, acted at Court, Christmas 1588–9, Sc. 2, "Love doth cover heaps of cumbrous evils." In order to explain the nature of the satire in *Fair Em*, it is necessary to investigate a hitherto unnoticed identification of Worcester's 1586 company with the Admiral's, of the highest importance for stage history as determining the actors in Marlowe's early plays. On Twelfth Day 1585–6, "the servants of the Admiral and the Lord Chamberlain" acted at Court, *i.e.* the players of Lord Charles Howard, who held both these offices. Mr. Halliwell (*Illustrations*, p. 31) confused this Chamberlain with Lord Hunsdon, and takes the entry to refer to *two* companies. I sent him a correction of these and many other blunders, which he has never rectified, years ago—a fact which I should not notice had he not publicly complained that, with one or two exceptions, of whom I am not one, he had received no help of this kind. Of this Admiral's company in the plague year, 1586, there is no trace in London; but in that year, and that year only, a company travelled under the protection of the Earl of Worcester. They were licensed for this travel on 14th January, and were at Leicester in the course of the year (Shakespeare Society's Papers, iv.); their names were R. Browne, J. Tunstall (Dunstan), E. Allen, W. Harryson, T. Cooke, R. Jones, E. Browne, R. Andrews; all of whom were licensed, together with hired men, T. Powlton and W. Paterson, "Lord Harbard's man," *i.e.* a member of the company of Herbert Earl of Pembroke: a scratch company evidently, but containing names of celebrated London actors. In 1587 and 1588, the Admiral's men acted in London publicly, and at Christmas 1588–9 at Court. On 3d January 1588–9, Alleyn and Jones (acting evidently for the company) dissolved partnership, and Alleyn bought up their properties and play-books. In November the Admiral's men were playing about the City, and not at the Curtain, where they had probably produced *Tamberlain, Faustus, Orlando, Alcazar,* and *Marius and Sylla;* and in their Court performance on 23d December were reduced to showing "feats of activity." In 1590 R. Brown and Jones went abroad and acted at Leyden in October. They returned, and on December 27 and February 16 the Admiral's men acted at Court for the last time before the reconstitution of their company in 1594. Already R. Brown, J. Broadstreet, T. Sackville, and R. Jones had obtained a pass from Lord C. Howard, the Admiral, their patron, to travel to Germany by way of Holland, and a company acted there till 1617 under Sackville. Jones returned to England and joined the reconstituted Admiral's company under Allen in 1594. Alleyn had never relinquished the title of Admiral's servant, even when in Lord Strange's service in 1593. Putting these facts together, can there be any doubt that the service under Worcester was merely temporary, and that in the list of 1586 we have that of the principal actors in the Admiral's company? Mr. R. Simpson, to whom we owe so much as a discoverer of problems to be solved, and so little for their solution, rightly stated that *Fair Em* was a satirical play, and that Manvile (or Mandeville, the lying traveller) meant Greene, and Mounteney the aspiring Marlowe. He was wrong in identifying Valingford with Shakespeare—he was Peele (valing, an old castle or peele—*Camden*)—and doubly wrong in making William Conqueror Kempe. Robert of Windsor, his travelling name, points to Robert Browne; and it was to Browne's company that Marlowe and Peele had been attached, not to Kempe's. The names William Conqueror and Marquess Lubeck were probably names of characters which had been acted by Browne and Jones, perhaps in the play of *William Conqueror*, which was on the stage as an old play in 1593. Fair Em of Manchester is no doubt, as Mr. Simpson says, Lord Strange's company of players.

1622 [often, but wrongly, dated c. 1591].

The Birth of Merlin, or The Child hath Found his Father, was published in 1662 as "written by W. Shakespeare and W. Rowley." Rowley probably revised the play for a revival c. 1622, but in the main it is manifestly by another hand. The comic scenes with Joan Goto't may be Rowley's, but the serious parts are palpably Middleton's. I owe the suggestion of his authorship to Mr. P. A. Daniel. A ballad on the subject was entered on 10th May 1589, S. R. In ii. 3*b* iii. 6 we have some very interesting imitations of Shakespeare. Cutting out the Rowley additions in iii. 1. 4, I would ask the reader to carefully compare the remaining parts of ii. 3*b*, beginning with *Aurel.* "Artesia, dearest love," iii. 2. 3. 5. 6, with such passages of Shakespeare as they call to memory: *e.g.* iii. 2, "This world is but a mask," &c., with *As You Like It*, ii. 7. 139, &c., and iii. 3. 1–6 with *Lear*, iii. 2. 1–9. Compare especially the definition of a crab as "a creature that goes backward" in ii. 3, with *Hamlet*, ii. 2. 206, "if like a crab you could go backward." Crab as the name of an animal does not occur elsewhere in Shakespeare. I believe the early plays on this subject, *Vortiger*, 4th December 1596, and *Uter Pendragon*, 29th April 1597, in Henslowe's Diary, to be alluded to by Jonson in his Prologue to *Every Man in his Humour*, 1601—

"To make a child now swaddled to proceed
Man: and then shoot up *in one beard and weed*
Past threescore years."

1592.

June. *A [Merry] Knack to Know a Knave* was acted as a new play at the Rose by Edward Alleyn and his company (*i.e.* Lord Strange's) "with Kempe's *Merriments of the Men of Gotham.*". The introduction of Honesty as a principal character points to R. Wilson the elder as the author. It was certainly not written by Greene and Nash, as Mr. Simpson supposes. Besides this play and a number of revivals, mostly of plays of the Queen's company (see my *Shakespearian Study*, p. 88), Lord Strange's men acted this season certain new plays : on March 3, *1 Henry VI.;* April 11, *Titus and Vespasian* (these have been already noticed) : Apri l28, *2d. Tambercame;* May 23, *The Taner of Denmark;* and in 1593, January 5, *The Gelyous [Jealious] Comedy;* January 30, *The Guise* (*i.e.* Marlowe's *Massacre of Paris*).

1594.

July 24, *Locrine* was entered S. R. and published in 1595 as "newly set forth, overseen, and corrected by W. S." I see no reason to infer that W. S. is William Shakespeare. The play was written, according to Mr. Simpson, by Tilney in 1586. I rather think for him by G. Peele. Shakespeare has no concern with it further than the letters W. S. indicate.

1595 [possibly 1599].

A 'Larum for London, or The Siege of Antwerp, was acted about this time. It was published in 1602, but entered S. R. 29th May 1600. The title at once points it out as a moralising play, of the same class as *A Looking-Glass for London;* didactic as to politics. I believe it to be by the same author, T. Lodge. The fear of a Spanish invasion is evident in the play. In July 1595 the Spaniards made a descent on Cornwall and burned Mouse Hole, Neulin, and Penzance. This is the most likely time for any real danger to London from the Spaniards to have been apprehended. Lodge, probably in the next year, wrote *The Taming of the Shrew* (afterwards altered by Shakespeare) for the Chamberlain's company. The seldom-used word *villiaco*, found in this play, occurs in *2 Henry VI.*, iv. 8, in the part I assign to Lodge.

1596.

The Life and Death of Sir Thomas More was certainly acted in this year. That this also was a political play is evident from the numerous alterations made in the MS. by E. Tylney, Master of the Revels. He specially objected to all passages directed against the French; and cut out entirely Scene 1, the insurrection scene. This must have alluded too closely to events of the time. Now on 29th June 1595 there was an insurrection of the London Prentices, suppressed by the then Lord Mayor just in the same way as that in the play by Sheriff More. (See Maitland and Stowe under that date.) Moreover, in October 1595 Hartford was imprisoned in the Tower for contempt, and threatened with loss of his title, just as More is in the play, which was no doubt acted while he was in prison (Aikin's *Elizabeth*, chap. xxiv.) I have previously noted the certainty of this play being acted by the Chamberlain's players, T. Goodale being one of the actors. It was probably written chiefly by Lodge ; but some scenes, such as Scene 2 with the Lifter and Scenes 9, 10, with Faulkner and the players, bear unmistakable marks of another hand, the same, I think, as the author of *Lord Cromwell*. It is a singular play, containing a comedy, Scenes 1–10, and a tragedy, Scenes 11–18, in one. This leads me to conjecture that it is the same play as was played by the Paul's children before James and the King of Denmark, 30th July 1606. This contained a comedy and tragedy, and was called *Abuses*. I need hardly say that this title is specially appropriate to *Sir T. More*. It pleased the kings, as was to be expected, more than it did the authorities under Elizabeth. We know that some plays of the Chamberlain's company passed into the hands of the Paul's boys, *e.g. Satiromastix*. The part of Justice Suresby is probably the one alluded to in *The Return from Parnassus*, iv. 3, where Kempe tells Philomusus (Lodge) that his face " would be good for a foolish mayor or a foolish justice of peace." In the same scene,

Studioso (Drayton) is made to recite from *Richard III.* and *Jeronymo*, both which plays were still acted by the Chamberlain's men in 1599; so that Drayton was looked on in 1602 as a tragedian, Lodge as a comedian. This agrees with Meres' classification of them in 1598. Nevertheless it is certain that both of them produced both tragedies and comedies.

1597–9.

The Merry Devil of Edmonton, acted at the Globe, and therefore still on the stage in 1599, was closely connected with the early form of *1 Henry IV.*, in which Falstaff was called Oldcastle. (see *supra*, p. 33). Coxeter says that it was ascribed in an old MS. of the play to Michael Drayton. No doubt it was written by him. The character of the Host, and indeed all the play, are so like parts of *Sir John Oldcastle*, which we know to have been partly written by Drayton, that it is not possible to doubt the identity of authorship. That play was written by Munday (i. 1; v. 2—end), Wilson (? i. 2; ii. 3; iii. 4), Hathaway (? iii. 1; v. 1), and Drayton, who probably was the plotter and chief composer. The *Merry Devil* was entered S. R. 22d October 1607. The entry on 5th April 1608 refers to the prose history by Thomas Brewer. Nevertheless that entry has been confidently adduced by Mr. Halliwell and others as proof that Drayton did not write the play (see Halliwell's *Dictionary of Old Plays* under *Merry Devil*): which as printed is evidently greatly abridged. All the part relating to Smug's taking the place of St. George as the sign of the inn, for instance, which is found in the prose story, must have been cut out, though an allusion to it is left in the end of the play. This alteration was probably made c. 1603–4, as in the *Black Book* (S. R. 22d March 1604) a revival of the play contemporaneous with *The Woman Killed with Kindness* is alluded to. It remained popular even to 1616: Jonson's prologue to *The Devil is an Ass* calls it "your dear delight." That play is of a somewhat similar nature, founded on the adventures of a devil incarnate; so also are Dekker's *If this be not a Good Play the Devil's in it*, and Haughton's *Grim the Cobler of Croydon, or The Devil and his Dame* (6th May 1600). In this last, which gives a posterior limit of date, Robin Goodfellow calls himself "merry devil," and is no doubt intended as a satire on Drayton, as is also the Robin Goodfellow of *Wily Beguiled*, 1597. In *Sir Giles Goosecap* by Chapman, the continued usage by Goosecap of the phrases "tickle the vanity on't" and "we are all mortal" points to Drayton as the person ridiculed under that name; while in *2 Henry IV.*, ii. 1. 66, Falstaff uses the exact phrase of Smug in scene 3 of "tickling the catastrophe." Another point of connection with Shakespearian satire of this date is found in the term Hungarian, scene 8, which occurs in *Merry Wives*, i. 3. 23, and nowhere else in Shakespeare. The great similarity of the Hosts in these two plays has been often noted. There is much confusion in the Christian names in our present version of the *Merry Devil*, an indication of revision. Drayton's first connection with the Chamberlain's company was in my opinion his writing the Induction for *The Taming of the Shrew* in 1596, afterwards altered by Shakespeare. *The Merry Devil* was entered as Shakespeare's on S. R. 9th September 1653, probably on account of the similarity of title with *The Merry Wives of Windsor;* and this similarity does point to a connection, though not of authorship, between these plays. The Oldcastle play, acted 6th March 1600 at Lord Hunsdon's, was probably *The Merry Devil*.

1594.

The Seven Deadly Sins, an old play plotted for the Queen's company by Tarleton, was revived. I have had already occasion to refer to the plot of this play, which is extant at Dulwich College.

1598-9.

A Warning for Fair Women was entered S. R. 17th November 1599, and printed as "lately divers times acted" by the Chamberlain's men. Its title, so like *A Looking-Glass for London* and *A 'Larum for London*, its didactic character, its Induction, with History, Tragedy, and Comedy for actors, so like that to *Mucedorus*, and its style and metre all point to Thomas Lodge as the author. As a murder-play it should be compared with *Arden of Feversham*, *The Yorkshire Tragedy*, and *Two Tragedies in One*. Plays on similar subjects, such as *Page of Plymouth*, by Dekker and Jonson, September 1599; *The Tragedy of Merry*, by Haughton and Day, December 1599; *The Tragedy of Orphans*, by Chettle, November 1599; and perhaps *The Stepmother's Tragedy*, by Dekker and Chettle, October 1599, were very abundant just at this time. This seems to be Lodge's final original production for the stage.

1598-9.

Every Man in his Humour in its first form, with the Italian names, in the latter part of 1598, and his *Every Man out of his Humour* in the spring of 1599, both by Jonson, were acted by the

Chamberlain's men. Jonson then left them and wrote for the children of the Chapel.

1601.

Satiromastix was written by Dekker against Jonson's *Poetaster* for the Chamberlain's men, and acted first by them and afterwards by the Paul's boys.

1601.

The Chronicle History of Thomas Lord Cromwell was entered S. R. 11th August 1602. This is clearly a political play, in which the career of Cromwell Earl of Essex shadows forth another Earl of Essex, of much greater interest to an audience of 1601. One scene, iii. 2, reminds us strongly of scene 9 in *Sir T. More;* and the whole play is very like the part of *Sir John Oldcastle* assigned by me to Drayton. In Act iv. the Chorus apologises for the omission of Wolsey's life. That had, in fact, been treated already by Chettle in August 1601, and by Chettle, Munday, Drayton, and Smith in November 1601, in two plays for the Admiral's men. Drayton's last work for them was done in May 1602 and *Cromwell* was probably acted in June. The second edition, 1613, had " by W. S." on the title. This was clearly an attempt, like the "by W. Sh." in the 1611 edition of the older *John*, to father the play on Shakespeare after his retirement from theatrical life. It has been supposed that Wentworth Smith is indicated. This is most unlikely. Smith was a hack writer for Henslowe, 1601–3, not one scrap of whose work was ever thought worth publishing; and that he, at the same date that he was a "novice" in the Admiral's, should have been an independent author for the Chamberlain's, is one of the plausible figments that will not be received by any one acquainted with stage history. If W. S. are authentic initials, W. Sly is a more likely claimant.

1603.

The London Prodigal was published in 1605, with the name of William Shakespeare on the title-page. This surely shows some connection of Shakespeare with its authorship. It is true that in 1600 his name had been attached to *Sir John Oldcastle* in one of the editions then printed, and that he could not have written, or been concerned with the writing of, that play; but the peculiar relation in which it stands to his historical plays places it in a very different category from a play which was acted by his own company, and over the publication of which he may be supposed to have had some control, direct or indirect. Perhaps he "plotted" it. At the same time it should be noticed that the publisher, Butter, was the same man who issued the Quarto of *Lear* in 1608, which was certainly derived from an authentic copy, however carelessly printed; while Pavier, who published *Oldcastle*, was notoriously an issuer of surreptitious and piratical editions. This play is certainly by the same hand as the *Cromwell*. In iii. 3, "And where nought is the king doth lose his due," with which compare *Cromwell*, ii. 3, "And where nought is the king must lose his right," is taken from Nash's *Unfortunate Traveller* (p. 15, Grosart's reprint), "When it is not to be had the king must lose his right." Compare, also, "Pardon, dear father, the follies that are past," v. 1, with *Cromwell*, iv. chorus, "Pardon the errors are already past," and the passing of St. George's inn in i. 2 with the *Merry Devil* plot. The date of production is certainly 1603. The words "under the King," ii. 1, and the allusion to Armin the actor, who took the part of Matthew Flowerdale, "So young an armin," v. 1, forbid an earlier date. This last allusion, by the bye, has never previously been explained. On the other hand, the allusions to Cutting Dick, ii. 2, *The Devil and his Dame*, iv. 2 (Mar. 1600), and to "wanton Cressid," v. i. (1602), would lose much effect at a later date. The name Greenshield was adopted from this play in the "comical satire" of *Northward Ho*, 1605, as Frescobald was in *The Honest Whore*, 1603, from *Cromwell*.

1603.

Sejanus, by Jonson, was acted this year. Jonson had returned to the Chamberlain's men from the Admiral's, for whom he wrote after leaving the Chapel children in 1601; but this play being a political satire on Leicester got the company into trouble, and he again left them for the children of the Revels. See *supra*, p. 49.

1604.

The Malcontent, by Marston, was acted "with the additions played by the King's Majesty's servants" by Webster, and entered S. R. 25th July. This play belonged to the Revels' children, and was appropriated in retaliation for their playing *Jeronymo*, which was the property of the King's men. (See the Induction.) Compare p. 52.

1604.

Gowry, already noticed, was performed this year.

1603-4.

The Miseries of Enforced Marriage, by George Wilkins, was entered S. R. 31st July 1607. It was founded on the life of Mr. Caverley, the hero of *The Yorkshire Tragedy*, and the play ends with a reconciliation before October 1603, when his third child was born, and dating about January or February, just before the accession of King James. This play was written before 1605. Mr. P. A. Daniel discovered the identity of story in it and in *The Yorkshire Tragedy*. The share of G. Wilkins in the authorship of *Timon* and *Pericles* has already been noticed. He left the King's company for the Queen's in 1607, before publishing the present play. He is not the G. Wilkins who died in 1603: Mr. W. C. Hazlitt's statement in his *Handbook* to that effect is a mistake.

1605.

A Yorkshire Tragedy, founded on the same story, was certainly acted soon after the execution of Caverley, 5th August 1605. The murdered children were buried in April. The prose account of Caverley's trial was entered S. R. 24th August, and the story of his life was printed by V. S.

PLAYS BY OTHER AUTHORS. 303

(Valentine Simmes) in the same year. The play was entered S. R. 2d May 1608, and printed as by William Shakespeare. I cannot think that this was unauthorised. Compare the parallel instance of *The London Prodigal.* Was the author his brother Edmund; and did Shakespeare assist in or revise his work? (See p. 60.) The "young mistress" of Scene 1 is the Clare Harcup of the *Enforced Marriage,* and her decline is inconsistent with her death in that play, but in accordance with facts. Together with three other probably similar short plays it was acted as *All's One, or one of the Four Plays in One.*

1605.

Volpone or the Fox, by Jonson, was acted in this year.

1605-6.

Mucedorus, an old play, originally written, I think, for the Queen's company by T. Lodge, was revived under exceptional circumstances, with additions at Court. From the added part at the end of the play it appears that "a lean hungry neagre (meagre) cannibal," "a scrambling raven with a needy beard," had written "a comedy" for the King's players, containing "dark sentences pleasing to factious brains," and that information had been given to "a puissant magistrate," and that the players feared "great danger or at least restraint" in consequence. Moreover, this "unwilling error" had been lately "presented" to the King: nevertheless, not being "boys," but "men," they had avoided the "trap," apologised, and been pardoned. The only known new comedy, not Shakespeare's, produced by the King's men between 1604 and 1610 was Jonson's *Fox*. It contains a good deal, even in its present state, that must have been unpalatable at Court, especially on monopolies and spies; and Jonson altered his plays so much after performance for publication, that it is dangerous to draw conclusions as to what the play may have originally contained. One thing in it, however, was particularly "obnoxious to construction," the miraculous "Oglio del Scoto," which, in the case of one who was this same year imprisoned for satirising the Scots in *Eastward Ho*, might well be taken as a gird at the Scotch King's miraculous charisma in treating for the King's evil. It is to the *Eastward Ho* affair that the "trap for boys, not men," alludes; and the meagreness and "needy beard" plainly indicate Jonson as the "raven" (Corbaccio) who wrote the comedy. In accordance with this view stands the fact that on the Christmas succeeding this unfortunate performance of 1605-6 there was no Court masque produced by Jonson. The date hitherto assigned to the "additions" in *Mucedorus* has been 1610, because the edition of that year was issued as it was acted before the King on Shrove Sunday night. But there was no Court performance in the 1609-10 winter on account of the plague. The date 1610 is therefore impossible; the words on the title were probably repeated in the usual way from the 1606 edition, of which, though mentioned in Beauclerc's *Catalogue*, 1781, no copy unfortunately is extant. Of the authorship of the original play, with its Induction, "cooling-card" mark, and many similarities to *Marius and Sylla*, there can be no doubt: it was written by Lodge. Who wrote the "additions" in 1605-6 it would be hard to say: perhaps Wilkins.

1607-11.

The Revenger's Tragedy by Cyril Tourneur (?) was entered S. R. 7th October 1607, and probably acted not long before. The Second *Maiden's Tragedy*, licensed in 1611, which we know to have been acted by the King's men, was probably by the same author.

In 1610 Jonson returned to the King's men

(he had been writing for the Revels' children since he left, after producing *Volpone*), and his *Alchemist* was acted in that year; in 1611 his *Cataline*, and Beaumont and Fletcher's *Philaster, Maid's Tragedy,* and *King and no King;* c. 1612 Webster's *Duchess of Malfy* was produced. The further prosecution of this subject belongs to a life of Fletcher rather than of Shakespeare.

SECTION VII.

EARLY ENGLISH PLAYS IN GERMANY.

THE importance of the performance of English plays in Germany and its bearings on our own stage history has never been duly estimated. This is owing to the fact that the groups of such plays have not been treated as wholes, only isolated references to single dramas having been occasionally made by our critics. I must here confine myself to such groups as have reference to the productions of Shakespeare. In 1626–7 a company of Englishmen acted at Dresden, and a list of their performances has fortunately been preserved (Cohn, *Shakespeare in Germany*, p. 115). This company appears from their christian names to have been the Company of the Revels, which broke up in 1625 in the plague-time. In the *Runaway's Answer*, 1625, to Dekker's *Rod for Runaways*, which was directed against those who left London for fear of the plague, the players say, " We can be bankrupts on this side and gentlemen of a company beyond the sea: we burst at London and are pieced up at Rotterdam." The 1626 Dresden company were Robert Pickleherring [R. Lee] and two boys; Jacob der Hesse, and Johan Eydtwardtt (two Germans); Aaron the dancer (probably a German Jew); Thomas die Jungfrau [T. Basse], John [Cumber], William the wardrobe-keeper (probably a German), the Englishman, the Redhaired, and four boys. The other members of the Revels' company can be traced in England; and although Robert, Thomas, and John are common christian names, they are not to be found in conjunction in any other list of English players of the date. The plays acted by these men were the following:—

1. *Duke of Mantua and Duke of Verona.* Comedy.
2. *Christabella.* C.
3. *Amphitryon.* C.
4. *Romeo and Julietta.* Tragedy. [Founded on Shakespeare's play of 1591; extant in German MS., and printed by Cohn.]
5. *Duke of Florence.* Tragi-Comedy. [Not Massinger's play, which is of ten years' later date.]
6. *King of Spain and ViceRoy of Portugal.* C. [Kyd's *Jeronymo,* c. 1588.]
7. *Julius Cæsar.* T. [Query, the old play men-

tioned by Gosson in 1580, or the Admiral's play of 1594, or Shakespeare's, or the Admiral's of 1602, or the Oxford of 1606, or Chapman's, or the old play on which Chapman's is founded? The last most likely.]

8. *Crysella.* C.
9. *Duke of Ferrara.* C.
10. *Somebody and Nobody.* T. C. [Printed in German, 1620; extant in an altered form, by Heywood in my judgment, as played by Queen Anne's men in English; published c. 1609. In its original form acted c. 1591.]
11. *King of Denmark and King of Sweden.* T. C. [*Clyomon and Clamydes.* ? by R. Wilson, c. 1585.]
12. *Hamlet, Prince of Denmark.* T. [From Kyd's old play, c. 1589; extant in modernised MS. in Germany; printed in Cohn. The Induction with Night and the Furies is quite in Kyd's manner.]
13. *Orlando Furioso.* C. [Greene's play, c. 1587.]
14. *King of England and King of Scotland.* C. [Greene (and Lodge)'s *James IV.*, 1591.]
15. *Hieronymo, Marshal of Spain.* T. [Kyd's *Spanish Tragedy,* c. 1588.]
16. *Haman and Queen Esther.* T. C. [Printed in German, 1620, from an English play acted in 1594 by the Chamberlain's men, but an *old* play then; originally not later than 1591. Compare the

interlude in Kirkman's *Wits*, which was probably founded on it. The German play ought to be made accessible to English readers.]

17. *The Martyr Dorothea.* T. [Perhaps from a play by Dekker and Massinger, revived for the Revels' company between 1619 and 1622. This is the only play in this list to which I can assign a definite date later than 1592. But were both taken from an older play?]

18. *Dr. Faust.* T. [Marlowe's play, 1588.]

19. *King of Arragon.* T. C. [Greene's *Alphonsus*, c. 1588.]

20. *Fortunatus.* T. [Printed in German, 1620, as *Comedy of Fortunatus and his Purse and Wishing Cap*, in which appear first three dead souls as spirits, and afterwards the Virtues and Shame. Evidently from the first part of *Fortunatus* by Dekker, as acted, 3d February 1596, as an *old* play. It was probably written c. 1591. This play like (16.) ought to be made accessible to English readers.]

21. *Joseph, the Jew of Venice.* C. [From another early play of Dekker's, c. 1591. The German version is extant in MS. in the Imperial Library at Vienna, and ought to be edited and translated. The Jew, however, is therein called Barabbas, and there are three suitors, as in Shakespeare's play, but no caskets. Dekker's play was entered 9th September 1653 on S. R.]

EARLY ENGLISH PLAYS IN GERMANY. 311

22. *The Dextrous Thief.* T. C.
23. *Duke of Venice.* T. C.
24. *Barrabas, the Jew of Malta.* T. [Marlowe's play, 1589.]
25. *Old Proculus.* C.
26. *Lear, King of England.* T. [From the old Queen's play, c. 1589. Yet it is strange that it should be called a tragedy. It would hardly be Shakespeare's play, as no other of so late date occurs in the list.]
27. *The Godfather.* T. C.
28. *The Prodigal Son.* C. [Printed in German, 1620. Translated in Simpson's *School of Shakespeare*. Probably from an old play revived by Heywood for Derby's men c. 1599, but originally founded on Greene's *Mourning Garment*, 1590, and written (for what company?) c. 1591. So I conjecture.]
29. *The Graf of Angiers.* C.
30. *The Rich Man.* T. [Acted on 17th September 1646 as *The Rich Man and the Poor Lazarus*. Perhaps from a very old play by Ralph Radcliffe before 1553; more likely from the Moral by the player (? R. Wilson) in Greene's *Groatsworth of Wit*, 1592, who wrote the Moral of *Man's Wit* and the dialogue of *Dives*, and played in *Delphrigus*, *The King of Fairies*, *The Twelve Labors of Hercules*, and *The Highway to Heaven*.]

It appears from this list that while only one, if any, of these plays, *Dorothea*, which was probably taken with them by the Revels' company in 1625, can be assigned to a comparatively late date with certainty, the majority are early productions, anterior to 1592. Bearing in mind that there were a large number of plays published before 1626 which might have been used without fear of any opposition from companies in England, it is clear that in Germany the preference was given to older plays, which must have been imported at an early date, either by Leicester's players in 1586, by Pembroke's in 1599, or Worcester's [Admiral's] in 1590 and 1592. Leicester's returned to England in 1577 and Pembroke's c. 1601; but Worcester's, or rather a detachment from the Admiral's, were permanently established in Germany. E. Brown and R. Jones indeed came back to England; but Thomas Sackville and John Broadstreet are traceable in Germany, the latter to 1606 and the former to 1617. There is little doubt that the *Hamlet* and *Romeo*, in their German versions, are from early plays, anterior to 1592. This conclusion is confirmed by the list of plays published in Germany in 1620, "acted by the English in Germany at Royal, Electoral, and Princely Courts:"—

1. *Queen Esther and Haughty Haman.* C. [16. in previous list.]
2. *The Prodigal Son,* "in which Despair and Hope are cleverly introduced." C. [28. in previous list.]
3. *Fortunatus and his Purse and Wishing Cap,* "in which appear first three dead souls as spirits, and afterwards the Virtues and Shame." C. [20. in previous list.]
4. *A King's Son from England and a King's Daughter from Scotland.* C. [*Serule and Astræa;* probably the same as *Serule and Hypolita,* acted 1631.]
5. *Sidonia and Theagine.* C.
6. *Somebody and Nobody.* C. [10. in previous list.]
7. *Julio and Hypolita.* T. [Query, *Philippo and Hypolita,* acted as an *old* play at the Rose, 9th July 1594; similar in plot to *The Gentlemen of Verona.*]
8. *Titus Andronicus.* T. [Not our extant play, but the *Titus and Vespasian* acted by Lord Strange's men, April 1592.]
9. *The Beautiful Mary and the Old Cuckold.* A merry jest.
10. In which the clown makes merry pastime with a stone.

I am not acquainted with Ayres's plays; but it appears from Cohn (p. 64) that among them are

Mahomet the Turkish Emperor (from Peele's play, c. 1591), *The Greek Emperor at Constantinople and his daughter Pelimperia with the hanged Horatio* (Kyd's *Spanish Tragedy*, 1588); *Valentine and Orson* (from an old English play S. R. 23d May 1595); *Edward III., King of England, and Elisa Countess of Warwick* (from Marlowe's play, 1590: Philip Waimer had already dramatised the same subject at Danzig in 1591); *The Beautiful Phenicia* (on the same story as *Much Ado*, and strongly confirming the identity of that play with *Love's Labour's Won*, 1590: Cupid enters in person, and shoots Count Tymborus, the Benedick of the German version); *The Two Brothers of Syracuse* (from the *Comedy of Errors*, c. 1590); *The Beautiful Sidea* (containing some incidents showing that it came from some source in common with that of the *Tempest*, but certainly not from that play direct); and *King of Cyprus* (founded on the same story as *The Dumb Knight* by Machin and Markham, c. 1607). Cohn does not give exact dates of authorship, but is of opinion that we should not assign to any a year later than 1600; and in 1605 Ayres died. Here again we meet with the same phenomenon—acquaintance with many English plays of date anterior to 1592; but not with any one that can be shown to be later. No doubt Ayres's knowledge of English plays was obtained from the Worcester's (Admiral's) company, who went over in 1590-2.

Yet further, in the tragedy of *An Adulteress* by Duke Henry Julius of Brunswick, printed 1594, we find the plot of *The Merry Wives* almost identically reproduced (see Cohn, p. 45, &c.) I do not see, however, so much likeness between his *Vincentius Ladislaus* and *Much Ado*.

As regards Shakespearian chronology, it results from this examination of English plays in Germany that there is no positive evidence of English plays of later date than 1592 having been acted there before 1625; that there is evidence that many (a score at least) of date not later than 1592 were acted between 1592 and 1626; that these plays were probably among those imported by Worcester's (Admiral's) players in 1592; and that in the list are contained *The Comedy of Errors, Romeo and Juliet, The Merry Wives, The Gentlemen of Verona,* and *Love's Labour's Won, i.e.* every play by Shakespeare except *Love's Labour's Lost,* that is in this treatise placed at a date not later than 1592; besides Kyd's *Hamlet,* Marlowe's *Edward III.,* and other plays with which Shakespeare was indirectly connected.

APPENDIX.

TABLES.

APPENDIX.

In Table I. I give the dates of the Stationers' Registers entries of Shakespeare's plays as collected in 1623, the printers and publishers of the earliest extant edition of each, and the dates of all known subsequent editions anterior to the 1623 Folio. A. appended to a date means Anonymous, *i.e.* published without the author's name; F. means that the edition was used by the Folio editors as copy to print from. The relative popularity of the plays will be in some measure seen by a glance at this table. The most popular were *Richard III.* (six editions in sixteen years); *1 Henry IV.* (six editions); *Edward III.* (five editions in twenty years); *Richard II.* (four editions in nineteen years); *Henry V.* (three editions in nine years). All these were Histories. Next to the Histories rank the Tragedies *Hamlet, Romeo and Juliet,* and *Pericles:* the other great tragedies, *Lear, Othello,* and the Comedies being decidedly less to the popular taste than the Histories. The entries of change of copyright will be found in their places in Table V.

Table II. gives similar information for every known extant play not of Shakespeare's authorship in which he may have been an actor or reviser. *Edward III.* appears in both these tables. The extreme popularity of *Mucedorus* is very noticeable.

Table III. gives the number of Court performances in each year for such companies as are known to have been playing in London. From this table it is evident that up to 1591 the Queen's men were the most important of all; in other words, that Greene was the chief Court stage poet, and held the position formerly occupied by Lyly, who wrote for the Chapel children before the public theatrical companies had obtained the prominent place. His chief rival was Marlowe of the Admiral's company. But after 1591 Lord Strange's company takes the lead and keeps it, which means that Shakespeare was the principal Court stage writer till 1611. This throws new light on the relations of Greene, Shakespeare, and their respective companies. But this table comprises, in fact, a compendium of the whole stage history of the time; and as the current versions of this history by Collier, Halliwell, and others are replete with blunders, it may be well to give a very short summary of the results of my investigations—proofs, where lengthy, of some minor details being necessarily reserved for a future publication. Column i. concerns one company only: as Lord Leicester's it was acting in London in 1585; in 1586 it was acting on the Continent; in 1587-8 it was travelling about England; after Leicester's death it began in 1589 to act in London, and was patronised by Lord Strange, who became Earl of Derby in 1593: after his death in 1594, Henry Carey, Lord Hunsdon, the Lord Chamberlain, became its

APPENDIX.

patron, who died in 1596; they then passed to his heir, George Carey: in 1603 they were patented as the King's men, and retained that title till the closing of the theatres.

Column ii. The Admiral's men were abroad from 1591 to 1594; in 1603 they were assigned to Prince Henry, and after his death in 1612 to the Palsgrave. The Earl of Hertford's men, who appear once in this column, were not a regular London company, but probably invited to play this once at Court while the Admiral's were abroad, in consequence of the Queen having been entertained by Hertford in the preceding year's progress.

Column iii. Queen Elizabeth's company, formed 1583, took the lead till 1591: they only reappear in conjunction with Sussex in 1593-4, when both companies vanish from the London stage. About 1599 Derby's company appears in London: it became Worcester's in 1602, and was assigned to Queen Anne in 1603.

Column iv. The Earl of Oxford's "boys" were in London in 1586; they travelled in the plague year, and are almost certainly the same company who reappear in London in 1589 as Pembroke's. By Marlowe's aid they prospered a year or two, but after his death became insignificant, and are only dimly traceable to 1600.

In 1597 the Chapel children are stated to have occupied Blackfriars, but till 1600 no play is traceable to them. In 1603-4 they were reorganised as the Children of the Revels, and again in 1610 as a new company under the same name: in 1612 they were again reorganised as the second Lady Elizabeth's company, the first of that name, set up in 1611, having broken up.

x

Column v. The Paul's boys were inhibited c. 1590, re-established 1600, finally put down 1607.

The Duke of York's men were established 1610, and at Prince Henry's death in 1612 took the name of the Prince of Wales' men.

The reader will observe that never more than five companies existed contemporaneously; and scarcely ever more than two of considerable importance. The statements of Collier and Halliwell are grossly exaggerated.

In Table IV. every entry of a play that I can find in the Stationers' Registers is extracted with all necessary fulness. The only point requiring explanation is that the capital letters after the publishers' names indicate the names of the licensers:—T. = Tylney; B. = Sir G. Buck; S. = Segar, his deputy; A. = Sir John Astley; H. = Sir Henry Herbert; T. = Thomas Herbert, his deputy; Bl. = Blagrave, also his deputy. Where the Master of the Revels or his deputy was not the licenser, the insertion of the Wardens' names, &c., would have needlessly encumbered the tables. The spelling has been modernised, except in proper names, &c., where it is of advantage to retain the old forms. These tables afford for the first time complete means of estimating Shakespeare's influence, in I. on the reading public positively; in II. as compared with his co-workers; in III. at Court; in IV. as compared with writers for other companies.

Table V., of transfers of copyright, is, I fear, in spite of much labour, incomplete. Notifications of omission will be welcome and duly acknowledged with gratitude.

TABLES.

TABLE I.—QUARTO EDITIONS

Date, S. R.		For whom Entered, S.R.	Name of Play.
1593-4	Feb. 6	John Danter	Titus Andronicus
1593-4	Mar. 12	Thomas Myllington	York and Lancaster, I.
...	...	...	Richard Duke of York
1595	Dec. 1	Cuthbert Burby	Edward III.
...	...	...	Romeo and Juliet (1)
1597	Aug. 29	Andrew Wise	Richard II.
1597	Oct. 20	Andrew Wise	Richard III.
1597-8	Feb. 25	Andrew Wise	1 Henry IV.
1598	July 22	James Roberts	Merchant of Venice.
...	...	...	Love's Labour's Lost
...	...	...	Romeo and Juliet (2)
1600	Aug. 4	...	As You Like It
1600	Aug. 14	"Set over" to Thomas Pavier	Henry V.
1600	Aug. 23	Andrew Wise and William Aspley	{ Much Ado about Nothing { 2 Henry IV.
1600	Oct. 8	Thomas Fisher	Midsummer Night's Dream
1600	Oct. 28	Thomas Haies	Merchant of Venice.
1601-2	Jan. 18	John Busby (with assignment to Arthur Johnson)	Merry Wives of Windsor.
1602	April 19	Thomas Pavier	1, 2 Henry VI. and Titus Andronicus
1602	July 26	James Roberts	Revenge of Hamlet (1)
...	...	...	Hamlet (2)
1602-3	Feb. 7	James Roberts	Troylus and Cressida
1607	Nov. 26	Na. Butter: Jo. Busby	King Lear
1608	May 20	Edward Blount	{ Pericles { Anthony and Cleopatra
1608-9	Jan. 28	Ri. Bonion; Hen. Whalley	Troylus and Cressida
...	...	...	Pericles
1621	Oct. 6	Thomas Walkley	Othello

APPENDIX.

OF SHAKESPEARE'S PLAYS.

	Printer and Publisher of Earliest Edition Extant.	Dates of Extant Editions.					
a	By J. R. for Edward White	...	1600A.	...	...	1611A.	...
b	By Thomas Creede for Thomas Millington	1594A.	1600A.	...	...	...	1619A.
c	By P. S. for Thomas Millington	1595A.	1600A.	...	...	...	
d	... for Cuthbert Burby	1596A.	1599A.	...	1609A.	1617A.	1625A.
e	By John Danter	1597A.	...	...	...	...	...
f	By Valentine Simmes for Andrew Wise	1597A.	1598	...	1608	1615 F.	...
g	By Valentine Sims for Andrew Wise	1597A.	1598	1602	1605	1612	1622
h	By P. S. for Andrew Wise	1598	1599	1604	1608	1615 F.	1622
i	By J. Roberts	...	1600	...	...	...	...
j	By W. W. for Cuthbert Burby	1598	...	...	...	...	...
k	By Thomas Creede for Cuthbert Burby	...	1599A.	...	1609A. F.	...	...
l	"Stayed" with the two following plays. Not printed.	...	...	...	...	...	...
m	By T. Creede for T. Millington and J. Busby	...	1600A.	1602A.	1608A.	...	...
n	By V. S. for Andrew Wise and William Aspley	...	1600 F.	...	...	...	...
		...	1600	...	...	...	...
o	... for Thomas Fisher	...	1600	...	...	...	...
	By James Roberts	...	1600 F.	...	...	...	...
p	By J. R. for Thomas Hayes	...	1600 F.	...	...	...	...
q	By T. C. for Arthur Johnson	...	1602	...	...	...	1619
r	By assignment from Thomas Millington	...	...	...	...	...	...
s	... for N. L. and John Trundell	...	1603	...	...	...	...
t	By J. R. for N. L.	...	...	1604	1605	1611	...
u	"To print when he hath gotten sufficient authority for it." Not printed.	...	...	...	...	...	...
v	... for Nathaniel Butter	...	...	...	1608 bis	...	...
w	Not printed.	...	...	...	...	...	...
x	By G. Eld for R. Bonion and H. Whalley	...	...	...	1609 bis	...	...
	... for Henry Gosson	...	...	...	1609 bis	1611	1619
z	By N. O. for Thomas Walkley	...	...	...	...	...	1622

APPENDIX.

TABLE II.—QUARTO EDITIONS OF OTHER PLAYS PERFORMED BY SHAKESPEARE'S COMPANY.

Date.		For whom Entered.	Name of Play.	Extant Editions.
1593-4	Jan. 7	R. Jones	A Knack to Know a Knave	1594
[1594	July 20	T. Creede	Locrine	1595]
1595	Dec. 1	C. Burby	Edward III.	1596, 1599, 1609, 1617, 1625
...	...	W. Jones	Mucedorus	1598, 1606, 1610, 1613, 1615, 1619, 1629, 1634, 1639, &c.
1599	Nov. 17	W. Aspley	Warning for Fair Women	1599
1600	April 8	W. Holme	Every Man out of his Humour	1600 (printed for N. Ling)
1600	May 27	J. Roberts	Cloth Breeches and Velvet Hose	These plays were stayed, sufficient authority for their printing not being forthcoming
1600	May 29	J. Roberts	Alarum to London	
1601	Aug. 14	C. Burby and W. Burre	Every Man in his Humour	1601
...	...	E. White	Massacre of Paris	n.d.
1600	Nov. 11	I. Barnes	Satiromastix	1602
...	...	W. Ferbrand	Alarum for London	1602
1602	Aug. 11	W. Cotton	Lord Cromwell	1602, 1613
1604	July 2 & 5	W. Aspley and T. Thorpe	Malcontent	1604
1604	Nov. 2	E. Blunt	Sejanus	1605
...	...	N. Butter	London Prodigal	1605
1607	July 31	G. Vincent	Miseries of Enforced Marriage	1607, 1611, 1629, 1637
1607	Oct. 7	G. Elde	Revenger's Tragedy	1607
1607	Oct. 22	A. Johnson	Merry Devil of Edmonton	1608, 1617, 1626
...	...	...	Volpone, or the Fox	1607
1608	May 2	T. Pavier	Yorkshire Tragedy	1608, 1619
...	...	J. Wright	Fair Em	1631

APPENDIX. 327

Year	I.	II.	III.	IV.	V.	Total
	Leicester's	Admiral's	Queen's	Oxford's	Paul's	
1584-5	0	0	5	1	0	6
1585-6	0	1	1	0	0	2
1586-7			Plague Year			0
1587-8		0	3	0	1	4
1588-9	*Strange's* 0	0	2	0	3	7
1589-90	0	2	2	0	3	7
1590-1	0	2	2	0		7
1591-2	6	*Hertford's* 1	5	0	*Sussex's* 1	9
1592-3	3		1	*Pembroke's* 2		5
1593-4			Plague Year			5
1594-5	*Chamberlain's* 2	*Admiral's* 0		0		0
1595-6	5	0	*Total* 19	0		2
1596-7	6	2		0		5
1597-8	4	0		*Total* 3		6
1598-9	3	2	*Derby's* 1	*Chapel* 1	*Paul's* 1	6
1599-00	3	3	0			3
1600-1	3	3	*Worcester's* 0	0		6
1601-2			*Richard II.* played for Essex faction.			
1602-3	2	4	*Q. Anne's* 2	1 *Revels* 0	0	8
1603-4	*King's* 2	*P. Henry's* 3	2	1	0	0
1604-5	9	4	1	2	0	5
1605-6	4	8	1	0	0	16
1606-7	10	6	0	0	2	15
1607-8	12	6	0	0		19
1608-9	13	4	0	0	*Total* 10	18
1609-10	12	3	Plague Year		*D. of York's* 1	17
1610-1	15	4	3	2 *Revels* 0	3	15
1611-2	22	4	4	1 *L. Eliz.* 1	4	1
1612-3	28	1	0	2 *Revels* 3	2	25
				2 *L. Eliz.* 2		35
						36
1613-4	7	*Palsgrave's* 0	2	1	*P. Charles'* 0	11
1614-5	0	0	0	0	0	1
1615-6	0	0	0	0	0	0
Totals	169	58	14	13	10	297

TABLE IV.—ENTRIES OF PLAYS IN THE STATIONERS' REGISTERS, 1584-1640.

Date.	For whom Entered.	Name of Play.
1584 April 6	Thomas Cadman	Sappho by Lyllye: "if he get ye comedy lawfully allowed to him."
Nov. 12	Thomas Hackett	Fedele et Fortuna. The deceits in love discoursed in a Commedia of ii Italian gent. and translated into English.
1585 April 1	Gabriel Cawood	Tityrus and Galatea. A Comedy.
1588 Oct. 28	Richard Jones	Pageant before Martin Calthrop, L. Mayor, 29th Oct. 1588, by G. Peele. "Upon condition that it may be licensed."
1590 July 31	Richard Jones	A comedy of the pleasant and stately moral of the three Lords of London.
Aug. 14	Richard Jones	The two comical discourses of "Tomberlein the Cithian shepparde."
1591 July 26	Richard Jones	The Hunting of Cupid, by G. Peele, M.A. of Oxford. "Provided always that, if it be hurtful to any other copy before licensed, then this to be void."
Oct. 4	Mrs. Broome, widow of William Broome	Endimion, Galathea, Midas; three comedies played before her Majesty by the children of Paul's.
1592 April 3	Edward White	The tragedy of "Arden of Faversham and Blackwall."
Oct. 6	Abel Jeffes	The Spanish Tragedy of "Don Horatio and Bellmipeia."
Nov. 20	Edward White	The tragedy of "Salamon and Pereceda."
1593 July 6	William Jones	The troublesome reign and lamentable death of Edward II. King of England, with the tragical fall of proud Mortimer.

1593	Oct. 8	Abel Jeffes	The Chronicle of K. Edward I. surnamed Longshank, with his return out of the Holy Land: with the life of "Leublen," rebel in Wales, with the sinking of Queen Elinour. An enterlude.
	Oct. 19	Symond Waterson	The tragedy of Cleopatra.
	Oct. 23	John Danter	The life and death of Jack Straw. An enterlude.
	Dec. 7	John Danter	The history of Orlando Furioso, one of the 12 peers of France. A playbook.
1593–4	Jan. 7	Richard Jones	A Knack to Know a Knave, newly set forth, as it hath sundry times been played by Ned Allen and his company, with Kempe's applauded merriments of the men of Goteham. A comedy.
	Jan. 26	Nicholas Ling and John Busbye	Cornelia : Thomas Kydd being the author.
	Feb. 6	John Danter	A noble Roman history of Tytus Andronicus.
	Mar. 5	Thomas Creede	The looking glass for London, by Thomas Lodg and Robert Greene, gent.
	Mar. 12	Thomas Myllington	The first part of the Contention of the two famous houses of York and Lancaster, with the death of the good Duke Humphrey and the banishment and death of the Duke of Suffolk, and the tragical end of the proud Cardinal of Winchester, with the notable rebellion of Jack Cade and the Duke of York's first claim unto the crown.
1594	May 2	Peter Shorte	A pleasant conceited history called the "Tayming of a Shrowe."
	May 13	Thomas Creede	The Pedlar's Prophesy. "A pleabook."
	May 14	Thomas Creede	The Famous Victories of Henry V., containing the honourable battle of Agincourt.
	May 14	Thomas Creede	The Scottish story of James IV., slain at Flodden, intermixt with a pleasant comedy presented by Oboron King of Fairies.

ENTRIES OF PLAYS—continued.

Date.	For whom Entered.	Name of Play.
1594		
May 14	Edward White	The History of Friar Bacon and Friar Boungaye.
	[previously entered to Adam Islip, whose name is crossed out]	The most famous Chronicle History of Leire King of England and his three daughters.
		The famous history of John of Gaunte, son to King Edward III., with his Conquest of Spain and marriage of his two daughters to the Kings of Castile and Portugale, &c.
		The Book of David and Bethsaba.
May 17	Thomas Gosson	A Pastoral pleasant comedy of Robin Hood and Little John.
		The Famous Chronicle of Henry I., with the life and death of Bellin Dunn, the first thief that ever was hanged in England.
May 17	Thomas Millington	The famous tragedy of the Rich Jew of Malta.
May 24	John Danter	The wounds of Civil War lively set forth in the True Tragedies of Marius and Scilla.
May 28	Cuthbert Burbye, by consent of John Danter	The history of Orlando Furioso. "So often as the same book shall be printed, the said John Danter to have the imprinting thereof."
June 8	Cuthbert Burbey	The Cobbler's Prophesy.
June 18	Cuthbert Burby	Mother Bumbye. An enterlude.
June 19	John Danter	Godfrey of Bulloigne, with the Conquest of Jerusalem. An enterlude.
June 19	John Danter	The life and death of Heliogabilus. An enterlude.
June 19	Thomas Creede	The tragedy of Richard III., wherein is shown the death of Edward IV., with the smothering of the two princes in the Tower, with a lamentable end of Shore's wife and the conjunction of the two houses of Lancaster and York. An enterlude.

APPENDIX. 331

1594	July 20	Thomas Creede	The lamentable tragedy of Locrine, the eldest son of King Brutus, discoursing the wars of the Britons, &c.
1595	April 1	Cutbert Burbye	The Pynder of Wakefeilde. An enterlude.
	April 16	Raphe Hancock	A pleasant conceipt called an Owlde Wife's tale. An enterlude.
	May 10	John Hardye	The tragedy of Ninus and Semiramis, the first monarchs of the world.
	May 23	Thomas Gosson / Raffe Hancock	} Valentine and Orsson, played by her Majesty's players. An enterlude.
	Sept. 22	Robert Fynche	A woman in the moon.
	Nov. 24	William Blackwell	The true tragical history of King Rufus I., with the life and death of Belyn Dun, the first thief that ever was hanged in England.
	Nov. 26	Cutbert Burbye	The most rare and pleasant history of A Knack to know an honest man.
	Dec. 1	Cutbert Burby	Edward III. and the Black Prince, their wars with King John of France.
1595–6	Jan. 20	Thomas Gosson / John Danter	} The first part of the famous history of Chinan of England.
1597	Aug. 29	Andrew Wise	The tragedy of Richard II.
	Oct. 20	Andrew Wise	The tragedy of King Richard III., with the death of the Duke of Clarence.
1597–8	Feb. 25	Andrew Wise	The history of Henry IV., with his battle of Shrewsbury against Henry Hottspurre of the North, with the conceited mirth of Sir John Ffalstoff.
1598	July 22	James Robertes	The Marchaunt of Venyce, or otherwise called the Jewe of Venyce. Provided it be not printed without license first had from the Lord Chamberlain.
	Aug. 15	William Jones	The blinde begger of Alexandrya. "Upon condition that it belong to no other man."

ENTRIES OF PLAYS—continued.

Date.		For whom Entered.	Name of Play.
1598	Oct. 5	William Aspley	The tragic comedy of Celestina, wherein are discoursed in most pleasant style many philosophical sentences and advertisements very necessary for young gentlemen, discovering the sleights of treacherous servants and the subtile carriages of filthy bawds.
	Oct. 5	[William] Ponsonbye	The tragi-comedy of the Vertuous Octavia, by Samuell Brandon.
1599	Aug. 28	{ John Oxombridge John Busbie	The first and second part of Edward IV. and the Tanner of Tamworth, with the history of the life and death of Master Shore and Jane Shore his wife, as it was lately acted by the right honorable the Earl of Derby his servants. Two plays.
	Nov. 17	William Aspley	A Warning for Fair Women.
1599— 1600	Feb. 20	William Aspley	Old Fortunatus in his new livery. A comedy.
1600	Mar. 28	Cuthbert Burby	The play of Patient Grissell.
	Mar. 31	William White	A famous history called Valentine and Orsson, played by her majesty's players.
	April 8	William Holme	A comical satire of Every man out of his Humour.
	May 27	[James] Robertes	A moral of Cloth Breeches and Velvet Hose, as it is acted by my Lord Chamberlain's servants. "Provided that he is not to put it in print without further and better authority" [than the Wardens'].
	May 29	[James] Robertes	The Allarum to London. "Provided that it be not printed without further authority."
	July 24	Richard Oliff	Two plays or things; the one called The Maid's Metamorphosis: the other Give a man luck and throw him into the Sea.

APPENDIX. 333

1600	Aug. 11	Thomas Pavier	The first part of the history of the life of Sir John Oldcastell, Lord Cobham. The second and last part of the history of Sir John Oldcastell, Lord Cobham, with his martyrdom. The history of the life and death of Captain Thomas Stucley, with his marriage to Alexander Curtis his daughter, and his valiant ending of his life at the battle of Alcazar.
	Aug. 14	[Cuthbert] Burby Walter Burre	Every man in his humour. A book.
	Aug. 23	Andrew Wise William Aspley	Much Ado about Nothing The second part of the history of King Henry IV, with the humours of Sir John Ffallstaff. Written by Master Shakespere. Two books.
			[The following entries occur in another part of the Registers:—My Lord Chamberlain's men's plays entered.
	May 27 May 27	[James] Robertes J[ames] Robertes	A moral of cloth breeches and velvet hose. Allarum to London.
	Aug. 4	...	As you like it. A book. } To be Henry V. A book. } stayed.] Every man in his humour. A book.
	Sept. 8	Ffelix Norton	The comedy of Much Ado about nothing. A book.
	Oct. 7	Richard Olyffe	Jack Drum's entertainment, a comedy, as it hath been divers times acted by the Children of Paul's. The Wisdom of Doctor Dodepole, played by the children of Paul's.
	Oct. 8 Oct. 23 Oct. 28	Thomas Ffyssher Richard Oliffes Thomas Haies	A Midsummer Night's Dream. The weakest goeth to the walls. A book called The book of the Merchant of Venice." "By consent of Mr. Roberts."

APPENDIX.

ENTRIES OF PLAYS—*continued.*

Date.		For whom Entered.	Name of Play.
1600	Oct. 28	[Cuthbert] Burby / Walter Burre	Sommer's last Will and Testament, presented by William Sommers.
	Nov. 25	William Wood	Love's Metamorphosis, written by Master John Lylly, and played by the Children of Paul's.
	Dec. 1	[William] Leake	The Downfal of Robert Earl of Huntingdon, after called Robin Hood.
	Dec. 1	[William] Leake	The Death of Robert Earl of Huntingdon, with the lamentable tragedy of Chaste Mathilda.
1600–1	Jan. 7	Thomas Busshell	The play of Doctor Faustus.
	Mar. 1	John Harrison, jun.	God speed the plough.
1601	May 23	Walter Burre	Narcissus, the fountain of Self Love.
	July 3	Edward Alde	The true history of George Scanderbarge, as it was lately played by the right hon. the Earl of Oxenford his servants.
	Aug. 3	William White	A comedy of A Woman will have her Will.
	Oct. 24	Matthew Lownes	The first and second parts of the play called Anthonio and Melida. "Provided that he get lawful license for it."
	Nov. 11	Thomas Ffyssher	The untrussing of the Humorous Poets, by Thomas Decker.
	Dec. 21	John Barnes	Poetaster, or his arraignment.
1601–2	Jan. 18	Mathewe Lownes / John Busby	An excellent pleasant and conceited comedy of Sir John Ffaulstof and the merry wives of Windesor [assigned to Arthure Johnson at same date].
1602	June 7	Edward Aldee	Blurt Master Constable.
	July 26	James Robertes	The Revenge of Hamlett Prince Denmark, as it was lately acted by the Lord Chamberlain his servants.

APPENDIX. 335

1602	Aug. 11	William Cotton	The life and death of the Lord Cromwell, as it was lately acted by the Lord Chamberlain his servants.
1602-3	Feb. 7	[James] Robertes	Troilus and Cresseda, as it is acted by my Lord Chamberlain's men. "When he hath gotten sufficient authority for it."
1604	April 30	Edward Blunt	The works of William Alexander of Menstrie, containing the Monarchic Tragedies.
	July 5	William Aspley Thomas Thorpe	} The Malcontent, Tragicomaedia. An interlude. [Crossed out and re-entered.]
	Nov. 2	Edward Blunt	The tragedy of Sejanus, written by Benjamin Johnson.
	Nov. 9	Thomas Man, jun.	The humours of the Patient Man, the Longing Wife, and the Honest Whore.
	Nov. 29	[Simon] Waterson	} The tragedy of Philotus, written by Samuel Daniell.
	Dec. 4	Edward Blunt	The life and death of Cavaliero Dick Boyer.
1604-5	Feb. 8	Nathaniel Butter	The history of Richard Whittington, his low birth, his great fortune, as it was played by the Prince's servants.
	Feb. 8	Thomas Pavyer	The Fair Maid of Bristoe, played at Hampton Court by His Majesty's players.
	Feb. 12	Nathanaell Butter	King Henry VIII. An enterlude. "If he get good allowance before he begin to print it."
	Mar. 2	Henrie Rockett	Westward Hoe, presented by the children of Paul's. A comedy. "Provided that he get further authority before it be printed." [Crossed out.]
1605	May 8	Simon Stafford	The Tragical history of King Leir and his three daughters, as it was lately acted. Assigned [at the same date] to John Wright, "provided that Simon Stafford shall have the printing of this book."
	June 26	John Hodgetes	The Dutch Courtesan, as it was lately presented at the Blackfriars. "Provided that he get sufficient authority before it be printed."

APPENDIX.

ENTRIES OF PLAYS—continued.

Date.		For whom Entered.	Name of Play.
1605	July 5	Nathaniel Butter	'If you know not me you know nobody.
	Sept. 4	William Aspley, Thomas Thorp	Eastward Ho. A comedy.
	Sept. 14	Nathaniel Butter	The second part of If you know not me you know [no]body, with The Building of the Exchange.
	Oct. 16	John Wright	The Return from Pernassus, or The Scourge of Simony, publicly acted by the Students in Saint John's College, in Cambridge. An enterlude.
	Nov. 26	[Simon] Waterson	The Queen's Arcadia, presented by the University of Oxon in Christchurch.
1605–6	Jan. 10	Edward Blounte	A comedy called Sir Gyles Goosecap, "provided that it be printed according to the copy whereunto Master Wilson's hand is at."
	Mar. 12	John Trundell, William Cotton	Nobody and Somebody.
	Mar. 12		The Flanne. A play. "Provided that he shall not put the same in print before he get allowed lawful authority.
	Mar. 17	Eliazar Edgar	The Wonder of Women, or the tragedy of Sophonisba.
1606	May 13	John Trundell, John Busbye	The Fleare. A comedy. "Provided that they are not to print it till they bring good authority and license for the doing thereof." [Trundel's share was transferred to A. Johnson, Nov. 21, and Buck's license obtained to print.]
	June 5	John Wright, Nathanael Ffossbrook	Julius Cæsar's Revenge.
	Nov. 12	Clement Knighte	Wily Beguiled.
1606–7	Feb. 23	[Simon] Waterson	Lingua. A comedy. [Assigned to J. Waterson, 19th Aug. 1635.]

APPENDIX.

ENTRIES OF PLAYS—*continued*.

Date.	For whom Entered.	Licenser.	Name of Play.
1607			
April 10	Francis Burton	B.	The tragical life and death of Claudius Tiberius Nero.
April 20	Nathanael Butter } John Trundell	B.	The Whore of Babilon.
April 24	Henrie Rockett	B.	The Fair Maid of the Exchange.
May 9	Arthur Johnson	B.	The Phenix.
May 15	Arthur Johnson	B.	Michaelmas Term. A comedy.
May 20	Eleazar Edgar } Robert Jackson	B.	The Woman hater, as it hath been lately acted by the Children of Paul's.
June 3	William Aspley	B.	The tragedy of Busey D'Amboise, made by George Chapman.
June 29	John Busbye } Arthur Johnson	T.	Cupid's Whirleygigge. A comedy.
June 29	John Wright	B.	The travels of the three English Brothers, as it was played at the Curtain. A play.
July 31	George Vyncent	B.	The misery of inforced Marriage. A tragedy.
Aug. 6	George Elde	B.	The Puritan Widow. A comedy.
Aug. 6	George Elde	B.	Northward Ho.
Aug. 6	Thomas Thorp	B.	What you will. A comedy.
Oct. 7	George Elde	B.	The Revenger's Tragedy. } Two plays. A Trick to catch the Old one.
Oct. 12	John Browne } John Helme	B.	The Family of Love, as it hath been lately acted by the Children of His Majesty's Revels. A play.
Oct. 16	John Wright	B.	The tragedy of Pope Alexander VI., as it was played before his Majesty.

Y

APPENDIX.

ENTRIES OF PLAYS—continued.

Date.		For whom Entered.	Licenser.	Name of Play.
1607	Oct. 22	Arthur Johnson	B.	The Merry Devil of Edmonton. A play.
	Nov. 26	Nathaniel Butter / John Busby	B.	Master William Shakespeare his history of King Lear, as it was played before the King's Majesty at Whitehall upon Saint Stephen's night at Christmas last by His Majesty's servants playing usually at the Globe on the Bankside.
1607–8	Mar. 22	Richard Bonyon	B.	The Five Witty Gallants, as it hath been acted by the Children of the Chapel. A play.
1608	Mar. 28	Richard Moore	B.	A most witty and merry conceited comedy called Who would a' thought it, or Law Tricks.
	April 12	John Helme	B.	Humour out of Breath.
	April 21	Thomas Thorpe	B.	The characters of two Royal Masques invented by Ben. Johnson.
	April 29	Thomas Man, jun.	B.	The second part of the Converted Courtesan, or Honest Whore.
	May 2	[Thomas] Pavyer	...	A Yorkshire Tragedy, written by Wylliam Shakespere.
	May 20	Edward Blount	B.	Pericles, Prince of Tyre.
	June 3	John Busby / Nathanael Butter	B.	A Roman tragedy called the Rape of Lucrece.
	June 5	Thomas Thorp	B.	The Conspiracy and Tragedy of Charles Duke of Byronn, written by George Chapman.
	Oct. 4	Walter Burre / Eleazer Edgar	S.	A mad World, my maysters.
	Oct. 6	John Bache	B.	The Dumb Knight. A play.

APPENDIX. 339

1608	Nov. 25	Nathanael Butter	B.	The tragedy of Mustapha and Zangar.
1608–9	Jan. 26	Henry Walleys Richard Bonion	S.	The Case is altered. [Bartholomew Sutton is added to the two other publishers on 20 July 1609.]
	Jan. 27	Jeffrey Charlton	S.	Bonos Nochios. An interlude. Craft upon Subtilty's back. An interlude.
	Jan. 28	Richard Bonion Henry Walleys	S.	The history of Troylus and Cressida.
	Feb. 22	Richard Bonion Henry Waller	S.	The masque of Queens celebrated, done by Benjamin Johnson.
	Mar. 10	John Busby, jun.	S.	The tragedy of the Turk, with the death of Borgias, by John Mason, gent.
1610	June 12	John Browne	...	Chester's Triumph in honor of the Prince, as it was performed upon S. Gregory's day in the aforesaid city.
	Sept. 20	John Browne John Busby, jun.	B.	Epicoene, or the Silent Woman, by Ben. Johnson.
	Oct. 3	Walter Burre	B.	The Alchemist, made by Ben Johnson.
	Oct. 31	Thomas Thorpe	B.	Histriomastix, or the Player Whipped.
	Nov. 9	Robert Wilson	B.	Ram Alley, or Merry Tricks.
1611	Sept. 14	John Stepneth	B.	The tragedy of the Atheist.
	Oct. 14	William Barrenger	B.	The Golden Age, with the lives of Jupiter and Saturn.
	Nov. 23	John Budge	B.	A Woman is a Weathercock. A comedy.
1611–12	Feb. 1	William Barrenger	B.	A Christian turned Turk, or the tragical lives and deaths of the two famous pirates Ward and Danseker, as it hath been publicly acted. Written by Robert Daborn, gent.
	Feb. 15	Edward Blunte	B.	A play-book, being a Tragi-comedy called the Nobleman, written by Cyril Tourneur.

ENTRIES OF PLAYS—continued.

Date.	For whom Entered.	Licenser.	Name of Play.
1611–12 Feb. 15	Edward Blunte	B.	The Twins Tragedy, written by Niccolls. A tragedy.
1612 April 17	[John] Browne	B.	The Revenge of Bussy D'Amboys. A tragedy.
		B.	The Widow's Tears. A comedy. Both written by George Chapman.
1614 Dec. 17	Richard Hawkins	B.	The tragedy of the Fair Mariamne, Queen of Jewry.
1614–5 May 23	Richard Redmer	B.	Hog hath lost his Pearl.
1615 Feb. 21	Robert Lownes	B.	The Valiant Welshman.
April 18	Walter Burr	...	Ignoramus, Comoedia prout Cantabrigie acta coram Jacobo, &c.
April 24	Josias Harison	B.	The Hector of Germany, or the Palsgrave "is a harmless thing". [These four words have been struck through with a pen.]
April 24	Josias Harison	...	Cupid's Revenge.
April 28	Nicholas Okes	...	Albumazar. A comedy acted before His Majesty at Cambridge, 10 Mar. 1614[–5]. [Assigned at same date to Richard Woodriffe.]
Aug. 14	Richard Redmere	...	The Honest Lawyer. A play.
1615–6 Mar. 19	Miles Patriche	B.	The Scornful Lady, written by Francis Beaumont and John Fletcher.
1618 April 20	John Parker	B.	The Marriages of the Arts, written by Barth. Holyday, M.A. A comedy.
June 3	Barnard Alsope	...	See me and see me not, by Dabridgcourt Belgier. A poem.
Aug. 7	[Edward] Blounte	B.	A King and no King. A play.¶

1619	April 28	[Richard] Higgenbotham } [Francis] Corstable }	B.	The Maid's Tragedy. A play.
	July 10	[John] Brown	B.	The Temple Masque, anno 1618.
	Oct. 17	Richard Meighen	B.	Swetnam the Women Hater arraigned by Women. A comedy.
1619-20	Jan. 10	Thomas Walkley	...	Philaster. A play.
	Jan. 15	John Trundle	...	The life and death of Guy of Warwick, written by John Day and Thomas Decker.
1620	May 22	Laurence Chapman	B.	Two Merry Milkmaids. A play.
	July 4	George Purslowe } John Trundle }		A courtly masque, or the The World Tost at Tennis, acted at the Prince's Arms by the Prince his highness' servants.
1621	Sept. 18	John Norton	B.	The Pilgrim of Casteell, or the Fortunes of Llamphilus and Nisa. "Not to be printed until he bringeth more sufficient authority."
	Oct. 6	Thomas Walkley	B.	The tragedy of Othello, the Moor of Venice.
	Dec. 7	Thomas Jones	B.	The Virgin Martyr. A tragedy.
1621-2	Feb. 22	Matthew Rodes	B.	A tragedy of Herod and Antipater, by Gervase Markham.
1622-3	Jan. 20	Edward Blackmore } George Norton }	A.	Sforza, Duke of Millaine, made by Master Messenger. A play.
1623	Sept. 3	Francis Grove	A.	A book of Jigs containing three books or parts.
	Nov. 8	[Edward] Blounte } Isaac Jaggard }	...	Master William Shakspeer's Comedies, Histories, and Tragedies, so many of the said copies as are not formerly entered to other men.
	...		...	Comedies : The Tempest.
	...		...	The Two Gentlemen of Verona.
	...		...	Measure for Measure.

ENTRIES OF PLAYS—continued.

Date.	For whom Entered.	Licenser.	Name of Play.
1623 Nov. 8	[John] Harrison Edward Blackmore	...	The Comedy of Errors. As you like it, All's well that ends well. Twelfe Night, The Winter's Tale. Histories: The third part of Henry VI. Henry VIII. Tragedies: Coriolanus, Timon of Athens, Julius Cæsar, Macbeth, Anthonie and Cleopatra, Cymbeline.
1623–4 Mar. 12		H.	The Bondman, by Philip Messenger.
1624 June 28	John Wright	...	The Spanish Jepsye.
1626 April 14	John Waterson	...	The Staple of News. A comedy.
1627 April 8	Robert Milborne	...	Apollo Shroving. A comedy.
1627–8 Feb. 27	John Marriott	H.	The tragedy of Lodovick Sforza, Duke of Millan, by Robert Gomersall.
1629 June 2	Henry Seile	H.	The Lover's Melancholy, by John Ford, gent.
Nov. 13	Jaspar Emerye	H.	The Duchess of Suffolk, written by Thomas Drue. A play.
1629–30 Jan. 1	Ephraim Dawson	H.	The Collonell, written by William Davenant, gent.

APPENDIX. 343

1629-30 Jan. 10	John Waterson	H.	The Crewel Brother, written by William Davenant.
		H.	The Just Italian, by the same.
Feb. 26	John Grove	H.	Hoffman, the Revengeful Father. A play.
Feb. 27	Raph Mabbe	H.	The Grateful Servant, by James Shirley. A play.
Mar. 22	John Waterson	H.	The Spanish Bawd. A play.
1630 Mar. 26	John Marlott	H.	The Runegado, by Philip Messenger. A play.
April 8	[Francis] Constable	H.	Aristippus and the Pedler.
April 8	—— Allott	H.	The Chast Mayd of Chepeside. A play.
April 16	[Francis] Constable	H.	The Pedler, by R. Davenport. A comedy.
		H.	The Battle of the Affections, or Love's Lodestone. A play.
June 29	[Nathaniel] Butter	H.	The second part of the Honest Hoore, by Thomas Decker.
Sept. 13	Andrew Crooke	H.	A comedy in Latin called Loyola, by Doctor Hackket.
Nov. 8	[Henry] Seile	H.	Match me in London, by Thomas Decker. A play.
1630-1 Feb. 9	[Robert] Milborne	H.	A comedy in Latin called Pedantius.
Feb. 25	[Francis] Constable	H.	The School of Complement, by James Shirley.
1631 April 17	Thomas Alchorne	H.	New Inn, written by Ben: Johnson. A comedy.
April 25	William Sheeres	H.	Scicelides, acted at Cambridge. A play.
May 16	John Jackman	H.	The Wonder of a Kingdom, by Thomas Decker. A comedy. [Entered again under 24 Feb. 1635-6 to N. Vavasor, "dated 7 May 1631."]
May 16	John Jackman	H.	The Noble Spanish Souldier, by Thomas Deckar. A tragedy. [Entered again under 9 Dec. 1633 to N. Vavasor, "anno 1631."]
May 18	[Thomas] Harper	H.	Caesar and Pompey, by George Chapman. A play.
June 16	Richard Royston	H.	The Fair Maid of the West, 1st and 2d part. A comedy.
Sept. 7	[Richard] Meighen	H.	Amarath the Turk. A play.

APPENDIX.

ENTRIES OF PLAYS—continued.

Date		For whom Entered.	Licenser.	Name of Play.
1631	Sept. 7	[Richard] Meighen	H.	The tragedy of Bajazet II., or the Raging Turk.
	Sept. 28	[Richard] Thrall	H.	Ffraus honesta.
	Nov. 12	[Michael] Sparkes	H.	A flora show at Norwich.
	Nov. 19	John Waterson	H.	The Emperor of the East. A playbook.
	Nov. 24	[Francis] Constable	H.	A new wonder, or a Woman never vexed. A comedy by William Rowley.
1631–2	Jan. 16	[John] Waterson, jun.	H.	The Maid of Honor, by Philip Massinger. A play.
	Jan. 26	John Grove	H.	The Leaguer. (The reformations to be strictly observed: may be printed not otherwise expressed by the foresaid words) [*sic*]. A comedy.
	Feb. 9	William Cooke	H.	The Changes, or Love in a Maze, by Master Sherley. A comedy.
1632	Mar. 24	Nicholas Vavasor	H.	The Northern Lass, by Master Broome. A comedy.
	Mar. 30	Francis Constable	H.	The Fatal Dowry. A tragedy.
	May 9	Andrew Crooke	H.	A tragedy in Latin called Roxana.
	June 13	[Humfrey] Robinson	H.	The Rival Friends, by Peter Hausten. A comedy.
	Sept. 27	[Thomas] Harper	H.	All's lost by Lust, by William Rowley. A tragedy.
	Nov. 2	William Sheares	H.	The Costly Whore. A Comedy.
	Nov. 9	William Cooke	H.	A dialogue of Riches and Honor, by J. S.
	Nov. 10	[Henry] Seile	H.	Alaham, by Fulke Lord Brooke. A tragedy.
			H.	A new way to pay old debts, by Philip Massinger. A comedy.
1632–3	Nov. 20	Nicholas Vavasor	H.	The Jew of Malta. A tragedy.
	Jan. 15	William Sheares	H.	A match at Midnight. A play.

APPENDIX. 345

1632–3	Jan. 15	William Cooke	H.	The witty fair one, by James Shirley. A play.
	Jan. 21	Hugh Beeston	H.	Love's Sacrifice, by John Ford. A tragedy.
	Mar. 19	William Cooke	H.	The Bird in the Cage, by James Shirley. A comedy.
1633	Mar. 28	Hugh Beeston	H.	The Broken Heart, by John Ford. A tragedy.
	June 15	[Richard] Meighen	H.	The Fine Companion, by Shackerley Marmyon. A play.
	July 15	Nicholas Okes	H.	The Traveller, by Master Heywood. A comedy.
	Aug. 1	—— Allott	H.	Fuimus Troes, or the True Troians, represented by the gentlemen students of Magdalen College in Oxford.
1633–4	Feb. 24	Hugh Beeston	H.	Perkin Warbeck, by John Ford. "Observing the caution in the license." A tragedy.
1634	April 8	John Waterson	H.	The two Noble Kinsmen, by John Fletcher and William Shakespeare. A tragi-comedy.
	April 17	John Spenser	H.	Bellum grammaticale, by Master Spense.
	June 25	Nicholas Oakes	Bl.	A maidenhead well lost. A play.
	Oct. 28	Benjamin Fisher	H.	The Witches of Lancashire. A play.
	Nov. 3	William Cooke	H.	The Traytor, by James Shirley. A play.
1634–5	Jan. 19	John Benson	H.	The Shepherd's Holiday, by J. Rutter. A tragi-comedy.
1635	Sept. 30	John Crouch	Bl.	The Queen's Masque, or Love's Mistress, by Master Haywood. A play.
	Dec. 7	[John] Marriott	H.	The Great Duke of Florence. A comical history, by Philip Massinger.
1635–6	Feb. 4	[Richard] Meighen	H.	The Platonic Lovers, by William Davenant. A play.
	Feb. 4	[Richard] Meighen	H.	The Wits, by William Davenant. A play.
1636	June 17	Robert Raworth	H.	A challenge for Beauty, by Haywood. A play.
			Bl.	The history of Anniball and Scipio, by Thomas Nabbes. A play.
	Aug. 6	Charles Greene	El.	A moral masque, by Thomas Nabbes.

ENTRIES OF PLAYS—continued.

Date.		For whom Entered.	Licenser.	Name of Play.
1636-7	Mar. 29 [P 23] Mar. 25	{[John] Waterson John Benson} James Beckett	T. T. ‡	The Elder Brother, written by John Fletcher. A comedy. The Royal King and the Loyal Subjects, by Master Heywood. A comedy.
1637	April 13	{Andrew Crooke William Cooke}	T.	Hide Park, by James Shirley. A comedy.
	April 26	[John] Waterson	T.	{The Lady of Pleasure. } By James Shirley. Two plays. The Young Admiral.
			T.	The Valiant Scot. A tragedy.
	Oct. 18	{Andrew Crooke William Cooke}	...	The Example, by Master Shirley. A play.
	Nov. 15	William Cooke	...	The Gamester, by James Shirley. A play.
	Nov. 28	John Okes	...	A Shoemaker is a gentleman, with the life and death of the Cripple that stole the weathercock of Paul's, by William Rowley. A comedy.
1637-8	Jan. 29	Thomas Walkley	H.	The Cid, a tragi-comedy translated out of French by Master Rutter.
	Feb. 3 Feb. 15	[Henry] Seile John Okes	...	The Fancies, by John Ford. A play, The Martyred Soldier, with the life and death of Purser Clinton, by H. Shirley.
	Mar. 5 Mar. 12	John Okes Henry Sheapard	...	The Lost Lady. A play. The wisewoman of Hogsden, by Thomas Haywood. A play.
	Mar. 13 Mar. 13	{[Andrew] Crooke William Cooke} [Andrew] Crooke	...	The Duke's Mistress, by James Shirley. A play. The Conspiracy. A play.

APPENDIX. 347

1637–8	Mar. 13	[Andrew] Crooke, John Crooke, Richard Searger	The Royal Master, by James Shirley. A play.
	Mar. 14	[Henry] Seile	A Latin Comedy called Naufragium Joculare, by Abraham Cowley. A Pastoral Comedy called Love's Riddle, by Abraham Cowley, whilst he was King's Scholar in Westminster School. A Latin Comedy called Cornelianum Dolium, by T. R.
1638	Mar. 30	[Thomas] Harper, [Thomas] Slater	Tottenham Court, by Thomas Nabbes. A play.
	April 5	Charles Greene	Aglaura, by Sir John Sucklin, Knight. A play.
	April 18	Thomas Walkley	Covent Garden, by Thomas Nabbes. A play.
	May 28	Charles Greene	The Spring's glory, by Thomas Nabbes. A book.
	June 23	Charles Greene	The Seven Champions of Christendom, with the life and death of Jack Straw and Wat Tyler, by John Kirke. A play.
	July 13	John Oakes	Phillip Chalbott, Admiral of France, and the Ball, by James Shirley. A book.
	Oct. 24	[Andrew] Crooke, William Crooke	Arviragus and Philicia, first and second parts. A play.
	Oct. 26	John Crooke, Richard Serger	The Tragedy of Cleopatra, and Julia Agripina, Emperess of Rome. } Two plays.
	Oct. 26	Thomas Walkley	The Lady's Trial, by John Ford. A play.
	Nov. 6	Henry Sheapard	The Sophister. A comedy.
	Nov. 7	[Humphry] Mozeley	Argalus and Parthenia, by Henry Glapthorne. A play.
1638–9	Jan. 11	[Daniel] Fakeman	Monsieur Thomas, by Master John Fletcher. A comedy.
	Jan. 22	[John] Waterson	The unnatural Combat, by Phillip Massinger. A tragedy.
	Feb. 14	[John] Waterson	Imperiale. A tragedy.
	Mar. 1	[Thomas] Harper	A new trick to cheat the Devil, by Master Damport. A book or comedy.
1639	Mar. 28	Humphrey Blundon	

APPENDIX.

ENTRIES OF PLAYS—*continued*.

Date.	For whom Entered.	Name of Play.
1639		
April 12	William Cooke	The Maid's Revenge, by James Shirley. A play.
April 25	[Andrew] Crooke / William Cooke	Nightwalkers. / Opportunity. / Love's Cruelty. / The Coronation. / Wit without money. } 5 plays.
June 18	John Okes	The Knave in Grain, or Jack Cottington. A play.
July 8	Laurence Blaicklock	The Bride, by Thomas Nabbes. A play.
July 29	William Cooke	The Humorous Courtier, by James Shirley. A play.
Sept. 23	George Hutton	Albertus Wallenstein, late Duke of Friedland, by Henry Glapthorne. A tragedy.
Oct. 3	Daniel Frere	Messalina, the Roman Empress, by N. R. A tragedy.
Oct. 4	John Crooke / Richard Sergier	The Bloody Brother, by J. B. A tragedy.
Nov. 4	Daniel Frere	Unfortunate Mother, a tragedy by Thomas Nabbes. A play.
Nov. 20	Daniel Frere	The Rebellion, by Thomas Rawlins. A play.
Nov. 29	John Williams / Francis Egglestone	The Arcadia. A Pastoral. / Love's Cruelty, by James Shirley. A Tragedy. Entered before to Master Crooke.
1639–40 Jan. 31	[William] Leake	The Strange Discovery, by J. G., gent. A tragi-comedy.
Feb. 14	William Cooke	The Tragedy of Saint Albons, by Master James Shirley. A play.
Feb. 20	John Benson	The Masque of the Gypsies, by Benjamin Johnson.

Date		Publisher	Title
1639-40	Mar. 11	John Williams / Francis Egglestone	The Antiquary. A comedy. / Look to the Lady, by James Shirley. A comedy.
	Mar. 19	[Francis] Constable	Sparagus Garden. } Three plays, by Rich. Brome. / The Antipodes. / Wit in a Madness.
	Mar. 20	[Andrew] Crooke / Richard Seirger	The Masque of Augurs. / Time Vindicated. / Neptune's Triumphs. / Pan's Anniversary, or The Shepherd's Holiday. Four masques, by Benjamin Jonson.
1640	April 2	William Cooke	The Queen of Arragon, by William Habington, Esquire.
	April 2	[Andrew] Crooke	The Swaggering Damosell, by Master Chamberlayne. A comedy.
	April 4	[Francis] Constable	The Prisoner, by Master Killegrey. A tragedy.
	April 27	[Francis] Constable	The Lady's Privilege, by Henry Glapthorne. A play. / Wit in a Constable, by Henry Glapthorne. A comedy.
	April 28	[Richard] Whitaker	Saint Patrick for Ireland. } Two plays, by James Shirley. / The Constant Maid.
	May 22	Widow Wilson	The Hollander, by Henry Glapthorne. A comedy.
	May 22	John Okes	Love's Masterpiece, by Thomas Haywood. A comedy. / Claracilla, by Master Killegray. A play. / Christianetta.
	Aug. 4	[Andrew] Crooke	The Jewish Gentleman. / A New Academy or Exchange. / The Lovesick Count. } Six plays, by Richard Broome. / The Covent Garden. / The English Moor, or Mock Marriage.

TABLE V.—TRANSFERS OF COPYRIGHT IN PLAYS, 1584-1640.

Date.			Name of Play.	To whom Transferred.
1584	April	1	Campaspe	1591, Oct. 4, Galathea re-entered. 1597, April 12, Sappho and Campaspe transferred from T. Cadman to Joan Brome. 1601, Aug. 23, Sappho, Campaspe, Endymion, Midas, Galatea, from Mrs. Brome, deceased, to G. Potter. 1632, all six published together by E. Blount.
1585	April	6	Galatea	
1584			Sappho	
1591	Oct.	4	Midas } Endymion	
1594	Jan.	18	Mother Bombie	
1592	Oct.	6	Spanish Tragedy	1599, Aug. 13, Spanish Tragedy and Edward Longshanks assigned from A. Jeffes to W. White. 1600, Aug. 14, Henry V., Spanish Tragedy, Edward Longshanks, Jack Straw, Looking-glass for London, "formerly printed," set over to T. Pavier. 1602, April 19, 1 & 2 Henry VI. assigned from T. Millington to T. Pavier. 1626, Aug. 4, Henry V., Spanish Tragedy, Sir John Oldcastle, and "Master Pavier's right in Shakespere's plays, or any of them," assigned by Mrs. Pavier to E. Brewster and R. Bird. 1630, Nov. 8, his interest in Henry V., Sir John Oldcastle, York and Lancaster, and Yorkshire Tragedy assigned by Mr. Bird to J. Cotes.
1593	Oct.	8	Edward Longshanks	
1593	Oct.	23	Jack Straw	
1593-4	Mar.	5	Looking-glass for London	
1593-4	Mar.	12	i York and Lancaster ii York and Lancaster	
1595	Aug.	11	Sir John Oldcastle	
1600	Aug.	4	Henry V. "stayed"	
1608	May	2	Yorkshire Tragedy	
1600	July	24	Maid's Metamorphosis	1600, Oct. 23, Jack Drum assigned from F. Norton to R. Oliff. 1615, Nov. 6, Jack Drum, Weakest to the Wall, and Maid's Metamorphosis, from Mrs. Oliff to P. Knight. 1617, Oct. 18, Weakest to Wall and Maid's Metamorphosis assigned from P. Knight to R. Hawkins. 1627-8, Mar. 1, King and no King, Philaster, and Orthello assigned from T. Walkley to R. Hawkins. 1629, Oct. 27, Maid's Tragedy from Heggenbotham and Constable to R. Hawkins. 1638, May 29, all the group except Jack Drum from Hawkins to Mead and Meredith. 1638-9, Jan. 25, the same from them to Leake.¹
1600	Sept.	8	Jack Drum's entertainment	
1600	Oct.	23	Weakest goeth to the wall	
1618	Aug.	7	King and no King	
1619	April	28	Maid's Tragedy	
1619-20	Jan.	10	Philaster	
1621	Oct.	6	Othello	

APPENDIX.

Year	Date	Title	Notes
1599	Aug. 28	1 & 2 Edward IV.	1599–1600, Feb. 23, his moiety in 1 & 2 Edward IV. assigned from J. Busby to H. Lownes. 1627, May 30, his share in Poetaster and Anthonie and Mellida assigned by T. Lownes to H. Lownes and R. Young. 1628, Nov. 6, his interest in Poetaster, 1 & 2 Jane Shore, and Anthony and Melida assigned by H. Lownes to G. Cole and G. Latham. 1630, Dec. 6, their interest in the same play assigned by them to R. Young.
1601	Oct. 24	Antonio and Mellida	
1601	Dec. 21	Poetaster	
1597	Aug. 29	Richard II.	1603, Jan. 25, set over from A. Wise to M. Low.
1597	Oct. 20	Richard III.	
1597–8	Feb. 25	1 Henry IV.	
1600	Aug. 14	Every Man in his humor	1605, Aug. 6, Sejanus assigned by E. Blunt to T. Thorpe. 1610, Oct. 3, Sejanus and Vulpone assigned by T. Thorpe to W. Burre. 1612, Sept. 28, Silent Woman assigned by J. Browne to W. Burre. 1622–3, Feb. 17, D'Ambois' Revenge assigned by Mrs. Browne to J. Marriott. 1630, July 3, Narcissus, Mad World, Alchemist, Silent Woman, Ignoramus, assigned by Mrs. Bur to J. Spencer. 1630, July 20, Ignoramus entered for G. Edmondson and J. Spencer (with Spencer's consent). 1635, July 4, all the seven plays by Jonson were entered for Stansby by virtue of a note bearing date 1621, June 10, under the hands of W. Burre and M. Lownes. *N.B.* Stansby printed the Jonson folios 1616, 1631.
1601	May 23	Cynthia's Revels (Narcissus)	
1604	Nov. 2	Sejanus	
1607		Volpone	
1608	Oct. 4	A mad world, my Masters	
1610	Sept. 20	Silent Woman	
1610	Oct. 3	Alchemist	
1611		Catilina	
1612	April 17	D'Ambois' Revenge	
1615	April 18	Ignoramus	
1594	May 2	Taming of a Shrew	1606–7, Jan. 22, the first three were entered for N. Ling, with C. Burby's consent. 1607, Nov. 19, all four were set over to J. Smythick. Mr. Halliwell in his Outlines omits the Shrew entry.
1598		Love's Labour's Lost	
1599		Romeo and Juliet	
1602	July 26	Hamlet	

352   APPENDIX.

TRANSFERS OF COPYRIGHT—*continued*.

Date.	Name of Play.	To whom Transferred.
1594 May 28	Orlando	1609, Oct. 16, assigned by Mrs. Burby to Welby. 1617-8, Mar. 2, by Welby to Snodham. 1625-6, Feb. 23, by Mrs. Snodham to W. Stansby. 1638-9, Mar. 4, the first four by Mrs Stansby to Bishop. Only half shares in the two last plays are concerned in these entries.
1595 April 1	George a Greene	
1595 Dec. 1	Edward III.	
1600 Aug. 14	Every man in his humour	
1600 Oct. 28	Summer's last Will and T.	
1600	The Shoemaker's Holiday	1610, April 19, assigned from V. Symms to J. Wrighte, and agreed that "Symms shall have the workmanship of the printing thereof for the use of the said J. Wrighte during his life, if he have a printing house of his own."
1600-1 Jan. 7	Dr. Faustus	1610, Sept. 13, assigned from T. Bushell to J. Wright. 1611, Dec. 16, Edward II. assigned from W. Jones to R. Barnes. 1615-6, Jan. 5, Dr. Doddipoll from Mrs. Oliffe to H. Bell. 1617, April 17, Edward II. from R. Barnes to H. Bell. 1638, Sept. 4, both plays from Henry and Moses Bell to Haviland and J. Wright.
1593 July 6	Edward II.	
1600 Oct. 7	Dr. Doddypoll	
1600 Dec. 1	1 & 2 Robin Hood	1616-7, Feb. 16, all assigned from Leake to Barrett. 1626, April 3, Cromwell and Fawn from Mrs. Barrett to Parker. 1638, Sept. 4, all the plays from Parker to Haviland and J. Wright.
1602 Aug. 11	Lord Cromwell	
1605-6 Mar. 12	The Fawn	
1598 Sept. 17	Mucedorus	1618, Sept. 17, assigned by Mrs. Jones to J. Wright. 1613, April 19, "a half part" in the two last plays, all Edgar's interest in the Courtesan (which was entered originally to Hodgetts), and the whole of Sophonisba assigned from E. Edgar to J. Hodgetts.
1605 June 26	Dutch Courtesan	
1605-6 Mar. 17	Sophonisba	
1607 May 20	Woman hater	
1608 Oct. 4	A Mad World, my M.	

APPENDIX.

Year	Date	Title	Notes
1615	Aug. 14	The Honest Lawyer	1622-3, Jan. 11, assigned by R. Woodriffe to T. Barlow.
1607	April 24	Fair Maid of Exchange	1616, April 9, assigned by Mrs. Rocket to N. Bourne. 1635-6, Feb. 27, by Bourne to G. Edwardes.
1615	April 24	} Cupid's Revenge	1617, May 8, Scornful Lady assigned by M. Patrich to T. Jones. 1619, April 15, Cupid's Revenge and the Palsgrave by J. Harrison to T. Jones. 1633, Oct. 24, all six plays by T. Jones to Matthews.
1615-6	Mar. 19	The Palsgrave	
1621	Dec. 7	Scornful Lady	
1624		Virgin Martyr	
1633		Nero	
1600	Oct. 28	The Heir	
1607	Oct. 12	Merchant of Venice	1619, July 8, L. Hayes, inherited from T. Hayes, his father.
1608	April 12	Family of Love	1621, Sept. 2, Tu quoque and Fair Quarrel assigned by J. Trundle to T. Dewe. 1627, Dec. 3, all four plays by Mrs. Helme (and T. Dewe?) to W. Washington. 1628, May 21, the last three by him to Flesher.
1614		Humor out of Breath	
1617		Greene's Tu Quoque	
1607	Oct. 22	Fair Quarrel	
1592	April 3	Merry Devil of Edmonton	1624, June 21, assigned by A. Johnson to F. Faulkner.
1592	Nov. 20	Arden of Feversham	
1594	May 14	Salomon and Bersheba	1624, June 29, assigned by Mrs. White to E. Aldee. [The Leire entered with these was not the old play, but a prose history now lost.] 1640, April 22, Bacon, Robin Hood, and The Owl assigned from Mrs. Aldee to Oulton.
		} F. Bacon and F. Bungay	
	?	} Robin Hood and Little John	
		The Owl (not extant; written 1613)	
1608	Oct. 6	The Dumb Knight	1610, Nov. 19, assigned by J. Bache to R. Wilson.
1603		Nero (in Latin)	1626, Sept. 4, Nero and Woman's a Weathercock transferred from J. Budge to Allott. 1630, Nov. 16, Blount's interest in Shakespeare assigned to Allott. 1631, Sept. 7, Staple of News assigned by J. Waterson to Allott. 1637, July 1, all the group from Mrs. Allott to Legatt and A. Crook. [*N.B.* 1 Henry VI. is called 3 Henry VI., Troylus is omitted, and Anthony included in the 1630 entry.]
1611	Nov. 23	Woman's a Weathercock	
1614		Bartholomew Fair	
1622		Share in Shakespeare Folio	
1626	April 14	Staple of News	
1629		Roman Actor	
1630	Mar. 26	Aristippus	
1633	Aug. 1	True Trojans	

APPENDIX.

TRANSFERS OF COPYRIGHT—*continued*.

Date.		Name of Play.	To whom Transferred.
1623	Nov. 8	Share in Shakespeare Folio	1627, June 19, Jaggard's share assigned by Mrs. Jaggard to T. Cotes and R. Cotes. 1628, Dec. 8, H. Walley's share assigned to R. Meighen. 1629, Oct. 12, assigned by C. Knight to T. Knight. 1635-6, Mar. 8, by T. Knight to Alchorn.
1609	Nov. 12	Faithful Shepherdess	
1606		Wily Beguiled	
1601-2	Jan. 18	Merry Wives of Windsor	1629-30, Jan. 29, assigned by A. Johnson to Meighen.
1607	May 9	Phoenix	
1607	May 15	Michaelmas Term	
1607	June 29	Cupid's Whirligig	
1594	June 19	Four London Prentises	
1611-2	Oct. 14	Golden Age	
1613		Silver Age	1630, Aug. 2, assigned by N. Okes to J. Okes.
1632		Iron Age	
1615	April 28	Albumazar	
1611		Roaring Girl	1630-1, Feb. 10, assigned by T. Archer to H. Perrey. 1634, Sept. 15, White Devil and Insatiate Countess assigned by H. Perrey to H. Taunton. 1633, May 9, assigned by M. Rhodes to F. Smith. 1633, Aug. 3, by F. Smith to T. Lambert. 1633-4 Jan. 2, by T. Lambert to F. Smith again.
1612		White Devil	
1613		Insatiate Countess	
1621-2	Feb. 22	Herod and Antipater	
1606-7	Feb. 23	Lingua.	1635, Aug. 19, assigned by S. Waterson to J. Waterson.
1607	July 31	Misery of enforced M.	1637, April 28, assigned by Mrs. Vincent to R. Thraile.
1607	Oct. 22	Merry Devil of E.	1624, June 21, assigned by A. Johnson to F. Faulkner.

APPENDIX. 355

1608	Nov. 26	Mustapha.	1632, Nov. 10, assigned by N. Butter to J. Seile.
1619-20	Jan. 15	Guy of Warwick.	1620, Dec. 13, assigned by J. Trundle to T. Langley.
1620	May 22	Two Merry Milkmaids.	1623, Sept. 13, assigned by L. Chapman to M. Walbanke.
1622-3	Jan. 20	Duke of Milan.	1623, May 5, Norton's share assigned to Blackmore.
1639	June 18	Knave in grain.	1639, Oct. 22, assigned by J. Okes to J. Nicholson as "new vampt" [which is not part of the title, as Mr. Halliwell supposes].
1630		Picture	
1600	April 8	Every Man out of his Humor	1634, Aug. 8, assigned by T. Walkley to J. Waterson.
1629		Wedding	1638, April 28, assigned by Smethwick to Bishop.
1629-30	Feb. 26	} Grateful Servant	1637, Sept. 25, assigned by J. Grove to W. Leake.
1631-2	Jan. 26	Hoffmann	
1637-8	Mar. 5	Holland's Leaguer	
		Lost Lady	1638, Sept. 24, assigned by J. Okes to J. Coleby. 1640, Sept. 5, by J. Coleby to R. Roiston.
1604-5	Feb. 12	Henry VIII. (When you see me, &c.)	
1605	July 5	1. If you know not me, &c.	
1605	Sept. 14	2. If you know not me, &c.	
1607	Nov. 26	Lear	
1608	June 3	Lucrece, Roman tragedy	1639, May 21, assigned by N. Butter to Flessher.
1630	June 29	2. Honest Whore	

At this point we lose the aid of Mr. Arber's reprint of "The Stationers' Registers," which does not extend beyond 1640. It is, however, necessary to continue our notes to 1660, the date of the reopening of the theatres, because even at that date entries were made attributing plays to Shakespeare. The following memoranda have no pretence to completeness, and are compiled (pending an opportunity of examining the registers themselves) from the much-abused *Biographia Dramatica*, which is, nevertheless, much more useful than the abbreviated compilation made from it (retaining nearly all its errors) by the scissors of Mr. Halliwell, and published by him as *A Dictionary of Old English Plays*. Two of these entries are so important for dramatic history that they are printed in parallel columns, with the list of MSS. once in the possession of John Warburton, the Somerset Herald, but mostly destroyed by his cook. From these it will be seen at a glance that three-fifths of his collection consisted of the remainder of Moseley's stock, which contained the majority of old unprinted MSS. extant in 1660.

From these S. R. entries, taken as a whole, the reader will find that the total number of extant plays originally produced between 1576, when theatres were first opened, and their closing in 1642, is less than 500. Nor have we reason to believe that they ever numbered more than 2000 or so. Nearly all worth preserving has been preserved. The gross exaggerations of Halliwell and Collier on this matter depend on their estimating the number of contemporaneous theatres and companies at some fifteen. They really never exceeded five. They also neglect the facts that many so-called new plays were mere revisions of the old ones, "new vamped" versions slightly altered; and that the inferior theatres depended largely on extemporaneous performances, of which only the plots were committed to writing. In the palmy days of the Admiral's company, Henslow brought out a new play once a fortnight, but this was undoubtedly an exceptional instance. The best companies, such as the King's, and after them the Queen's, produced one in about two months. Taking all this into consideration, 2000 is a liberal estimate; 20,000 is a number that could only be dreamed of by an inaccurate writer intent on effect rather than truth. And of this 2000 not more than a quarter would be worth preserving: indeed, of those preserved many are quite valueless. The few good ones lost are such as *The Jeweller of Amsterdam*, suppressed for political reasons; or the original *Henry VIII.*, destroyed by fire or other accident.

In these Supplementary Lists names of authors wrongly attributed are printed in *italics*, and names of plays occurring both in Warburton's list and Moseley's entries are *asterised*.

1646. Sept. 4, were entered, The Spartan Ladies, by Ludovic Carlell; The Corporal and the Switzer, by Arthur Wilson; The Fatal Friendship, by Burroughes.

1653. Sept. 23, The Bondwoman.

1653. Nov. 29 (by R. Marriot), The Black Wedding; Castara, or Cruelty without Lust; The Conceits; The Divorce; The Florentine Friend; A Fool and her Maidenhead soon parted; The Law Case; The Noble Ravishers; The Paraside, or Revenge for Honor, by *Henry Glapthorne*; Pity the Maids; The Proxy, or Love's Aftergame; The Royal Choice, by Sir Robert; Stapylton; Salisbury Plain; Supposed Inconstancy; The Woman's Law; Woman's Masterpiece; The Younger Brother.

1654. April 8, The Apprentice's Prize, by Brome and Heywood; The Life and Death of Sir Martin Skink, with the Wars of the Low Countries, by Brome and Heywood; The Jeweller of Amsterdam, or the Hague, by Fletcher, Field, and Massinger; The Maiden's Holiday, by Marlowe and Day (see Warburton's list).

APPENDIX.

SUPPLEMENTARY TABLE OF MOSELEY'S ENTRIES IN 1653 AND 1660, AND WARBURTON'S LIST.

Plays entered 9 Sept. 1653.	Authors.	Plays in the Warburton MSS.	Authors.	Plays entered 29 June 1660.	Authors.
*Philenzo and Hippolito. C.	P. Massinger	*Philenzo and Hippolito. C.	P. Massinger		
		*Antonio and Vallia. C.	P. Massinger	*Antonio and Vallia. C.	P. Massinger
		*The Parliament of Love. C.	W. Rowley	*The Parliament of Love	W. Rowley
*The Spanish Viceroy, or The Honor of Women. C.	P. Massinger	The Judge. C.	P. Massinger		
		*The Honor of Women. C.	P. Massinger		
*Minerva's Sacrifice, or The Forced Lady. T.	P. Massinger	*Minerva's Sacrifice. T.	P. Massinger		
*Believe as you list. C.	P. Massinger	*The Forced Lady. T.	P. Massinger		
The Italian Nightpiece, or Unfortunate Piety	P. Massinger	*Believe as you list. C.	P. Massinger	*Believe as you list. C.	P. Massinger
The Wandering Lovers, or The Painter. C.	P. Massinger				
*The Very Woman, or The Woman's Plot [or the Prince of Tarent.] T. C.	P. Massinger	*The Woman's Plot. T. C.	P. Massinger	*A right Woman	Beau. and Flet.
*The Noble Choice, or The Orator. T. C.	P. Massinger	*The Noble Choice. T. C.	P. Massinger		
		*The Tyrant. T.	P. Massinger	*The Tyrant. T.	P. Massinger
The Prisoner, or The Fair Anchoress [of Pausilippo]. T. C.	P. Massinger	Alexias, or The Chaste Gallant. T.	P. Massinger		
		*Fast and Welcome. C.	P. Massinger	*Fast and Welcome. C.	P. Massinger
		*The four honorable Loves. C.	W. Rowley	*The four honored Loves. C.	W. Rowley
The Fool without Book	W. Rowley	*The Nonesuch. C.	W. Rowley	*The Nonesuch. C.	W. Rowley
*The Second Maiden's Tragedy		*The Second Maiden's Tragedy	G. Chapman		

APPENDIX. 359

Title	Author	Title	Author	Title	Author
		*Yorkshire Gentlewoman and her sons	G. Chapman	*The Yorkshire Gentlewoman and her son	G. Chapman
		*The Fatal Love		*Fatal Love, a French tragedy	G. Chapman
		*The King of Swedland	T. Dekker	*Gustavus, King of Swethland	T. Dekker
		*Jocondo and Astolpho	T. Dekker	*The tale of Jocondo and Astolpho. C.	T. Dekker
		*An ill beginning may have a good end. C.	J. Ford	*An ill beginning has a good end, and a &c. C.	J. Ford
		*The London Merchant. C.	J. Ford	*The London Merchant. C.	J. Ford
		*The Royal Combat. C.	J. Ford	*The Royal Combat. C.	J. Ford
*Beauty in a Trance	J. Ford	*Beauty in a Trance	J. Ford		
*The Governor	Sir C. Formido	*The Governor	Sir C. Formido		
		*The Duchess of Fernandina. T.	H. Glapthorne	*The Duchess of Fernandina. T.	H. Glapthorne
		The Vestal. T.	H. Glapthorne	The Noble Trial.	H. Glapthorne
		*Nothing impossible to Love. T. C.	Sir R. Le Greece	*Nothing impossible to Love. T. C.	Sir R. Le Greece
		*Love hath found out his eyes	T. Jordan	*Love hath found out his eyes	T. Jordan
		*The Crafty Merchant, or The Soldiered Citizen, [or Come to my country house], or The Merchant's Sacrifice	S. Marmion [W. Bonen]	*The Soldiered Citizen	
*The Puritan Maid, the Modest Wife, and the Wanton Widow. C.	T. Middleton	*The Puritan Maid, the Modest Wife, and the Wanton Widow. C.	T. Middleton		
*The Widow's Prize. C.	W. Sampson	*The Widow's Prize. C.	W. Sampson		
The history of Cardenio.	Fletcher and *Shakespeare*	A play	W. *Shakespeare*	Iphis and Ianthe, or A marriage without a man	W. *Shakespeare*
*Henry I. and Henry II.	*Shakespeare* and Davenport	*Henry I.	W. *Shakespeare*		

APPENDIX.

SUPPLEMENTARY TABLE—continued.

Plays entered 9 Sept. 1653.	[Authors.	Plays in the Warburton MSS.	Authors.	Plays entered 29 June 1660.	Authors.
*The Inconstant Lady. C.	[Query, is Duke Humphrey a version of 2 Henry VI.?] A. Wilson	*Duke Humphrey. T.	W. Shakespeare	*Duke Humphrey The history of King Stephen	W. Shakespeare W. Shakespeare
The Lovesick Maid, or The Honor of Young Ladies	R. Brown	*The Inconstant Lady. C.	A. Wilson		
The Jew of Venice	T. Dekker	The Fair Favorite	Sir W. Davenant	The Faithful Friends	Beau. and Flet.
The Woman's Mistake	Drue & Davenport	The Bugbears C.	J. Geffrey	The history of Madoc, King of Britain	F. Beaumont
The Duke of Guise	H. Shirley	A Mask	R. Govell		
		The History (Tragedy) of Jobe.	R. Greene	The Fatal Brothers. T.	R. Davenport
The Dumb Bawd	H. Shirley	The Queen of Corsica. T.	F. Jaques	The Politic Queen, or Murther will out	R. Davenport
Giraldo the Constant Lover	H. Shirley	The Maiden's Holiday	C. Marlowe		
The Spanish Duke of Lerma	H. Shirley	St. George for England	Wil. Smith	The Prodigal Scholar. C.	T. Randall
The Countryman	Anonymous	Works	Sir J. Suckling	The Christmas Ordinary	Trin. Coll. Oxon.
The King's Mistress	Anonymous	'Tis good sleeping in a whole skin	W. Wager		
The Politic Bankrupt, or Which is the best Girl?	Anonymous	An enterlude	R. Wood		
		The Flying Voice.	R. Wood		
		The City Shuffler	Anonymous		
		The Fairy Queen.	Anonymous		
		The Great Man.	Anonymous		
		The Lovers of Loodgate	Anonymous		
		Orpheus	Anonymous		
		The Spanish Puecas	Anonymous		
		Demetrius and Marsina, or The imperial Impostor and unhappy Heroine			

INDEX.

INDEX OF PLAYS AND AUTHORS CONNECTED WITH SHAKESPEARE'S COMPANY BEFORE 1611.

Author.	Play.	Pages.
Anonymous	Alarum for London	See Lodge.
,,	Cloth Breeches and Velvet Hose	326.
,,	Cromwell, Earl of Essex	42, 145, 146, 298.
,,	Edward III.	See Shakespeare.
,,	Fair Em	See Wilson.
,,	Gowry	152, 301.
,,	Hester and Ahasuerus	93, 116, 309.
,,	Jealous Comedy	See Shakespeare.
,,	Knack to Know a Knave	16, 109, 290.
,,	Locrine	See Peele.
,,	London Prodigal	54, 148, 154, 299.
,,	Merry Devil of Edmonton	See Drayton.
,,	Mucedorus	See Lodge.
,,	Oldcastle	See Drayton.
,,	Richard, Duke of York	See 3 Henry VI.
,,	Seven Deadly Sins	See Tarleton.
,,	Sir Thomas More	27, 127, 292.
,,	Spanish Maz	53.
,,	Tambercam, 2d part, acted 28 April 1592.	
,,	Taming of a Shrew	See Kyd.
,,	Taner of Denmark, acted 23 May 1592.	
,,	Titus and Vespasian	16, 109, 313.
,,	Warning for Fair Women	See Lodge.
,,	York and Lancaster	See 2 Henry VI.
,,	Yorkshire Tragedy	53, 54, 154, 158, 302.
Dekker	Satiromastix	36, 43, 45, 298.
Drayton	Merry Devil of Edmonton	31, 58, 131, 139, 157, 294.
,,	Oldcastle, Sir John	41, 78, 140.
Fletcher	Henry VIII.	See Shakespeare.
,,	Two Noble Kinsmen	252.
Jonson	Alchemist	65, 81, 163.
,,	Every man out of his humour	36, 37, 79, 137, 297.

2 A

INDEX OF PLAYS—*continued.*

Author.	Play.	Pages.
Jonson	Every man in his humour	34, 39, 40, 79, 140, 297.
,,	Jeronymo (additions)	52.
,,	Sejanus	49, 80, 147, 151, 301.
,,	Volpone	50, 54, 56, 80, 154, 303.
Kyd	Hamlet	See Shakespeare.
,,	Jeronymo (Spanish Tragedy)	16, 52, 151, 308.
,,	Taming of a Shrew	19, 23, 28, 99, 116, 117, 129.
Lodge	Alarum for London	27, 126, 291.
,,	Mucedorus	56, 156, 303.
,,	Warning for Fair Women	35, 136, 297.
Marlowe	Edward III.	See Shakespeare.
,,	Guise (Massacre of Paris)	16, 112.
,,	Henry VI.	See Shakespeare.
,,	Richard, Duke of York	See 3 Henry VI.
,,	Richard III.	See Shakespeare.
,,	Titus Andronicus	See Shakespeare.
,,	York and Lancaster	See 2 Henry VI.
Peele	Edward I.	14.
,,	Locrine	24, 120, 291.
Rowley	Birth of Merlin	289.
Shakespeare	All's well that ends well	42, 111, 142, 216.
,,	Anthony and Cleopatra	58, 157, 158, 161, 244.
,,	As you like it	36, 38, 39, 138, 140, 208.
,,	Coriolanus	60, 160, 244.
,,	Cymbeline	57, 156, 162, 246. ✓
,,	Edward III.	19, 23, 118, 127, 282.
,,	Errors, Comedy of	13, 26, 105, 125, 178.
,,	Hamlet	19, 23, 42, 49, 50, 99, 117, 142, 146, 148, 149, 227, 309.

INDEX OF PLAYS—*continued.*

Author.	Play.	Pages.
Shakespeare	1 Henry IV...	30, 32, 130, 134, 198.
,,	2 Henry IV...	32, 130, 199.
,,	Henry V.	35, 38, 40, 138, 140, 206.
,,	1 Henry VI...	16, 109, 255.
,,	2 Henry VI...	39, 98, 115, 145, 263.
,,	3 Henry VI...	19, 23, 39, 110, 126, 145, 271.
,,	Henry VIII...	68, 170, 250.
,,	Jealous Comedy (Merry Wives)	16, 19, 39, 112.
,,	John	27, 127, 196.
,,	Julius Cæsar	39, 42, 214.
,,	Lear	53, 58, 156, 157, 237, 311.
,,	Love's Labour's Lost	11, 32, 103, 133, 202.
,,	Love's Labour's Won	13, 104.
,,	Macbeth	28, 43, 55, 56, 57, 128, 155, 238.
,,	Measure for Measure	52, 153, 234.
,,	Merchant of Venice	30, 41, 129, 134, 141, 197.
,,	Merry Wives of Windsor	39, 139, 145, 210.
,,	Midsummer Night's Dream	18, 26, 41, 126, 181.
,,	Much Ado about Nothing	33, 40, 134, 140, 204.
,,	Othello	52, 153, 235.
,,	Pericles	58, 61, 158, 161, 245.
,,	Richard II.	26, 32, 42, 126, 132, 143, 187.
,,	Richard III.	23, 32, 118, 132, 176, 275.
,,	Romeo and Juliet	13, 27, 32, 38, 106, 128, 129, 191, 308.
,,	Taming of the Shrew	23, 40, 146, 224.
,,	Tempest	66, 163, 248.
,,	Timon of Athens	57, 156, 242.
,,	Titus Andronicus	23, 114, 116, 176, 280.

INDEX OF PLAYS—*continued.*

Author.	Play.	Pages.
Shakespeare	Troylus and Cressida	23, 44, 61, 136, 146, 160, 220.
,,	Twelfth Night	44, 111, 145, 219.
,,	Two Gentlemen of Verona	14, 106, 126, 188, 313.
,,	Winter's Tale	65, 163, 247.
Tarleton	Seven Deadly Sins	23, 296.
Tourneur	Revenger's Tragedy	58, 305.
Tylney	Locrine	See Peele.
Webster	Malcontent (Induction)	52, 151, 301.
Wilkins	Miseries of Enforced Marriage	49, 148, 302.
,,	Pericles	See Shakespeare.
Wilson	Fair Em	13, 104, 285.

NOTE ON THE ETCHINGS.

I have been asked to say a few words on the illustrations to this volume. The *Portrait of Alleyn* has been kindly permitted to be taken from the oil painting preserved at Dulwich College, and has not, it is believed, been previously engraved as a book illustration. It was thought that the reader would prefer a representation of this great actor, the first managing director under whom Shakespeare performed, to a reproduction of one of the many portraits of the poet himself, which have now become so hackneyed. For like reason, the *Font in which Shakespeare was baptized* has been obtained from a hitherto unreproduced original: an oil sketch made on the spot in 1853 by the world-known painter, Mr. Henry Wallis, and now in the artist's possession. It is with no little satisfaction that I find my work allowed to be associated with that of a painter so eminent, and with the name of one of the great poets for all ages, Mr. Robert Browning.

Printed by Ballantyne, Hanson & Co., Edinburgh and London.

www.ingramcontent.com/pod-product-compliance
Lightning Source LLC
Chambersburg PA
CBHW020313240426
43673CB00039B/790